YOU ARE NOT HUMAN

Jenny,
You are human!
Simon x
21/9/2018

YOU ARE NOT HUMAN
HOW WORDS KILL

SIMON LANCASTER

Biteback Publishing

First published in Great Britain in 2018 by
Biteback Publishing Ltd
Westminster Tower
3 Albert Embankment
London SE1 7SP
Copyright © Simon Lancaster 2018

ISBN 978-1-78590-407-3

10 9 8 7 6 5 4 3 2 1

A CIP catalogue record for this book is available from the British Library.

Set in Minion Pro and Futura

Printed and bound in Great Britain by
CPI Group (UK) Ltd, Croydon CR0 4YY

CONTENTS

To my mum and all the other humans

THIS IS NOT AN
INTRODUCTION...

It's an unexpectedly warm evening in February 2013 and hundreds of global art collectors, foreign investors and members of London's creative glitterati are making their way down St James's Street, London towards the pillared doors of Christie's auction house. For 250 years, this has been a place where millions of pounds have been spent with a literal blink of the eye or wave of the hand and tonight promises to be just such a night. Private collections and secret vaults around the world have been prised open for the Art of the Surreal auction. All the seats have been taken. The doorways are full. Dozens of people line the room, nervously checking their phones and biting their lips.

Jussi Pylkkänen, the Finnish global president of Christie's and auctioneer for the evening, gracefully welcomes everyone and briskly begins bidding on lot number 101 – a tiny oil painting called *Les Coquilles* by Max Ernst. The guide price was £100,000 to £150,000 but it ends up going for a breath-taking £433,250. Then, we head straight to lot number 102 – the Study for the *Head of the Virgin*, by Salvador Dalí – a fairly cursory and unattractive work which had been estimated to sell for £50,000 to £70,000 but ends up fetching £337,250. Lot number 103, *Volupté* by Francis Picabia, estimated at £80,000 to £120,000, ends up going for £229,250. It *is* going to be one of those nights. Pylkkänen smiles.

Now, it's time for lot 104. This is one of the star lots. Much of the pre-auction publicity has centred on this oil painting. All eyes in the room turn right, towards this grand, irregularly framed, world-renowned oil painting by René Magritte. There's no bowler hat in this painting, but there is an apple. Or, at least, I think it's an apple…

Magritte is probably one of the world's best-known surrealists. He was hugely influential on the London counterculture movement in the '60s. John and Yoko talked about him on their first date. In the '70s, his influence was evident on a number of album covers – from Pink Floyd to Jeff Beck. In the '80s, he inspired a Fleetwood Mac video and Paul Simon even wrote a song about him – 'René and Georgette Magritte with Their Dog After the War'.

Magritte was a rebel and subversive. In some ways, he was the precursor to Andy Warhol and 1950s Pop Art, constantly probing the ethics of capitalism, challenging the gap between reality and illusion. He was also a communist but, bizarrely, he came to inspire the biggest brand that has ever been known in the history of capitalism – but we'll come to that later. For now, let's take a look at his intriguing back story.

Magritte was born in Lessines in the province of Hainaut, Belgium in 1898 to Léopold Magritte, a tailor, and Régina (née Bertinchamps), a hatmaker. The oldest of three boys, his family had money but his upbringing was turbulent. His mother suffered severely with depression and attempted suicide a number of times. On one occasion, she tried to drown herself in the water tank upstairs in the attic. She was rescued but, after that, was forced to spend the rest of her life locked in her bedroom for her own protection. Life must have been filled with anxiety and anguish for young René, hearing his mother's cries from the next room. Finally, one night in 1912, she smashed down her bedroom door, fled from the house and made for the bridge that ran behind their family home. There, she flung herself in the raging River Sambre below. René Magritte was just fourteen years old.

When her bruised and battered corpse was discovered several days later, a mile downstream, she was returned to the family home and laid out in the family's front room. Her face had been covered with a blanket. A nurse probably did this to avoid traumatising young René, but it seems to have had precisely the opposite effect because for the rest of his life much of his artwork involved deliberately concealing or corrupting people's faces, as on the cover of this book. To see a human body with their face removed, blocked or distorted even slightly is profoundly shocking; it confounds our most primitive and basic expectations. Maybe Magritte's intention in depicting such shocking images was to recreate the feeling he had experienced when he first saw his dead mother.

Psychologists say a fascination with reality and illusion is common amongst those who are bereaved young: it is a consequence of them trying to reconcile their two conflicting worlds – the world they wish exists (in which their mother is still alive) and the world they know exists (in which their mother is dead). John Lennon shared this fascination with Magritte. His mother was also killed when he was young and he also found comfort in surrealism. As he said, 'Surrealism had a great effect on me because then I realised that the imagery in my mind wasn't insanity. Surrealism to me is reality.' Dancing upon the intersection between reality and illusion yielded many of Lennon's truly greatest works – 'Strawberry Fields Forever', 'Lucy in the Sky with Diamonds' and 'I am the Walrus'. It also proved immensely productive for Magritte.

The first piece of Magritte's oeuvre to catch the public eye was *The Treachery of Images*, produced in 1929 when he was just thirty years old. At first glance, this was just a simple classical picture of a pipe. But then beneath the pipe, in beautiful calligraphy, in a style which was immediately redolent of pre-school books used to teach children the alphabet – A is for Apple, B is for Banana, C is for Caterpillar – it said, '*Ceci n'est pas une pipe*'. This is not a pipe. Huh? So it was a pipe. But it was not a pipe. What did he mean?

Along with many of the other surrealist artists of the time – Picasso, Dalí, Ernst, Chirico, Miró and so on – he was exploring how easy it was to manipulate people's sense of perception through the corruption of words and images, or, as he put it, '*les mots et les images*'. He once postulated, 'An object is not so wedded to its name that one cannot find another name which suits it better.'

He tested this theory to the limit in one of his other pictures from this time: *La Clef des Songes* (The Key to Dreams), which was on display at London's Luxembourg & Dayan Art Gallery in a special exhibition of Magritte's works called

4

The Rule of Metaphor in summer 2018. This painting featured four instantly recognisable everyday items – a bag, a corkscrew, a leaf and a sponge – but three of them were described incorrectly. So, the bag was marked '*Le ciel*' (the sky). The corkscrew was marked '*L'oiseau*' (the bird). The leaf was marked '*La table*' (the table). The only picture that was marked accurately was the picture of a sponge – '*L'éponge*'. It was all very unsettling, because he was showing how easy it was to describe something as something it was not.

These works felt deeply relevant back in the 1920s and 1930s, with fascism on the rise and radios and cinemas all constantly spewing out propaganda. This was a world in which no one could be quite sure what was reality and what was illusion. Magritte wanted to expose what he saw as the inherent dishonesty of a capitalist and political system in which things could be readily misnamed and misdescribed with complete impunity. He once said all human activity was influenced by 'a bunch of sophism and lies'.[1] And this was a world he knew quite a lot about.

Magritte mastered his craft in advertising. He dabbled in commercial art throughout his life. The whole essence of advertising has always been based upon depicting things as something they are not. Cars are freedom. Chocolate is sex. Designer clothes equal power. Such deceptions remain ubiquitous today, but the claims that were made in Magritte's time were even more audacious. Tobacco companies actually claimed that cigarettes were good for your health. Old Gold adverts promised 'a TREAT instead of a TREATMENT'. Adverts for Lucky Strike cigarettes urged consumers, 'You need this throat protection.'

Magritte's paintings shone a light upon these everyday deceptions and distortions. But one of the most unsettling aspects of his works was that he deliberately emulated the appearance of children's books. By depicting a children's primer, Magritte was representing the ultimate voice of authority, but what that voice of authority was saying was patently wrong.

This work feels equally relevant today, in the age of Trump, alternative facts, fake news, Brexit, Boris, trolls and so on (this list is by no means exhaustive – feel free to add your own bêtes noires). This might explain the recent resurgence of interest in Magritte's work. Everyone today is fascinated by how easy it is to describe something as something it is not.

I've been a speechwriter for twenty years. Like Magritte, I've also spent a lot of time looking into the power that comes from mixing words and images. There was no actual financial storm: this was no act of nature, there were no real dark clouds, no downpour of rain. There was no actual Arab Spring: no blossom bloomed, no birds sang, no grass grew. When we save data to a cloud, we don't actually transmit our files to a fluffy white mass of condensed water vapour. Welcome to the mysterious world of metaphor, in which everything is something it is not.

Metaphors are fundamentally substituting one thing for another. The formula for a metaphor, if you like to think about things that way, is X=Y. For instance, we see ideas as containers, which we might 'unpack' or 'find holes in'. We see love as a flower that can 'blossom' and 'grow'. We talk about cash as water, with 'liquidity' and 'capital flows'.

Professors George Lakoff and Mark Johnson explored and examined a number of these conceptual metaphors in their groundbreaking 1980 book, *Metaphors We Live By*.

Many of these conceptual metaphors trace back to memories of our experience of childhood. For instance, we talk about good relationships as being 'warm'. The reason we see good relationships as warm is because, as babies, when we are being held and cuddled, our bodily temperature literally rises. So, the perfect relationship will always instinctively be perceived as warm.

Likewise, we can all accept the idea that life is a journey in which we 'move forward', even though we might 'trip up' or 'take a stumble'. People might speak about 'moving on' in their life, 'hitting an obstacle' or having 'someone by their side'. We're not literally going anywhere but we all understand what is meant.

If someone was to speak outside of these culturally accepted conceptual metaphors – e.g. to depict life not as a journey but as a table, with grooves, legs and a flat surface, we'd think them a bit odd. We might even challenge them on their way of thinking. But if we did challenge their metaphor, we would almost certainly do so without even mentioning the word metaphor. We'd probably just say, 'Hmm… I don't see things quite like that.' That's the way disagreements about metaphor are usually articulated. We argue about different perspectives rather than the language used.

Metaphors are far and away the most powerful element of political communication. They are the closest we have to being able to paint with words. Some say a picture is worth a thousand words. Yet a metaphor can paint a powerful picture that lasts a thousand years. The Iron Curtain. The Wind of Change. The Winter of Discontent.

I never cease to be amazed by how little people talk about metaphor, because it is almost impossible to speak for very long at all without using a metaphor. We use metaphors on average six times a minute or once every sixteen words.[2] Metaphors lie all around us in everyday discourse and they are very powerful. Metaphors are very *loaded*. Metaphors *plant* ideas in our minds. Our conversation is *littered* with metaphors.

Look at those metaphors I just used. Each of them paints a different image. These images could work for different audiences, depending on their perspectives. If I say metaphors are loaded, the picture I paint is that a metaphor is a gun. This might be appealing to someone who sees themselves under attack, taking a lot of 'flak' or regards themselves in a 'combative' argument at work. They might fancy that metaphor will help them. Maybe they could prepare some powerful 'bullet points' to 'shoot down' the 'other side's' argument.

How about if I say metaphors plant ideas? If I use that word, the image I'm creating is that metaphors are seeds. That picture might appeal to someone who saw themselves not so much in a war of words, but more in the slower and longer term 'cultivation' of ideas; someone who won't mind waiting for the metaphor to 'take root' or 'become embedded' and who is hoping that attitudes will then change more 'organically'. Thinking of images as seeds is a long-established way of thinking. Indeed, the very word propaganda is based upon the metaphorical notion that images are seeds which can be propagated.

But when I say our conversation is littered with metaphors, then I've conjured up a picture that metaphors are 'rubbish', 'worthless' and in all probability 'should be binned'. So that is a self-defeating image. Not one for a metaphor enthusiast like myself: I'll leave that one for the sceptics. But it's easy to see the everyday ease with which we speak in pictures to see things as things they are not. This facility is probably the single most important factor that distinguishes us as humans from other species. We look to the stars and see hope. We peer into the shadows and see death. We stare at the clouds and see bodies, birds or bunny rabbits. No other animal has this capacity. When a lion sees fire, it just sees fire. It's wholly literal. But a human can't look at anything for very long at all without superimposing something else on to it. When we look at fire, we can see emotion – the raging passion of love or the roaring flames of anger; we can see life – maybe the flame is dancing or perhaps it grows into a wild, ferocious, all-consuming beast; or we can see religion – the burning gates of hell or an awesome mighty god.[3]

Yuval Noah Harari argued in *Sapiens* that it was this unique capacity to see things as things they were not which gave *Homo sapiens* unparalleled domination of the planet. It was because we could look at fire, for example, and saw a God that we developed the capacity to create religions. This gave us the power to gather together in groups of hundreds of thousands or even millions where other primates had only previously been able to cooperate in numbers of around one hundred. By creating fictitious narratives, we gained unparalleled opportunities for cooperation and growth.

Neuroscientists have speculated that it might have been a

growth in the angular gyrus part of the brain that gave us this unique capacity for metaphorical thought. It seems to have grown to around eight times the size it is in other primates during the cognitive revolution 50,000 years ago, bringing our domination of the planet to completion. Our capacity for metaphor meant we could imagine where others could only see. It gave us our uniquely human qualities of invention, innovation and ingenuity.

Aristotle said that to be a master of metaphor was a sign of genius. Indeed, the very word intelligence derives from the Latin 'inter legere', which means to read across, which is fundamentally what we do with metaphor when we consider X to be Y. Many of the greatest intellectual breakthroughs in history have come through metaphorical insight. Adam Smith transformed everyone's conception of economics with his notion of an invisible hand of the market. James Watson and Francis Crick transformed our understanding of science and nature when they talked about the building blocks of DNA. More recently, Giacomo Rizzolatti transformed our understanding of neuroscience through his notion of mirror neurons. Metaphor is fundamental to our conception of the world. As Nietzsche argued, there is very little in the world which we do not comprehend through metaphor. It is fundamental to our perception, but it is also uniquely personal.

When I'm writing speeches for people, one of the first things I do is analyse their metaphors. This gives me all sorts of clues to their personal, political and private views. By understanding what they see in their mind's eye, I'm more likely to capture their voice and their views. For instance, one of my clients is fascinated by science. He forever talks about getting 'the elements' in place, 'formulas' for success and creating 'catalysts'. I don't see the world like that, but I know that he does, so that's how I'll write his speech. That's how he sees things. One of my other clients regularly speaks about 'raising the stakes', 'spinning the wheel' and 'keeping his cards close to his chest'. I don't doubt that on a Saturday night he might be found in some glitzy Piccadilly casino.

We can learn a lot about how someone sees the world by carefully listening to his or her metaphors. You can even get clues to what they're like in bed. People conceptualise sex in different ways. Some people see sex as football, talk about 'scoring', 'getting a hat-trick' and who could forget Alan Partridge's 'back of the net'? To others, sex might be a transformative process: the 'earth moved', I got my 'rocks off', I completely 'lost it'! To other people, it might be combat: you're 'banging' away, you 'shoot your load' or you 'fire blanks'. But if someone speaks about their penis as a 'weapon', it might put people off... Potential victims might well view it as dangerous.

Sex educator Al Vernacchio did a TED Talk in 2013 in which he suggested Americans should stop talking about sex as baseball ('first base', 'second base' etc.) because it is highly macho, and it implies fixed rules and winners and losers. He argued that instead, we should talk about sex as pizza, because everyone loves pizza and there are a million different ways to eat it.

It's not just someone's private life that you can investigate through their metaphors, you can also get clues to their political leanings. Tories use nature and personification metaphors twice as often as Labour supporters: they talk about 'the *heart* of our communities', Britain 'standing *tall* in the world' and Europe getting 'clogged *arteries*' – perhaps unsurprisingly, given they're a party that believes in laissez-faire economics and the power of the individual. Labour politicians use conflict metaphors twice as often as the Tories – they talk about '*fighting* for our rights', '*defending* public services from Tory *attack*' and 'getting resources to the *front line*' – again, not too surprising for a party born from revolutionary conflict. The Lib Dems favour journey metaphors: using them twice as often as the other parties, talking of '*moving forward*', being at a '*fork in the road*', taking '*a change in direction*' and so on – all quite natural for the party of progressives.

What's funny is how this view of the world manifests not just in the language but the imagery of the main parties. The Tory logo is the tree – nature. The Lib Dems' logo is the dove – symbolic of journey. And Labour's logo may now be the red rose, but this dates back to a period when their explicit strategy was to echo Tory language; who knows, maybe Jeremy Corbyn will soon dump the rose for something more traditional – a nice clenched fist or something.

As people's political allegiances can be detected through metaphor, so too can their professional perspectives. Many arguments at work can be traced back to different metaphorical perspectives. A good case study for this is the National Health Service, which is not only Britain's largest employer, with 1.3 million employees, it is also probably one of Britain's most fractious employers. The trouble is that everyone within the NHS has a wholly different perspective on what the NHS is and what it does. They all see things differently.

Politicians tend to view the NHS as a person. This is not surprising. They see the NHS as their child, their baby, one of the younger members of the family of state. Successive Health Secretaries have talked about making the NHS fitter and stronger, able to stand on its own two feet. They talk about the heart of the NHS, its values and beliefs, how it must step up. Look at how politicians from all parties gathered together to celebrate the NHS's seventieth birthday, paying tribute to Bevan and Beveridge, the founding fathers. Note it was the NHS's birthday that was celebrated, not the anniversary, and that we celebrated not the legislators but the founding fathers.

To managers in the NHS, this kind of talk sounds unbearably trite and unappealing. They don't want to see the NHS as a person because they want to be able to control it. So, they view the NHS not as a person, but as a machine, and more specifically a car in which they will drive change, accelerate reforms and put their foot down. They love this metaphor because it gives them the illusion of control. They can get all the components in place, issue toolkits and merrily go wherever they like on a whim, ordering compassion drives, dementia drives and efficiency drives.

This imagery is empowering for the managers because it puts them in the driving seat. It's not very attractive for clinicians, though, because, if the NHS is a car, that makes them nuts and bolts. So, trapped in a big machine from which they can't escape; not there to think: just to fulfil a function, no more, no less; and as soon as they fail to fulfil that function, they know that they will be removed and replaced without a second thought.

That metaphor infuriates them. They say the managers just don't get it. They have no idea what it's like on the frontline. With supreme irony, the very people who are in the business of saving lives most typically relate what they do to killing: doctors and nurses frequently see the NHS as a soldier. They battle cancer, beat disease and fight obesity.

This may be very helpful for them, but how does it make a patient feel? Who wants to see their body as a battleground? I have some personal experience of this. My eldest daughter Lottie is a type one diabetic. She was diagnosed when she was four years old. The language of diabetes is full of war metaphors – jabs, lancets, and shots of insulin. This was terrifying for Lottie. The doctors even gave her a comic prepared especially for children by the American Medical Association to explain diabetes called *What's Up with Ella?* It showed that when you eat you ingest little green aliens (sugar molecules), which are vicious invaders threatening to harm you, all you have to do is send in your superhero army (insulin) and they'll zap around your veins shooting down all the little green aliens. For a doctor, and I dare say, anyone who doesn't have diabetes, this is not a bad explanation of diabetes. It worked for me. It didn't work for Lottie. She hid under the table, begging us not to inject her. 'No, thank you, please!' she cried, using the best words she knew to win our approval.

My wife and I had to create alternative strategies. My wife works in communications as well – which invariably means that we're constantly manipulating the crap out of one another... However, every now and then we gang up on the kids and then we're a real force to be reckoned with: and so it was that we set about trying to make her medicine less scary. We knew we had to change the way diabetes appeared. The first thing we did was buy her a nice friendly looking medicine bag – 'DB' ('diabetic bag') – which featured on the side a big, beaming anthropomorphic giraffe. By making 'DB' her smiling pet, we gave her a sense of control. This was the opposite of the feelings invoked by the war metaphor, which left her feeling out of control and under attack.

This was not a case of super-sensitivity on our side. Christopher Hitchens described in his moving book *Mortality* a similar reaction when he was told he had cancer. Except it was instantly made clear to him that he didn't just have cancer, he was battling cancer.

'No well-wisher omits the combative image: You can beat this. It's even in obituaries for cancer losers, as if one might reasonably say of someone that they died after a long and brave struggle.'

To him, the whole idea seemed horribly inappropriate, particularly as he began chemotherapy.

Allow me to inform you, though, that when … kindly people bring a huge transparent bag of poison and plug it into your arm, and you either read or don't read a book while the venom sack gradually empties itself into your system, the image of the ardent soldier or revolutionary is the very last one that will occur to you. You feel swamped with passivity and impotence: dissolving in powerlessness like a sugar lump in water.[4]

You see the way his language is full of sweeping metaphors.

It's incredibly poetic, but this is much more important than that. Elena Semino of Lancaster University has conducted extensive research on cancer metaphors after losing her own father to the condition. She discovered that terminally ill patients who perceive they are at war with their cancer have lower survival rates than those that don't.[5] In May 2018, the Macmillan Cancer Charity produced a report called 'Missed Opportunities'; it showed that nearly two thirds of sufferers never talk to anyone about their fears of dying due to the pressure to present themselves as fighters.[6]

This is the thing: metaphors represent a mighty power in ways we can scarcely begin to imagine. They are like the invisible hand in all arguments, conception and perception, discreetly guiding and leading us, wholly outside of our conscious awareness. FMRI scanners show that the human brain struggles to tell the difference between metaphorical and literal thought: each is processed in the same way with the same speed, and neither has unconditional priority. There's even evidence that, in some cases, metaphorical meanings may be preferred to literal.[7]

That's why the metaphor frequently represents the single most important element in any sentence as well as the decisive turning point in any argument. We might be excited about 'taking a leap' and starting a new business, until a friend warns we might 'fall flat on our face'. We might say our new lover is the 'light of our life', before someone says, 'Ew! He's a creep.' We might believe that the house we're buying is 'heavenly' until we hear that next door are the 'neighbours from hell'. There's nothing literal about any of these pictures, but the imagery could stick in our mind for years.

Metaphors are also critical in political debates. Research shows that changing nothing more than the metaphor in a piece of text leads people to fundamentally different reactions on questions ranging from whether they will support foreign wars,[8] to what they think should be done about climate change,[9] to whether they will back preventative or punitive policies to deal with crime.[10]

But what's more extraordinary is that people deny the metaphor influenced them. They'll either say they didn't notice the metaphor or, if they did, they'll say it made no difference. That's what truly makes the metaphor so mighty: it's because people don't believe in its power that it is able to sneak in undetected, bypassing rational scrutiny. It is the nuclear bomb of all communication.[11] All of the other rhetorical devices – the rule of three, contrasts, and alliteration – are mere pea shooters in comparison.

Metaphors also have a profound power in business. Research shows that simply changing the metaphor can lead people to profoundly different views on whether a company's share price is going to go up or down.[12] If the metaphor of a living being is used to talk about a share (a person, a plant or an organism), people are more likely to think that share is going to go up.

So, for instance, if you said that, earlier today, shares in Sainsbury's 'leapt', 'climbed' or 'jumped' – or, that they 'stumbled', 'fell' or 'collapsed' – then people would be more likely to believe that those shares would go up. Why? Well, this is probably because we have a natural confidence in the innate ability of life forms to fulfil a given purpose. So, our instinctive mind might envisage the share price 'getting back on its feet', 'climbing back to its previous position' and even 'reaching up and touching new heights'. You see how the metaphor paints a picture which predisposes us towards a particular line of thought?

Compare that with a non-living metaphor. We could talk about shares as machines – so we might say that shares in GlaxoSmithKline 'were propelled higher', or 'driven up' – or, perhaps, they 'plummeted', or 'crashed'. But this kind of imagery would lead us to think the company would be less likely to succeed. Why? Well, maybe, people would envisage that sooner or later it would run out of fuel, need repair or require an upgrade. What we want to do ideally is to get in early with a business, providing seed capital, making sure that company has solid roots, watching it grow organically, seeing it branch out and then begin bearing fruits.

Oh yes, where were we? Fruit. We are back to Christie's in February 2013 and the sale of lot 104: Magritte's oil painting of an apple. The painting is big and bold, attractive and enticing, playful and childlike, in Magritte's characteristic style. And this is a very ordinary apple: rosy, plump and slightly marked. The painting is in the style of his other 'mots et images' works, so it is like a children's primer and, above the apple, in that carefully calligraphed text, is the legend 'Ceci n'est pas une pomme'. This is not an apple.

Bidding gets underway. It starts at a million. That is a lot of money. If Magritte were here today, he would almost certainly be filled with disgust, throwing scorn upon this vulgar display of wealth, condemning this capitalist hypocrisy, denying the special value accorded to art by the bourgeoisie as a simple means for asserting their superiority over their fellow man. Which brings me to the next part of Magritte's extraordinary story: about how it was that this radical communist came to inspire one of the most powerful brands ever to have existed in the history of capitalism.

It started in 1967. Paul McCartney was in the garden of his St John's Wood house, recording a song with the young Welsh singer Mary Hopkin, who had just won *Opportunity Knocks*. Someone knocked on the door. It was Robert Fraser, the flamboyant socialite art dealer. He had popped around to show Paul a piece of work that he thought he might like. He knew Paul was a fan of Magritte and he had in his hands the latest work which had come hot from the artist's Belgian studio: the ink was barely dry. Fabulous, said Paul. But let me finish off recording first. Leave it in the front room and I'll take a look later.

That evening, Paul went into his front room and there he saw, propped up against the dining table, this beautiful picture of a Magritte apple. The painting was *Le Jeu de Mourre*. It featured one of Magritte's signature apples: underneath it said simply, '*Au Revoir*'. It was, as it turned out, to be one of the last apple paintings that Magritte ever painted. McCartney instantly fell in love with it; he bought it and still owns it today.[13]

The memory of this painting came back to Paul a few months later when the Beatles were deciding what to call their new company. As he put it:

> We were sitting around at EMI, wondering, 'What shall we call this thing?' We were looking through names. A is for Apple. B is for Banana. C is for Caterpillar. And we

thought, Yeah! Like a schoolbook. A is for Apple. That should be the name of the company. Then I thought, Wow, that Magritte apple is very much 'an apple'. A big green apple, you know. I told the ad man about it.[14]

So it was that this Magritte painting ended up inspiring the Beatles' Apple Corps.[15] The 'Corps' was a further bit of word play – when we talk about corporations we are actually suggesting another metaphor: the idea that a corporation is a living being (the word corporation derives from the Latin *corpus* – meaning body) and, by abbreviating this to 'corps', McCartney threw in a little pun for good measure.

But the story doesn't end there… For millions of their fans around the world were then left enchanted as they watched that beautiful bright green Granny Smith apple – the new Apple logo – revolving around and around on the turntable. I remember doing so myself as a young boy in the 1970s listening to *Abbey Road*. It was beautiful. It looked so good you did want to eat it.

But at the same time that I was doing that, a young hippy inventor 5,000 miles away was doing the same thing. Working out of a garage in Palo Alto, California, Steve Jobs was a massive fan of the Beatles. He described them repeatedly as his model for business. And, just as the Beatles named their first company Apple, so Steve Jobs named his first company Apple, too.

Today, whilst Steve Jobs is no more, the company he founded lives on. On 2 August 2018, Apple became the world's first-ever trillion-dollar company to have existed in the whole of human history. Anyone who put seed capital into Apple in 1984 will have seen their investment grow by an eye-watering 40,000 per cent.[16] And the brand alone is worth $234 billion dollars. That's not the company which is valued at $234 billion, simply the brand – that little picture of the apple that I can see now in no fewer than six different places as I glance around my office. The Apple brand is 100,000 times as valuable as the Magritte painting, which ended up selling at Christie's Art of the Surreal auction for just shy of £3 million.

But you know what? Just as Magritte's painting *n'était pas une pomme*, so Apple is not a real apple. There are no real pips inside the Apple HQ in Cupertino, California. There is no real core to the company. No one's investment is literally bearing fruits. And if you try biting the apple on the back of your phone, you're just going to be left with a metallic taste in your mouth and sore teeth. Yet when we say Apple, we think Apple, we feel Apple. Fresh, fun, simple. Adam and Eve, Isaac Newton, the Beatles. But it's not real. It's an illusion. The apple has been the symbol for religious, scientific and cultural revolutions throughout history; today, it is the symbol of the technological revolution.

I'm not complaining. I think Apple is great. I have heaps of Apple products. Who cares if it's not really an apple? But isn't it extraordinary how easily we can say something is something it is not? It's fantastic, isn't it? But what would the consequences be if this power were deployed more cynically, in matters of life and death?

PIGGIES

Poena cullei (meaning 'penalty of the sack') must be one of the most cruel, depraved and unusual punishments ever to have been conceived in the history of justice. Practised in ancient Rome, it required that the criminal be stripped, scourged, and sewn into a sack made of ox skins together with a live snake, dog, monkey and cockerel. The sack was then lobbed into the river. Not only was this a horrific way to die – imagine having your flesh clawed, bitten and pecked in the darkness as you faced an inevitable death by drowning – it sent a clear message to everyone that the criminal was less than human. Each animal involved in *poena cullei* had a deep, symbolic meaning that became attached to the criminal: the monkey denoted that he was primitive, not evolved; the snake suggested he was untrustworthy and slippery; the dog implied he was dirty and diseased; the cockerel said he was stupid – bird-brained. It was the ultimate fall from grace. You were, as they put it, '*damnatus ad bestias*' – damned to the beasts.

This was not a punishment that was doled out lightly. *Poena cullei* was reserved especially for the uniquely heinous crime of patricide. In ancient Rome, there was no more wicked offence than that. Rome was the ultimate patriarchy. Fathers could, and frequently did, literally rule their households with an iron rod. They could merrily beat their wives and children, even murdering them and no one would much raise an eyebrow. But what could not happen under any circumstances was for a son to kill his father. Fathers demanded *pietas* – reverence. The whole of Roman society was based upon this ideal. The act of patricide was considered not just a crime against the family, but a crime against the whole institution of Rome.

So Sextus Roscius must have been a little bit worried, to say the least, when, in 80 BC, he was arrested and charged with his father's murder. His father, an immensely wealthy man who owned thirteen farms bordering the River Tiber just north of Rome, had been returning home from dinner with friends one night when he was captured, stabbed and brutally murdered. Sextus Roscius was arrested and charged with the crime. He needed a damn good lawyer to represent him, but there weren't too many of them around ancient Rome prepared to defend someone on a charge of patricide: it wasn't good for business. Plus, this case promised to be particularly challenging. Sextus Roscius's prosecutors were now in charge of administering his father's estate and stood to win ownership of it if he was found guilty. Any defence lawyer who proved too effective could well find his life was in danger. What lawyer would be crazy enough to step forward in such circumstances? Step forward, Marcus Tullius Cicero.

Today we all know Cicero as one of the greatest statesmen, orators and lawyers in history. At this stage, though, he was just a young fresh-faced lawyer, full of enthusiasm and talent, but with little real experience. He was acutely aware that this case could prove make or break for him. He wanted to win, but was under no illusions about the awesome challenge he faced. He knew a successful defence would require him to deploy all of his powers in rhetoric.

Cicero was a master of the art of persuasion. We know a great deal about his approach to the art, not simply because we can analyse his speeches, but because he wrote about his techniques across several volumes. He even wrote expert guides to speechwriting long before any other speechwriter had the temerity to produce another.* We know from these, in particular, that Cicero was a big fan of metaphor. He urged aspiring orators to be sparing in their use of most rhetorical devices (for instance, the rule of three, contrast and alliteration) but not metaphor, 'which he may possibly employ more frequently because it is of the commonest occurrence in the language of townsmen and rustic alike'.[17]

The case of Sextus Roscius was fully transcribed, so we can analyse the adroit manner in which Cicero used metaphor to manipulate opinion in the courtroom. He used metaphor both to elevate his client and to diminish the prosecutors, inverting their perceived status within Rome's all-important social hierarchy.

Addressing the prosecutors directly, he said, 'Some of you are geese, who only honk, and can do no actual harm while others are dogs who can bite as well as bark. We see that you are fed. In return, you should direct your attacks against those who genuinely deserve it.'[18]

---

* Simon Lancaster, *Speechwriting: The Expert Guide* (Hale, 2010). Available from all good retailers.

It's worth noting that this is not simile, it is metaphor. He's not saying they are like geese, he's saying they are geese. Some people get confused about the difference between simile and metaphor. A simile says that X is like Y, a metaphor asserts X *is* Y. Metaphors are much harder to object to than similes. In Forrest Gump, Forrest's mother (played by Sally Field) says to him, 'Life is a box of chocolates' and he thinks her profound. When Forrest quotes her later, he has transposed her message to simile. 'Life is like a box of chocolates': everyone thinks him a fool. Similes invite objections in ways that metaphors do not. That's what makes metaphors more powerful. It's like the difference between a CEO who says simply, 'Our company is like a football team,' which is likely to lead people to say no; and the CEO who says, 'Let's look at our goals for the year.'

In choosing the metaphor of animals, Cicero was flipping the whole case on its head. The case was based upon Sextus Roscius being less than human. Cicero was saying the prosecutors were less than human. To suggest someone was an animal in ancient Rome was to attack their very essence. It was to imply that whilst their appearance was human, their soul was animal. This was a belief based on ancient mythology and Aesop's fable about Zeus and Prometheus. As the legend went, when Zeus instructed Prometheus to put life on earth, Prometheus created humans and animals. But, when Zeus saw what he'd done, he decided there were too many animals and not enough humans. So Prometheus was instructed to give some of the animals the appearance of people. This meant there were some people who looked like humans but who actually had the souls of animals. So, when an animal metaphor was used against someone, it was not just an insult: rather, it purported to reveal the true essence of that person. *Pig. Bitch. Cow.*

Cicero's choice of metaphors in this trial was not random. Each one was carefully calculated to support his argument. When Cicero called the lawyers dogs, this was a savage insult. In ancient Rome, dogs were not regarded as man's best friend as they are today, but as man's sworn enemy. They were seen as foul, filthy creatures that roamed the streets, searching for corpses to feed on. When the people of Rome went to sleep at night, they would often hear these wild dogs barking and howling, tearing the flesh from the dead. Dogs were scavengers, and that was entirely the image Cicero wanted to superimpose upon the prosecutors as he made the case that they were just after Sextus Roscius's father's land. Cicero's message was clear: the prosecuting lawyers were disgusting, dirty scavengers who wanted to feed off a dead man.

The reference to geese was equally well conceived. This metaphor attacked the words they had used. Whilst geese make a lot of noise, they ultimately make very little sense. Again, a clear message: the prosecution case is dumb, stupid and illogical. The prosecutors have brains the size of birds.

Cicero also elevated his client. He turned the prosecution's claim that Sextus Roscius was a beast on its head. If his client was a beast, then he could not be guilty, because beasts never committed patricide; 'even wild animals live at peace with each other, thanks to the ties of birth and upbringing, and thanks to nature herself'.[19] So if he was guilty of patricide, he must be a beast. But if he is a beast, he can't be guilty of patricide, because beasts don't commit patricide. This is *Alice in Wonderland* logic.

He ended his long speech with an appeal to those who are

'tender-hearted by nature' not to 'lose all sense of humanity'. He claimed his client, like the jury and himself, was human, but that the prosecutors were not. This was the O. J. Simpson trial of its day and Cicero was Johnnie Cochran.

By using metaphor to illustrate his case – drawing on the everyday language of the townsman and rustic alike – Cicero won the case. He established himself as a man of immense rhetorical skill and ended up rising all the way to the top of Roman society, despite being neither a patrician nor a noble. But it was not all plain sailing. He made a few enemies on the way. In the power struggle that followed Caesar's death, he fell out spectacularly with Mark Antony and made a number of fiery, damning speeches against him. In one, he branded Antony a subservient, grovelling dog.[20] Antony was not impressed. He had Cicero captured and executed. After his death, Antony's wife Fulvia pulled out Cicero's tongue and jabbed it repeatedly with a hairpin to be sure that he could never again deploy his wicked powers of rhetoric.

Whether Cicero was right or wrong in his defence of Sextus Roscius, what is interesting is his extensive use of animal metaphors. Animal metaphors speak to our most primitive human instincts. We are hunters by nature; as Tennyson put it, 'red in tooth and claw'. The domination of animals by the human race in the Agricultural Revolution of 10,000 BC was a critical step in the development of humanity: by learning to command, control and kill animals, we acquired the land, space and resources in which to create cities, cultures and civilisations.

This obsession with animals explains why references to them are writ large through our language, in ways we scarcely realise. Indeed, the very letters you are looking at right now relate to our command of the animal kingdom. If you track back the evolution of our alphabet from the Kemetic to the Semitic, through Phoenician to Greek and Latin, you discover an array of animal and hunting symbolism.

The letter A actually started out in the world as an ox's head whilst N emerged from a snake, S grew from a tusk, Q began life as a monkey and the letter X was originally a symbol for a fish. Many of the other letters started out as depictions of hunting weapons. The letters F, U, V, W and Y came from hooks, Z came from an arrow, T came from a stick and the letter H was originally a rope.[21] Most of the remaining letters in our alphabet were depictions of some aspect of the human form: the letter E was a man shouting, I was an arm, K was a hand, O was an eye, P was a mouth and R was a head. So A is not for apple, A is for ox's head. There's an alternative children's primer waiting to be written there which is guaranteed to scare the life out of any child. But the reason letters started out like this was because the first writings were largely records of which animals were being captured, controlled and killed, by whom and how. So the very alphabet we know and love today started out as a record, and in some sense a celebration, of man's power over animals.

We remain endlessly fascinated by our relationship with animals today. Famously, we love watching kitten videos on YouTube – celebrations of our power over animals? It's no coincidence that some of the highest-grossing films in recent years have explored the relationship between mankind and animals: *Planet of the Apes*, *The Jungle Book* and *Beauty and the Beast*. The fact that these three films were all remakes of films that were hugely successful the first time around further demonstrates the insatiable appetite we have for such stories. Indeed, *Beauty and the Beast* is considered to be one of the oldest stories in history. The 'Animal Bridegroom' fairy tale, the story upon which it is based, is said to date back 3,000 years. It really is a tale as old as time.

We are also endlessly curious about the relative power between different animals. The question of which is stronger: lion or tiger, gorilla or bear, hippo or crocodile, still endlessly occupies children in playgrounds. It also occupied philosophers in the ancient world. There was always an idea that there was a natural hierarchy between humans and different animals. Aristotle was the first to have a serious shot at classifying and cataloguing this hidden hierarchy in 350 BC when he produced *Historia Animalium* (History of Animals). His work grouped particular animals together based on certain distinguishing features, e.g. that all birds have feathers. It was the grandest biological synthesis of its time.[22]

From this developed the notion of a 'Great Chain of Being'. The best visual depiction of this Great Chain of Being features in *Rhetorica Christiana* or The Rhetoric of Christianity, written by the Franciscan monk and polymath Didacus Valades in 1579. His book was written to help missionaries spread the word. This picture gave them a very clear image to communicate. There is a natural order in the world. Just as there are all sorts of inferior beings beneath us – Satan, soil, vegetation and animals – so there are all sorts of awesome beings above us, God almighty, the angels and archangels. There was an implicit contract in this picture. We must worship God, and in return for that worship, he will grant to us power over animals. This was an understanding of the relationship that ran through all of the Abrahamic religions and it seemed like a good deal.

But there's another aspect to it as well. This ominous, weighty-looking chain which runs right down from God almighty to the base of the earth symbolises that we are all slaves to this hierarchy: that it is completely, totally and utterly inescapable.

When you look at this picture now, 400 years on, it does indeed appear that it is inescapable. The Great Chain of Being remains 'indispensable to our understanding of ourselves, our world and our language', as Professors Lakoff and Turner put it in *More than Cool Reason*. Whether we're religious or not, we all still abide by all of the essential precepts of this picture. We all imagine there's some great force in the sky (God, Buddha or, more recently, Stephen Hawking). We all imagine there's something evil below (the devil, Beelzebub or just hot lava). We all also have a clear understanding of the relationship between the animals in this picture.

It is harder to think of more powerful and enduring imagery than that which is contained in this picture, part-icularly when it comes to social status. By positioning people at different points, we can instantly lift up those we do like, elevating them to the height of angels or gods, whilst bring-ing down those we don't like, reducing them to the status of lowlifes or dregs. With this image, we can produce feelings of awe and authority, family and familiarity, disgust and degra-dation, depending on our wishes.

And everyone would get it! We talk and think about ani-mals so much anyway that by referring to almost any animal on that picture you can instantly summon up a whole range of immediately recognisable meanings and associations. You call someone a cow, you're saying they're fat, stupid, docile, they're always eating, and basically, they're nothing more than useless hunks of flesh. But it goes beyond that too. You're also saying that they're fundamentally subor-dinate and inferior and that your life is worth more. And you're also saying your superiority over them is God's will.

It's a lot to get out of one syllable, isn't it? And that's only the beginning.

Everything that sits on the Great Chain of Being has this capacity to invoke powerful associations: the meaning of everything in that picture is so well engrained. Throughout history, people have always naturally sourced metaphors from this picture anyway, from Cicero to Shakespeare. Indeed, Shakespeare was a master of the art of dehumanisation. 'A pox o' your throat, you bawling, blasphemous, incharitable dog!' (*The Tempest*). 'Sblood, you starveling, you elf-skin, you dried neat's tongue, you bull's pizzle, you stock-fish!' (*Henry IV, Part I*). 'Poisonous bunch-back'd toad!' (*Richard III*).

This was clearly something Magritte had thought about as well. In his essays, he wrote that the bourgeoisie stratagem for preserving their class interests 'consists essentially in falsifying the natural relations between man and his world'. In his art, he regularly mixed humans with animals. He depicted men on leashes, women with horns and men with horses' heads. In *L'Invention collective*, he showed a woman's body washed up on a beach, with a fish's head. *Découverte* displays a beautiful naked woman, with feline patches of fur. *La Bonne Fortune* reveals a man in a suit with a pig's head. These are irresistibly arresting images and are amongst his best-known works.

the Beatles, probably inspired by Magritte, also spent a lot of time mixing humans with animals. I don't know if it was an ultimately aborted attempt to create another concept album in the mould of *Sgt Pepper* or simply all the drugs they were taking but, between the summer of 1967 and the summer of 1968, literally every single member of the Beatles wrote or recorded at least one song which explored the metaphor of humans as animals.

John Lennon wrote 'I Am the Walrus', 'Hey Bulldog' and 'Everybody's Got Something to Hide (Except For Me and My Monkey)'. He said that the latter song was about him and Yoko (she was the monkey), referencing the racist abuse Yoko had received.[23] Monkey is an old racist epithet for Asians, a simple short-hand way to depict them as subhuman. Lennon had used the term himself a couple of years previously after the Beatles had experienced a run-in with the police on their tour of the Philippines. After being accused of snubbing the Marcos family, they were literally kicked out of the country by Filipino police officers. Describing that altercation with officers which took place at the airport, Lennon said, 'We got kicked and pushed about by some monkeys and were very frightened.'[24]

Ringo Starr wrote 'Octopus's Garden' during a boating holiday with Peter Sellers, imagining a peaceful world away from the stresses of the Beatles. This song was not released until *Abbey Road* but, as George Harrison said:

I find very deep meaning in the lyrics ... All the things like 'resting our head on the sea bed' and 'We'll be warm beneath the storm ...' It's like this level is a storm, and if you get sort of deep in your consciousness, it's very peaceful. So Ringo's writing his cosmic songs without noticing.[25]

Paul McCartney wrote 'Rocky Raccoon' and 'Blackbird'. He explained 'Blackbird' was a song about the 'black people's struggle in the Southern states, and I was using the symbolism of a blackbird. It's not really about a blackbird whose wings are broken, you know, it's a bit more symbolic.' This beautiful song of hope for black people seemed to fit perfectly with the spirit of the American civil rights movement at that time. The principal line in 'Blackbird', 'You were only waiting for this moment to arise', sounded like a postscript to Martin Luther King's 1963 speech 'I Have a Dream' and a prelude to Maya Angelou's 1978 poem, 'Still I Rise'.

George Harrison wrote 'Piggies', which was about capitalists. Almost certainly inspired by a combination of Magritte's *La Bonne Fortune* and Orwell's *Animal Farm*, in Harrison's version the piggies didn't even pretend to be equal. The big piggies who picked on the little piggies were disgusting, lacking empathy and possibly cannibalistic. 'You can see them out for dinner, with their piggy wives, clutching forks and knives, to eat their bacon'. Harrison also included a call to action. 'In their eyes, there's something lacking. What they need's a damn good whacking'.

Many of these songs featured on their 1968 double album, *the Beatles*, known universally as *The White Album*. This was far and away the most conceptually advanced album they'd ever produced, both musically and linguistically. It was also the first album the Beatles put out on Apple. The album was plainly revolutionary and subversive from the get go: the album opened with the roaring sound of 'Back in the USSR' – a song which flipped on its head the then British Prime Minister Harold Wilson's 'I'm Backing Britain' campaign and became a celebration of communist Russia, making our arch enemy at the height of the Cold War appear cool and charming with Paul's jubilant, whooping rocking out à la Chuck Berry and the Beach Boys.

Most of the human/animal songs were bunched together halfway through side 1. 'Blackbird' and 'Piggies' shared extraordinary similarities: not only did they use the metaphor of humans as animals, they also combined a conservative style with a revolutionary message. Indeed, both were written in what must be the most conservative style imaginable: that of J. S. Bach. Paul McCartney admitted he based 'Blackbird' on Bach's chord progressions in 'Bourrée in E Minor'. 'Piggies', too, featured a harpsichord solo towards the end, which was redolent of a Bach prelude. The effect of the song was the same as a Magritte picture: lulling you in with the promise of familiarity, then hitting you with revolutionary lyrics. 'What they need's a damn good whacking'. The world was shocked. But the shock the world felt at hearing the fab four singing these subversive songs was nothing when they heard what Charles Manson had done in response to hearing this album.

Manson was an ex-convict from Cincinnati, Ohio. Having spent most of his life in federal facilities, in the late '60s this extraordinarily charismatic and charming figure created a quasi-communal cult in California. The commune comprised 100 or so mainly middle-class women who spent most of their time talking about philosophy, listening to music and taking acid. They came to be known as the Manson Family. When *The White Album* was released, Manson played the record to the Family over and over again. He knew what the lyrics meant. the Beatles were sending a message. It was a call to arms. The revolution was on.

On 25 July 1969, just nine months after *The White Album*'s

release, members of the Manson family went to the house of Gary Hinman, a music teacher and PhD student at UCLA, who they believed to be wealthy. After days of torture in which his ear was slashed, Hinman was stabbed to death. After the killing, one of the Manson Family wrote 'POLITI-CAL PIGGY' on the wall in Hinman's blood.

Less than two weeks after that, on the night of 8 August 1969, the actress Sharon Tate was hosting a dinner party at her Hollywood home when the house was invaded by members of the Manson Family. That night, five people, including Sharon Tate (who was eight and a half months pregnant at the time), were killed. The word 'PIG' was daubed on the front door of the house in Tate's blood.

Then, the following day, on 9 August 1969, two retail owners, Leno LaBianca and his wife Rosemary, were also brutally murdered by members of the Manson Family. This time, 'RISE' and 'DEATH TO PIGS' were written on the walls, whilst 'HEALTER SKELTER' (*sic*) was written on the refriger-ator door, all in Rosemary LaBianca's blood.

Manson explained his motives to the district attorney: 'It's the Beatles, the music they're putting out ... These kids listen to this music and pick up the message, it's subliminal.' In a 1970 interview with *Rolling Stone* magazine, he elaborated: 'The music is bringing on the revolution: the unorganized overthrow of the establishment. the Beatles know in the sense that the subconscious knows.' Manson explained that songs like 'Blackbird', 'Piggies' and 'Helter Skelter' foretold a bloody apocalyptic race war.[26] In court he said:

Is it a conspiracy that the music is telling the youth to rise up against the establishment because the establishment is rapidly destroying things? Is that a conspiracy? The music speaks to you every day, but you are too deaf, dumb and blind to even listen to the music ... Why blame it on me? I didn't write the music.

How a beautiful song like 'Blackbird' could inspire someone to kill is insane, but self-evidently it did play a role, given the appearance of lyrics at the crime scene. And it seems that, not only did the words of these songs inspire the fact of the killing, they even influenced the manner of the killing. The victims were forced to suffer a particularly protracted and agonising death because they were stabbed with forks and knives, in reference to the line in Harrison's song 'Clutching forks and knives to eat their bacon'. Rosemary LaBianca was stabbed forty-one times. Wojciech Frykowski, a screenwriter and one of the guests at Sharon Tate's dinner party, was stabbed fifty-one times. It's unimaginable how one human could inflict such inhumanity upon another.

But here's where the pernicious power of metaphor is really revealed: because although we all understand that killing humans is wrong, most of us believe that killing animals is fine. Indeed, for humans to kill animals is not only normal, many believe that is our natural imperative and our God-given right. It's the order of things.

Cognitive scientists are clear that our language, thought and behaviour are all interlinked: that the way we speak determines how we feel which, in turn, governs how we behave. So if we speak about people as piggies, we perceive them as pigs, which makes it permissible to treat them like pigs. In this way, the metaphor can turn the whole world on its head. It can make the abhorrent sound acceptable, the illegitimate sound legitimate and good people can turn evil. The danger is greater under the control of an authority figure like Manson.

You may have heard of the famous Milgram experiments in the early 1960s where the Yale psychologist Stanley Milgram tested how far people would sacrifice their morals, under orders from an authority figure. He told the participants they were taking part in a test which was exploring the role of punishments in learning. They were told to deliver electric shocks to people who got answers in a test wrong. The strength of those shocks would increase the more answers they got wrong. Milgram's experiment was devastatingly effective. He found that 65 per cent of people were prepared to administer a life-threatening electric shock.

In the 1970s, psychologist Albert Bandura reran the Milgram test, but this time with a significant variation. He wanted to test the role of dehumanisation in moral disengagement as well. So he reran the experiment, but he then split the participants into three different groups. For the first group, in what appeared to be an accidental side remark, the lab assistant muttered that the subjects 'seemed like a nice bunch of people'. With the second group, the lab assistant made no comment at all. With the third group, again in what appeared to be an accidental side remark, the lab assistant said, 'These people are animals.'

You wouldn't have thought such off-hand comments would make too much difference. And, at first, they didn't. Each of the three groups happily administered low levels of shock. But as the errors continued and the severity of the shocks was required to increase, a dramatic difference emerged. Despite continual errors, the first group of students went no higher than level 2 on the gauge. The second group of students went as high as level 5. The third group, though, who had been told that the subjects were animals, went to level 8 on the gauge. That's the power of dehumanisation. Just four words means four times the electric shock.[27] That's how easily the human becomes inhuman. You Are Not Human.

We all know that Hitler depicted the Jews as vermin and six million people were killed. Contemporaneous studies show that during the Holocaust the German people were largely aware what Hitler was doing but, because the dehumanisation had been so ruthlessly effective, they simply did not care. So the question I'm posing in this book is what if this dehumanisation was taking place in the world today? Would we know? Would we care?

I'm going on a journey to explore how different social groups are depicted in today's world, using the ancient picture in *Rhetorica Christiana* as my metaphorical guide, from bottom to top. So, who's right down at the bottom? Hell fire. We're back in the USSR.

TROLL

'The Russian disinformation campaign has already begun. There has been a 2,000 per cent increase in Russian trolls in the last twenty-four hours.' That was how Dana White, chief spokesperson for the Pentagon, responded when she was challenged about the success of America's latest Syrian bombing mission in her press conference on 14 April 2018. President Trump had tweeted the facts. 'Mission Accomplished!' Everything else was fake news: the product of Russian trolls.

Every physical war has always been matched with a war for information. Now, with most information flowing in this weird world of cyberspace it is much harder to control where it's coming from. American intelligence has been warning for some time about the malign influence of Russian trolls. As a 2017 Defence Intelligence Agency report put it:

Russia employs a troll army of paid online commentators who manipulate or try to change the narrative of a given story in Russia's favour. Russia's Troll Army, also known as the Internet Research Agency, is a state-funded organization that blogs and tweets on behalf of the Kremlin. Trolls typically post pro-Kremlin content and facilitate heated discussions in the comments sections of news articles. Their goal is to counter negative media and 'Western influence'. While the goal of some trolls is to simply disrupt negative content, other trolls promote completely false content.[28]

Whether or not you believe Dana White's extraordinarily impressive and precise calculation of a 2,000 per cent in crease in Russian trolls, one thing is certain: there's certainly been an exponential increase in the amount we're talking about Russian trolls. According to Google Trends, in April 2018, for the first time ever, there were more references on the internet to Russian trolls than to Russian dolls. And these Russian trolls were being blamed for pretty much everything – Brexit, Trump, fake news. But what do we mean when we talk about trolls?

Today, references to trolls invariably refer to people who are being provocative or offensive on the web, usually on social media. In my childhood, though, a troll was something completely different: it was a wicked subterranean demon that conjured up wicked spells and curses, the sort you found in fairy tales, like *Three Billy Goats Gruff* or in games like Dungeons and Dragons.

The original idea of trolls actually dates back to fourteenth-century Norse mythology. Trolls feature prominently in Scandinavian storytelling, one notable example being *The*

Snow Queen by Hans Christian Andersen, the book which inspired Disney's *Frozen*. *The Snow Queen* tells the story of a troll who distorts perception using a magic mirror. With that mirror, he can make good people appear bad and transform beautiful landscapes into boiled spinach. This is a fair depiction of what internet 'trolls' are alleged to do, but of course by depicting them as trolls, we are committing exactly the same crime for which we are condemning them. In fact, it's worse. It's not just distortion, it's demonisation. It's reducing them and plunging them straight to the bottom of the Great Chain of Being.

We've always been terrified by the idea there are demons in our midst. These fears have endured in various forms from the birth of the Abrahamic religions to the medieval witch-hunts of the sixteenth century through to the anti-communist witch-hunts of the US in the '50s, right up to *True Blood*, *Twilight* and *Stranger Things*. As David Frankfurter, Professor of Religious Studies at Boston University argues, defining people who are different to us as demons, sorcerers or vampires provides a source of instant horror and pleasure.[29] It's possibly because we can all see a little demon inside ourselves that this is such a source of fascination. And, of course, no conversation about the internet today is complete without reference to trolls.

'Troll' is a relatively new term in this context. It first appeared in 1992. The first time I noticed the word being used in a major national context was in 2014 when the story emerged about a woman from Leicester, Brenda Leyland, who had sent more than 400 offensive tweets about Gerry and Kate McCann, the parents of Madeleine McCann, the young girl who went missing from a holiday resort in 2007. Leyland was demonised across the front page of all of the newspapers for sending these tweets. She was widely described and condemned as a troll. But just days after the story came out, she took her own life in a Leicester hotel room.[30] That was the first time the word 'troll' appeared on my radar. Now it features all over the place; but, just recently, it's been all about the Russians.

I have to confess, in a strange kind of way, it feels peculiarly reassuring to hear the Russians being talked about as demons again. I grew up in an age of *James Bond* and *Rocky IV*, so this all feels very familiar, a bit like pulling on a pair of old slippers. It almost rouses a sense of nostalgia for my teenage years, those days of Sony Walkmans, cassettes and Kenny Everett shouting 'Let's bomb Russia' at Conservative Conference. It was back in the 1980s that this whole idea of the Russians being evil really got going, so let's wind the clock back and see how it all began.

Ronald Reagan's speech to the National Association of Evangelicals on 8 March 1983 came at a critical time. NATO had committed to massively increase their nuclear arsenal on the Western front, deploying an extra 464 USAF-109G ground-launched cruise missiles and 108 US Army Pershing II ballistic missiles, but there was intense public concern. It is easy to forget how different things were then: the Cold War was at its peak, tensions were running high, and the threat of nuclear war was very real and profound. Local authorities had actually issued guidance to households on what to do in the event of a nuclear assault (as I recall, it was basically to remove a door from its hinges, prop it up against a wall and then hide behind it – it didn't offer much comfort).

People were protesting all across Europe. Tens of thousands of women were camped out at Greenham Common. But it was not just in Europe that Reagan faced opposition, he faced difficulties at home as well. Across the White House, his party and right across the country, people were split.

The views of the church on such matters are critical in the States. God and the President are seen as inextricably intertwined, the President effectively regarded as God's emissary on earth, a theme to which we will return, but, on this issue, Reagan had already seen he could not bank on the church's support. The National Council of Churches and the Synagogue Council of America had already voted against further nuclear stockpiling. The National Conference of Catholic Bishops also seemed to be heading that way. The National Association of Evangelicals was the only group which remained undecided. They were split down the middle, with fiercely anti-communist conservatives on one side and vehemently anti-war Quakers on the other. Reagan, a Republican whose support was rooted in the Bible Belt, needed their backing. This was an argument he had to win. This issue could come to define his presidency. The speech would be critical.

Anthony R. Dolan, a Pulitzer Prize-winning former journalist, was given lead responsibility for writing the speech. In the States, speechwriting is not simply regarded as a work in poetry, it's an opportunity to make policy, to test and advance arguments: a chance to check for wonky planks in the thinking. Famously, it was during the writing of Lyndon B. Johnson's 1967 re-election speech that LBJ came to realise that his policy on Vietnam was flawed. After numerous drafts, he realised he simply couldn't make the case for escalating the conflict. A speech that was originally meant to announce an increase in the war effort ended up announcing a de-escalation. That's how high the stakes were.[31] The speech to the National Association of Evangelicals was critical, and it could go either way.

Anthony R. Dolan thought he had just the plan to help Reagan win this argument. He wanted Reagan to call the Soviets *evil*. He'd been trying to do that for over a year. He'd made his first attempt back in spring 1982 when he'd been working on a speech that Reagan was due to make to the British Parliament in the summer, at the special invitation of Margaret Thatcher. Dolan's first draft of that speech branded the Soviets evil on no fewer than five occasions. Cautious diplomats, however, had gone through the draft and removed each and every reference. In the end, the only nod to Dolan's strategy came in the form not of a statement, but a lame rhetorical question – 'Must freedom wither in a quiet, deadening accommodation with totalitarian evil?'

Curiously, Dolan's inspiration for the imagery of evil had originally come from Winston Churchill. To gain inspiration for Reagan's speech to the British Parliament, he'd flicked through some of Churchill's old speeches, including his famous 1946 'Iron Curtain' lecture, delivered in Fulton, Missouri. In that speech, Churchill had alluded to the impending battle between East and West as a battle between good and evil, through the more subtle imagery of a light and darkness metaphor. 'The dark ages may return … A shadow has fallen … I have, however, felt bound to portray the shadow … An iron curtain has descended across the Continent … The iron curtain which lies across Europe … Even in the darkest hours … These dark years of privation'.

Using the metaphor of dark and light was a vaguely ambiguous and characteristically British way of alluding to evil. Whereas American politicians can and frequently do explicitly invoke God and Satan in their rhetoric, any British politician that tried that would be out of a job quicker than you can say Tim Farron. We've had many openly atheist Prime Ministers and those who do have faith try to keep quiet about it. As Alastair Campbell famously said when he was Tony Blair's official spokesman, 'We don't do God.' Dark and light is our go-to way of invoking these things.

Dolan had no need for such restraint. In America, they don't just do God, they get Jesus, Mary and Joseph as well. With some nifty footwork, Dolan finally managed to get Reagan to deliver the speech he wanted – deploying that age-old speechwriter tactic of circulating the draft at the very last minute, so no one has any time to comment. And so it was that on 8 March 1983, just after 3 p.m., the President rose to make his speech to the National Association of Evangelicals with Dolan's draft before him.[32]

Reagan opened up with characteristic humility, levity and a self-deprecatory joke about the inherently unholy nature of most politicians. With the icebreakers out of the way, he moved to the important theme of his speech. Religious servitude meant freedom, and freedom meant religious servitude. It was religious servitude that had made America great, but their religion was under attack. It was under attack at home, with increased promiscuity and rising abortions which he announced a range of measures to tackle – cue sustained applause; and it was also under attack abroad. The audience clearly behind him now, his voice quivering with emotion, he got to the real meat of his speech.

We know that living in this world means dealing with what philosophers would call the phenomenology of evil and what theologians would call the doctrine of sin. There is sin and evil in the world, and we are enjoined by Scripture and the Lord Jesus to oppose it with all our might.

He quoted Lenin's scepticism about supernatural powers as proof the Soviets were evil. Then he went all Churchillian: 'We will never compromise our principles and standards. We will never give away our freedom. We will never abandon our belief in God. We will never stop searching for a genuine peace.'

He then shared a story that encapsulated the sacrifice believers might be called upon to make. He almost seemed filled with disbelief as he shared a story that really does defy belief.

A number of years ago, I heard a young father, a very prominent young man in the entertainment world, addressing a tremendous gathering in California... I heard him saying, 'I love my little girls more than anything... [But] I would rather see my little girls die now, still believing in God, than have them grow up under communism and one day die no longer believing in God.' There were thousands of young people in that audience. They came to their feet with shouts of joy. They had instantly recognised the profound truth in what he had said.

Having unleashed his emotional *pièce de résistance*, he brought his speech to a climax, sending a succession of powerful rhetorical waves crashing down upon the audience. He said communism was the 'focus of evil in the modern world...' He described the crisis as 'a spiritual one, at root. It is a test of moral will and faith.' He urged the audience to 'beware the temptation of pride to blithely declaring yourself above it all', which he said would be to 'ignore the facts of history and the aggressive impulses of an evil empire'. This was a 'struggle between right and wrong and good and evil ... a test of moral will and faith.'

When Reagan finished, the audience rose instantly to their feet and roared with approval. After his run-in with the diplomats over the House of Commons speech the year before, Dolan must have felt vindicated, and would have felt entitled to indulge himself in a little smug smile of self-satisfaction. It had clearly done the job. It wasn't diplomacy so much as drama, and it had been expertly delivered by one of the greatest political actors the world had ever known – which is exactly as it should be with political rhetoric.

John Yorke, who is Britain's top screenwriter, involved in many of Britain's top dramas, from *Life on Mars* to *East-Enders*, explained the connections to me.

The language of Reagan is the language of the Hollywood blockbuster. There is no more easily digestible narrative than simple good against evil. It powered the Westerns that were the bedrock of the studio system, just as it powered *Star Wars*, *Rambo* and *Fast and Furious*. Everyone identifies with the good guy and wishes to stop the bad guy.

It's ridiculously simplistic – reducing any enemy, whatever their complex motivations, to an 'other', a non-person. For if they are a non-person you cannot empathise with them. Binary narratives are deeply reductive and largely stupid. But they're also the most readily digestible and powerful form of story.

Drama is an essential dimension to political rhetoric, which is why there's a revolving door between the worlds of screenwriting and speechwriting. Peter Benchley was Lyndon B. Johnson's speechwriter before going on to write *Jaws* (even naughtily naming Jaws' first victim, Kintner, after his old White House boss). Jon Favreau left speechwriting for Barack Obama to pursue a screenwriting career in Hollywood. One of my old colleagues in Whitehall, James Dormer, went from writing speeches for Europe Minister Peter Hain to writing screenplays for Nicolas Cage…

Anthony R. Dolan could probably have gone on to write *Star Wars* after writing this speech.* But not everyone was impressed. Columnist Anthony Lewis wrote an article titled 'Onward, Christian Soldiers', in the following day's *New York Times* in which he described Reagan's strategy as 'primitive [and] dangerous'.

What is the world to think when the greatest of powers is led by a man who applies to the most difficult human problem a simplistic theology…? What must Soviet

---

* Indeed, in a sense he did. Just two weeks after the 'Evil Empire' speech, on 23 March 1983, Reagan delivered his now infamous 'Star Wars' speech, announcing plans for a space-based missile defence system which never quite got off the ground.

leaders think? However one detests their system, the world's survival depends ultimately on mutual restraint... For a President to attack those who disagree with his politics as ungodly is terribly dangerous.[33]

Lewis was right. The strategy was 'terribly dangerous' and real lives were at stake. For, whilst in Britain and America the Cold War was largely about rhetoric, in other parts of the planet, the Cold War was only too real.

Efraín Ríos Montt became President of Guatemala following a coup in March 1982. Montt was a member of a Christian fundamentalist church based in California, where Reagan had previously been Governor. Montt believed he was on a God-sent mission to wipe out communism. On his brutal march to power and in the months that followed he oversaw the killing of more than 200,000 Mayan Indian Guatemalans in what is now known as the Silent Holocaust. Attacks were unspeakably cruel. Babies were smashed into walls. Old men were thrown down wells. Girls were gang-raped. How could such crimes against humanity be committed in the name of God? The pastor of Montt's church explained: 'The army doesn't massacre Indians. It massacres demons, and Indians are demon possessed; they are communists.'[34]

It's not dissimilar to Manson logic, but Montt's stratagem came with the signed, sealed approval of the President of the United States. Ronald Reagan stood beside Montt on 4 December 1982 and declared him to be 'a man of great personal integrity'.[35] He said he knew that Guatemala was facing a 'brutal challenge from guerrillas', and vowed that the United States would support Montt's efforts 'to address the root causes of this violent insurgency.'[36] Later, on the very same day that Montt had stood beside Reagan to hear these words, Montt's elite forces headed out to a small hamlet called Dos Erres in the north of Guatemala and committed the most unbelievably savage and needlessly brutal attack.

Women who were pregnant had their bellies slashed and foetuses removed. An old woman was decapitated and her head was kicked around like a football. Children were thrown into the air and speared with bayonets. Men were hammered to death. One twelve-year-old girl described her experience: 'They started raping me ... I don't know how many times ... I lost consciousness ... The blood kept running ... Later I couldn't even stand or urinate.' Over 200 people were killed in all that night. And this was not an isolated episode. Amnesty International documented literally dozens of similar events occurring across Guatemala throughout the 1980s.

In 2011, four Guatemalan soldiers were sentenced to life imprisonment for the killings in Dos Erres.[37] However, one could argue that the person who really should have been held to account was the President who had ordered the attacks. Eventually, in 2013, thirty years after the event, an 87-year-old Ríos Montt was finally put on trial for genocide. Dozens of witnesses testified about rapes, massacres, forced displacement and other crimes. Montt was found guilty and sentenced to eighty years in prison but, before the ink was even dry on the ruling, the case was dismissed on technicalities. A new trial was ordered but that retrial never took place. Montt died on 1 April 2018.[38]

The demonisation of ethnic groups in Guatemala left behind a legacy. Rumours of Satanism remain rife and lynchings are common. This is the problem: you can't conjure up terrifying images of devils and demons one day and then expect them to vanish the next simply because you've gone. The images linger on, handed down from generation to generation.

Nothing better illustrates this than the story of Catarina Pablo, a young mother from Todos Santos Cuchumatán, a small village in the remote highlands of Guatemala. On 29 April 2000, Pablo was taking her young daughter out shopping in the market when a large black tour bus with dark tinted windows drove in. There were twenty-three Japanese tourists on board. Rumours had been circulating in the town for several days that Satanists were heading to the town, looking to steal children for use in some wicked satanic sacrifice. All-night prayer meetings were convened. Schools were closed.[39] The police assured citizens they had a plan for dealing with 'the dark forces' but as the villagers watched the bus roll in, they could not help but wonder, was this them?[40]

The tourists emerged from the bus. Moments later, Catarina looked down. Her daughter had vanished. Panic ensued. She called out for her child but there was no response. Friends and relatives called out. Still no reply. Within seconds, the locals were circling around the Japanese tourists waving their fists, demanding, 'Where's our child? What have you done?' The tourists were confused and bewildered. They didn't understand what was going on. The locals began pulling at the tourists' clothes and slapping them. 'Where's our child?' The locals grabbed their cameras and smashed them to the ground. The violence swiftly escalated. Crates were thrown. They started beating the tourists with sticks.

Shocked by how quickly the violence was escalating, the bus driver, Edgar Castellanos, tried to push everyone back on to the bus, but he was too late to protect everyone. One of the tourists, a forty-year-old property developer named Tetsuo Yamahiro, was pushed to the ground and kicked in the sides. Then someone took a rock and smashed it in his face. He was killed instantly.[41]

Edgar Castellanos pleaded for the other tourists to get back on the bus. They did, but then the locals started rocking the bus from side to side, throwing bricks at the windows. Someone grabbed Castellanos and brought him to the ground. They kicked him, beat him with sticks and hacked at him with machetes. Then someone poured gasoline over him and lit a match. Five hundred locals stood by and watched as he burnt to death before their eyes.

Then, Catarina felt a small hand slide into hers. She looked down and saw her daughter looking up at her with her big brown eyes. 'Mama?'

Three people were later charged with the murders – two men and a woman. All three were acquitted.[42] Judge Josue Felipe Baquiax explained, 'We simply couldn't condemn these people.'[43] He considered their actions defensible in light of Guatemala's terrible history. This is the thing, we're a long time on from Reagan's 'Evil Empire' speech but still the consequences rumble on. Anthony Lewis's article in the *New York Times* was right. Demonisation is 'terribly dangerous'.

Not that politicians will ever stop depicting their opponents as evil. The truth is that it's simply the most effective way to convince a nation that wants desperately to sit around on their sofas watching telly, eating nachos and sloshing back a big two-litre bottle of Coke that they have to get up and fight. Every generation needs its own definition of evil. It's the President who gets to call it. Twenty years after Reagan, that responsibility passed to George W. Bush. As he embarked on his round of demonisation, many would agree the depiction was absolutely apposite.

Many of us will never forget where we were when the Twin Towers fell in New York. 9/11 was a day that shook the whole world. Professor Lakoff, who grew up in New Jersey, captured the memories and images of that day in his powerful essay 'Metaphors of Terror', written just a few days after the attack.

> The devastation that hit those towers that morning hit me. Buildings are metaphorically people. We see features – eyes, nose and mouth – in their windows. I now realise that the image of the plane going into South Tower was for me an image of a bullet going through someone's head, the flame pouring from the other side, blood spurting out. It was an assassination. The tower falling was a body falling. The bodies falling were me, relatives, friends. Strangers who had smiled as they had passed me on the street screamed as they fell past me. The image afterward was hell: ash, smoke and steam rising, the building skeleton, darkness, suffering death.[44]

Many people around the world would share Lakoff's revulsion and reflections on that day. What we all saw was indeed an image of hell. So when President George W. Bush declared his war against terror, he could count on support from pretty much everyone around the world: Democrat and Republican, East and West, Christian and Muslim. But then Bush started extending his ambitions. He started stretching the demonisation far beyond the realms of the original perpetrators of the 9/11 attacks in pursuit of all sorts of other foreign policy objectives.

David Frum and Michael Gerson were responsible for crafting Bush's 2002 State of the Union address. Like Dolan twenty years earlier, they too sought inspiration in old speeches. They flicked through Franklin D. Roosevelt's old Second World War speeches, as well as Ronald Reagan's 'Evil Empire' speech. The phrase 'Axis of Evil' that they created for George W. Bush was basically a cut-and-shut job between these two sources of inspiration: the axis bit came from Roosevelt, the evil came from Reagan.

Karl Rove, Bush's senior adviser, loved it: he thought it was a signature phrase, giving the country 'a great mission', defining the problem 'in graphic, biblical terms without publicly committing to a particular solution'. Frum explained later that it was Gerson who demanded the speech contain 'theological language'.[45] Like Reagan's 'Evil Empire', the 'Axis of Evil' provided a brilliant rallying cry, turning a geopolitical ambition into a moral crusade.

The only trouble was that it was based on zero logic. There was no Axis of Evil. There was no alliance between Iran, Iraq and North Korea. The relationship between these three countries actually veered somewhere from absolute ambivalence to complete hatred. Frum himself acknowledged that the connection was flimsy. So the Axis bit was a bit dodgy, but so too was the reference to Evil.

Iran's relationship with America had actually been improving over the last few years. Secretary of State Madeleine Albright's formal apology to Iran in March 2000 for the United States' role in the overthrowing of Prime Minister Mohammad Mosaddegh back in 1953 had removed a major sticking point in their previously strained relationship. Moderates in the Iranian Parliament were keen to move forward from this and continue to strengthen their ties with the West. Iran had expressed early support for Bush's 'War against Terror'. They had helped the US with efforts to oust the Taliban from Afghanistan. Jack Straw, Britain's Foreign Secretary, had visited Tehran and been received warmly just weeks before Bush's 'Axis of Evil' speech.

Middle Eastern political experts Daniel Heradstveit and G. Matthew Bonham spoke to members of Iran's opposition to assess the full impact of that 'Axis of Evil' speech.

It has weakened the position of those who support a détente with the USA.

The Axis of Evil is a slap in the face of all those who trusted the USA.

When Bush used the term the Axis of Evil, it was as if he hit the moderate forces in Iran with a hammer.

Bush is pouring oil on the flames of anti-Americanism.

Iranians who were previously neutral to the USA have unfortunately changed their views and are now against the USA.[46]

And so it was that in Iran the public hostility to the United States which had been quelled in recent years resumed with renewed vigour. American flags were burnt and people marched, chanting 'Death to USA'.

By declaring Iran evil, they effectively guaranteed that Iran would call America evil in response. It is what the US psychologist and philosopher Sam Keen describes as 'adversarial symbiosis': where two enemies create a shared delusional system, a paranoia *à deux*. It is a phenomenon which can be observed in all walks of life. If a man calls woman a *bitch*, the woman is likely to reply that he's a *beast*. If police officers call members of a community *scum*, that community will probably reply by calling the police *pigs*. If people call politicians *snakes*, then those politicians will probably call them *trolls*. It's not very grown-up. It's playground politics. And this is the playground which President Trump now dominates, legs astride, a petrol can in one hand, a lit match in the other.

Later on, we will don waterproof clothing to wade through the metaphors of Mr Donald J. Trump – remember this is a man who rose to office on a 'drain the swamp' ticket – but he is of course a fan of demonisation. We shouldn't be surprised. His personal mentor was Roy Cohn, the controversial lawyer who prosecuted the McCarthy hearings in the 1950s, widely acknowledged to have framed Julius and Ethel Rosenberg for spying, a crime for which they were executed.[47] And Trump's political hero was Ronald Reagan. And, after years fronting *The Apprentice*, he was much more au fait with drama than diplomacy. And it showed.

In his very first speech to the United Nations on 19 September 2017, Trump addressed North Korea with a Reagan-like clarion call: 'If the righteous many do not confront the wicked few, then evil will triumph.' In a splendid example of adversarial symbiosis and rhetoric, Kim Jong-un quickly replied saying he would 'tame the mentally deranged US dotard with fire'. Everyone reached for their dictionaries and the world watched with wonder as shortly after, they became best friends. Then they weren't friends. Then they were again. Who knows what state their relationship will be in by the time you read this book.

Trump hasn't said too much about Putin. To be fair, their relationship would probably best be described in Facebook terms as 'it's complicated': this may explain his uncharacteristic ambiguity. But the US intelligence and defence establishment are being completely unambiguous in their depictions of Russia. For them, we are right back in the Cold War, Russia is evil again. There's lots of Russian trolls. And their view is also being echoed by the British government. Boris Johnson said that doing a deal with Putin was doing a 'deal with the devil'.[48]

It's all very confusing. I'm not quite sure what's happened. Twelve years ago, I was writing speeches for British Cabinet ministers, with full input and advice from the Foreign Office, heralding a new era of Russian–British relations, joking about *Teletubbies* being translated into Russian and waxing lyrical about our 'deepening and broadening' relationship.[49] Putin was President then just as he's President now. Was he good then and evil now? Do people really change that fast? Or is just that we want him perceptions of him to change?

I can't help but suspect that when political leaders demonise someone, in any sense or fashion, what they are really saying is: 'We disagree with them.' That's what the term 'troll' really means – this is someone I have a disagreement with – and it's not just being used in a geopolitical context; it's being used with alarming frequency by politicians on all sides, usually just as a way of silencing anyone who criticises or challenges them, thereby avoiding difficult debate and challenge. But the trouble is that when you label people trolls, you take away their humanity, delegitimise their opinion, and frequently leave them with no other choice than to get louder and louder, taking increasingly dramatic steps until those in power have no option but to listen.

This takes us on to the next chapter.

VEGETABLE

Kate James and Tom Evans cuddled up with their baby boy in the Maternity Ward of the Liverpool Women's Hospital and were absolutely besotted. Born on 9 May 2016, Alfie gurgled, giggled and did everything a little baby should. Kate and Tom were just eighteen and nineteen and, although Alfie was not planned, they were determined to be the very best parents they could. Tom had completed his apprenticeship to be a plasterer and, with extended families on both sides, they felt ready for anything.

The first sign something was not quite right with Alfie came when he was two months old. One of his pupils started drifting outward. The doctors said he had a divergent squint. Over the next few months, Kate grew increasingly concerned with his progress. She was worried he was sleeping too much, he didn't seem very interested in his toys and he wasn't responding properly to other people.

Then, on 14 December 2016 Alfie suffered a violent seizure. Kate and Tom rushed him to the Accident and Emergency

Department at Alder Hey Children's Hospital. The doctors checked him over and observed further seizures. They gave Alfie some sedatives. The sedatives seemed to work but then, two days later, Alfie suffered a rapid deterioration in his condition and fell into a deep coma.

He was transferred to the paediatric intensive care unit and put on to a life support machine. Over the weeks and months which followed, a succession of doctors came and examined him. It was clear that he had suffered some kind of devastating degenerative neurological disorder, but no one was quite clear what had happened and no one could give a cast-iron diagnosis.

The months went by. Tom, Kate and their extended family visited Alfie every day, stroking him, playing music to him, talking to him, surrounding him with love. The clinicians continued to support Alfie too: monitoring his condition and maintaining his life support system, but they were growing increasing sceptical about whether it was right for Alfie to live.

We don't know exactly when it was that the doctors first expressed their doubts to Tom about whether Alfie should live, or exactly what they said to him. But based on various statuses posted by the family on social media, they clearly had several conversations with Tom between November and December 2017, some of which he recorded at the time in Facebook updates.

The first warning came at the beginning of December when Tom posted that doctors intended 'to end [Alfie's] life by pulling plug' (*sic*) because Alfie was in a 'semi-vegetable state' (*sic*).*

---

* Although Tom reported the doctors had described Alfie in a 'semi-vegetable' state, I suspect from the subsequent medical reports that they probably said to him that Alfie was in a 'semi-vegetative' state.

Tom rejected this perspective. Alfie was clearly not a vegetable – semi or otherwise. Tom had a different view. Tom saw Alfie as a human being. And more than that, Tom saw him as a very special human being. Indeed, having seen Alfie continually defy doctors' expectations over the previous months, overcoming bouts of pneumonia and coughs, he saw Alfie as a fighter.

On 20 December 2017, Tom Evans posted another video, showing Alfie apparently conscious, rejecting outright the hospital's diagnosis.

He wrote the following status:

How can this be a semi vegetable state?? What is a semi vegetable state? Alfie we will fight for you we know you are aware of your surroundings and can felt [*sic*] us buddies and we will do all in our power to fight for your strong little life. #alfiesarmy #alfiesfight #alfiesright #alfiesbattle

That one status update encapsulates the different perspectives which lay on either side of this tragic argument about Alfie's life. Note how the two viewpoints were almost entirely dependent on metaphor. Of the fifty-two words in that status, seven were metaphorical: there were two vegetable metaphors and five war metaphors. These reflected the two different perspectives. Alder Hey viewed Alfie as a vegetable. Tom viewed Alfie as a soldier. The question was not which of these metaphors was true – neither was *literally*; the question was which of these metaphors would prevail. This is how many arguments are determined. The challenge is to come up with the metaphor that sticks.

It might seem peculiar that such an important decision of life or death can be reduced to metaphor; paradoxically, the more emotional the question we are grappling with, the more likely we are to turn to metaphor. Ask someone how old their mum is and they will just tell you. It's a simple factual question. Ask them what their mum means to them and they will invariably quickly turn to metaphor: 'She's the light of my life,' 'She's my rock,' 'She's an angel.' The presence of emotion stimulates our imagination. This brings out metaphor.

That's why metaphor is particularly prevalent in the language of healthcare. Not only because it's emotional, but also because what we're trying to describe is frequently intangible. The metaphor makes it concrete. It gives you a way to perceive it. Say you've got depression, you might perceive it as an animal (black dog), the devil (the demons have returned) or a burden (I've got the weight of the world on my shoulders)... The metaphor helps us make sense of the unknown. It provides certainty in place of ambiguity. This is why metaphor is so appealing in cases like this.

But in Alfie's case, there were two different metaphors and they were wholly in conflict. It was hard to see any room for compromise between such dramatically differing positions. How could a compromise be found when the issue was life or death? In the end, it was clear. It would have to go to the courts to decide.

In January 2018, Alder Hey applied to the High Court for permission to remove Alfie's life support machine. The case was allocated to the Hon Mr Justice Hayden in the Family Division. It was Mr Justice Hayden's responsibility to determine what should happen, in Alfie's best interests.

Medical experts from around the world came and gave evidence in the days and weeks that followed. Tom cross-examined many of the witnesses himself, preparing carefully, asking challenging and probing questions. Mr Justice Hayden clearly made great efforts to handle the case sensitively. He visited Alfie in hospital, at the request of Tom and Kate, and he said that when he arrived there he was greeted with great courtesy and warmth.

Then, on 20 February 2018, Mr Justice Hayden delivered the judgment Kate and Tom had been dreading. Acknowledging that his judgment would be devastating for Tom and Kate, he concluded: 'The continued provision of ventilation, in circumstances which I am persuaded is futile, now compromises Alfie's future dignity and fails to respect his autonomy. I am satisfied that continued ventilator support is no longer in Alfie's best interest.'

There were two words that stood out in Mr Justice Hayden's 12,000-word judgment: the idea that Alfie was in a 'semi-vegetative state'. The reason these two words stood out was simple: Mr Justice Hayden intended them to stand out. He put these words in bold and in italics, one of only two occasions he did so within the whole judgment. By using bold and italics, he made sure they demanded our attention. So let's give them that attention.

What does it mean to say someone is in a 'semi-vegetative state'? What does that mean? Is this a term that has any scientific, clinical or medical meaning? A search through *The Lancet* produces zero results. And if you Google the term 'semi-vegetative state', almost all references are in respect of the Alfie Evans case: 23,000 out of 28,000 references. A friend of mine who is a doctor informally surveyed a large group of his fellow doctors on an online medical forum. None of them had heard of the term either. One asked if 'the judge [had] become confused'.

I don't think Mr Justice Hayden had become confused. In this case, he was simply reporting the medical evidence which had been presented to the court. The term 'semi-vegetative' had come up twice in the hearings: once in the evidence of Dr Samuels (one of Britain's top paediatricians), and also in a report from the Bambino Gesù Hospital in Rome. Mr Justice Hayden was simply repeating their language, trusting the view of the experts.

But 'semi-vegetative' seems a peculiar phrase for medical experts to use. How can a baby be vegetative? My own science education stopped at GCSE Human Biology but even I know that human beings have a wholly different cellular make-up to vegetation. So what did the medical experts mean?

By describing Alfie's condition as vegetative, they were resorting to metaphor. It appears to have been Aristotle (yup, him again) who first developed the metaphorical idea that a brain had three parts: a vegetable, animal and human brain. This was used to signify loosely what we might now know as the instinctive, emotional and logical brain. By using this source, he was summoning up the same imagery of the natural hierarchy that we also see in the Great Chain of Being. It was a powerful reference point of course but, nevertheless, it was still only a metaphor and it was by no means the only metaphor for a brain. There is a wide variety of possibilities. For instance, Plato saw the three parts of the brain as chariot, horse and rider. More recently, psychologist Jonathan

Haidt has talked about the brain through the metaphor of the elephant and the rider, with the elephant being the unconscious. People often use technology metaphors for the brain: it might be the brain as a machine – hearing the cogs whirring, steam coming out his ears, got a screw loose; or the brain as a computer – resetting, downloading, going into shut-down.

So, with this array of metaphorical possibilities on offer, why was the metaphor of vegetation being used? What does that say about Alfie's condition? This is not just 'you are not human'. It's not even 'you are an animal'. As the Great Chain of Being shows, vegetable is beneath even animal.

So what's the effect of the vegetative metaphorical framing? What are the feelings that the metaphor of vegetation engenders? I know what it suggests to me: absolutely nothing. Not a bean. The idea of vegetation attracts no emotion or feeling in me whatsoever. Indeed, the very thought of vegetables and vegetation leaves me in a state of profound ambivalence. Whether they are on a plate, in a shop or six feet underground, I simply couldn't care less. And that's kind of the point really. Because we should care, shouldn't we? Is ambivalence a feeling we really want swirling around when we are debating an issue of life or death? Isn't speaking about a child as vegetation bound to remove compassion? Who was it that brought this way of thinking into mainstream medical discourse?

Meet Hellmuth Unger. Unger was born in 1891, the son of a construction worker from Nordhausen, a small industrial city between Leipzig and Hanover in Germany. Unger studied medicine and worked as an army doctor during the First

World War. Whilst in service, he was also active as a writer, sending reports in from the front line. However, in 1915, an injury brought his army career to a premature end. He returned to Leipzig and set up practice as an ophthalmologist, specialising in diseases of the eye.

During the 1920s, Unger built up his practice, but he continued writing plays, poems and articles. His passion was really in his writing so, as soon as he'd experienced his first taste of success, he closed his practice down. He went from being a literal doctor to become a spin doctor. In 1933, he started working for the newly established Enlightenment Office for Population Control and Racial Care, reporting in to the Reichsärzteführer, Gerhard Wagner. Wagner had been instructed to move public opinion on a particularly sensitive area of policy – euthanasia – seen as vital to achieving Hitler's vision of a clean and pure race.[50] Euthanasia was something which was attracting increasing support around the world at that time, including within intellectual circles in New York and London, but it was still very controversial. Even Hitler knew such a policy could only be introduced with careful preparation and clear public support.

So it was that, in 1936, Dr Unger came to write the novel *Sendung und Gewissen* or 'Mission and Conscience'. This tells the story of a woman with multiple sclerosis who is suffering terrible pain. She begs her husband, who is a doctor, to give her a fatal dose of morphine. Her husband, a loving man, obliges. He administers the fatal drug as a family friend plays romantic piano music in the background. It is, you might say, a good death ('euthanasia' derives from the Ancient Greek words for a good death – *eu* and *thanatos*).

But, following her death, her husband is charged with murder and brought to trial. His colleagues are prepared to invent an alibi for him, but he refuses to let them, defiantly insisting he has done nothing wrong. Before the court, he passionately argues that killing his wife was in her best interests. He implores them, 'Would you, if you were a cripple, want to vegetate further?' The court takes pity, agrees that the murder was an act of mercy and he is acquitted. The book ends with a quote from the Renaissance physician Paracelsus: 'Medicine is Love.'[51]

The novel was a massive success and was later made into a play and even a movie – *Ich klage an*, or 'I Accuse'.* When the film came out, fifteen million people went to see it.[52] It even won an award at the Venice Biennale and the director received a special bonus of RM 30,000 from Goebbels. But presumably Goebbels's award was less concerned with the film's artistic merits than its impact on public opinion. In that sense too, Unger's story was a roaring success and Hitler won the backing that he needed to execute his programme of euthanasia. Under 'Aktion T4', 70,000 German citizens were killed between 1939 and 1941. Their crime was to suffer such conditions as epilepsy and schizophrenia, and 5,000 children were also killed under this programme, for conditions ranging from Down syndrome to dyslexia.

One might have expected the language of vegetation to fall out of favour along with the Nazis, but it reappeared in 1972 when Scottish neurosurgeon Bryan Jennett and American

---

* In 2012, a French film *Amour* was released which covered similar theme to 'Mission and Conscience'. It went on to win multiple awards including Oscars, BAFTAs and the prestigious Palme D'Or award at the Cannes Film Festival.

neurologist Fred Plum wrote an article for *The Lancet* called 'A Syndrome in Search of a Name'. This article had set out to find a name for those patients whose 'responsiveness is limited to primitive postural and reflex movements'. Jennett and Plum concluded that these patients 'are best described in persistent vegetative state'.[53]

With this paper, Jennett and Plum hadn't just given the syndrome a name, they had established an incredibly potent way of seeing and thinking about such patients. They had created the canvas. It wasn't long before a number of others stepped forward, paintbrushes in hand, ready to add further details to this emerging picture.

In 1973, bioethics professor Joseph Fletcher lamented the 'incorrigible human vegetables eating up private or public financial resources in violation of the distributive justice owed to others'.[54] In 1976, the philosopher John Lachs expressed distress at the 'gardens that flourish in our major hospitals – the thousands of human vegetables we sustain on life-preserving machines. I cannot make myself believe that the unconscious vegetables in our hospitals are in any sense human.'[55]

When language changes, so do attitudes, and finally behaviour. So it was that just a year after the publication of Jennett and Plum's paper, the previously unthinkable occurred: two doctors at Yale University, Doctors Duff and Campbell, deliberately withheld treatment from forty-three babies born with 'birth defects'. All of the babies died. The doctors defended their decision in an article entitled 'Shall This Child Die?' in *Newsweek* on 12 November 1973. They admitted breaking the law, but argued that the law had to be changed to deal with such so-called '*vegetables*'. The doctors said, 'The public has got to decide what to do with vegetated individuals who have no human potential.'[56]

The article aroused a furious response, not least from Sondra Diamond, who was a counselling psychologist from Philadelphia and life-long sufferer of cerebral palsy. She wrote a letter to *Newsweek*, published on 3 December 1973.

I'll wager my entire root system and as much fertilizer as it would take to fill Yale University that you have never received a letter from a vegetable before this one, but, much as I resent the term, I must confess that I fit the description of a 'vegetable' as defined in the article, 'Shall This Child Die?' Due to severe brain damage incurred at birth, I am unable to dress myself, toilet myself, or write; my secretary is typing this letter. Many thousands of dollars had to be spent on my rehabilitation and education in order for me to reach my present professional status as a Counselling Psychologist. My parents were also told, 35 years ago, that there was 'little or no hope of achieving meaningful "humanhood" for their daughter'. Have I reached 'humanhood'? Compared with Doctors Duff and Campbell I believe I have surpassed it! Instead of changing the law to make it legal to weed out us 'vegetables', let us change the laws so that we may receive quality medical care, education, and freedom to live as full and productive lives as our potentials allow.[57]

Diamond won some sympathy from medics. Dr R. Lamerton, a medical officer at St Joseph's Hospice in London who was pioneering a new more compassionate approach to palliative care, wrote an article for the *Nursing Times* in 1974 entitled

'*Vegetables*?', in which he argued that the new language served no other purpose than to make clinicians despise those they were supposed to protect, pointing out that these names would inevitably reduce 'our whole willingness to care for them and give to them our best'. He particularly objected to how unscientific it was to talk about people as vegetables.

> What is scientific about it? Wherein does an unconscious man resemble a vegetable? Photosynthesis? Roots? Edibility? Science implies precise observation, confirmed by demonstration, leading to logical conclusions. I challenge anyone to demonstrate to me the vegetable attributes of a man.[58]

Despite Lamerton's objections, the vegetative metaphors prevailed; as the language became normalised, so perceptions of life became altered. The extent to which attitudes had shifted became obvious in the early '90s when a life-or-death decision was called for following the most horrific event ever to be witnessed in the history of English football.

On 15 April 1989, Liverpool had just begun playing Nottingham Forest at Hillsborough Stadium in the FA Cup semi-final when the most appalling crush occurred. The police had lost control outside. They opened a turnstile, allowing a large number of fans to come in. In images that still remain scorched deep on the national conscience to this day, ninety-four people were killed that day, and two more subsequently died from their injuries. A further 766 were injured and the many thousands more left traumatised.

One of those injured in the crush was eighteen-year-old Tony Bland, a Liverpool fan who had been near the front that day. His ribs were crushed, puncturing his lungs and depriving him of vital oxygen to the brain. After a year, the doctors diagnosed him in a 'permanent vegetative state'. Three years after that, and with no improvement in his condition, they applied to the High Court for permission to withdraw life support. It was a landmark case and became known as the 'right to die' case.

The case was controversial and generated a heated national debate. Finally, in a ground-breaking judgment delivered in November 1992, the president of the Family Division concluded there was 'no reasonable prospect' that Tony would emerge from his coma and that he should be allowed to die.[59] This was the first time in English legal history that a court had permitted a patient to die through the removal of life-prolonging treatment, including food and water. So it was that on 3 March 1993, Tony Bland became the ninety-sixth person to die as a result of the Hillsborough tragedy.

But Tony Bland was not the only person to be diagnosed in a permanent vegetative state after Hillsborough. So too was Andrew Devine, but Devine's life support machine was not turned off. In 1994, five years after the disaster and one year after the death of Tony Bland, Devine's family were convinced they had seen him following a moving object with his eyes. He continued to show further signs of consciousness and, by March 1997, he had started communicating with his family again using a 'yes' and 'no' switch.[60] Today, Devine lives at home with his parents. His life is difficult – there is no doubt about that – but he is aware of his surroundings, he enjoys touch, he can eat pureed food on his own and his family describe him as 'the centre of the family and the glue which holds us together'. He even went to the twenty-fifth anniversary commemoration of the Hillsborough disaster at Anfield.[61]

When Devine first emerged from his permanent vegetative state, the medical profession was astonished. Dr Keith Andrews, director of medical and research services at the Royal Hospital for Neuro-disability, said at the time that it was a unique case.[62] But there have since been other cases of people emerging from these so-called 'permanent vegetative states'. Some of these were referenced in a 2003 *British Medical Journal* paper. One of these cases included the extraordinary story of a 27-year-old man who had been diagnosed in a permanent vegetative state who woke up to say, 'I want to eat sushi and drink beer.'[63]

Some estimates suggest that as many as one in five diagnoses of PVS are wrong.[64] How can anyone truly be sure what's going on behind closed eyelids? Adrian Owen, a neuroscientist at Western University, is one person who thinks there might be more than meets the eye. In 2014, working with Lorina Naci, then of the University of Western Ontario, he put twelve healthy volunteers in an fMRI scanner and showed them an eight-minute edited version of the Alfred Hitchcock film *Bang! You're Dead!* The film is filled with dramatic tension, depicting a young boy wandering around his neighbourhood with a partially loaded gun, pointing the weapon at people and pulling the trigger. Owen then played the same film to a 35-year-old man who had been in a vegetative state since age seventeen, monitoring his brain activity on a scanner. The fMRI scanner revealed almost identical responses in his brain to that which had been observed amongst the healthy people.[65]

This is an area where there is clearly some doubt. Indeed, Tony Bland's father, Allan, had doubts about his son. He said, 'I used to think that he pulled a face when his fingers were extended to have his nails cut, despite Dr Howe's explanation that Tony could not possibly feel anything.'

The trouble is that it is very hard to challenge doctors. We all naturally struggle to challenge anyone in authority, as Milgram showed. Neuroscientists have shown that when we are listening to people who we perceive to be expert the part of our brain that deals with critical scrutiny effectively shuts down. This is likely to be exacerbated with doctors. The MORI veracity index shows doctors are one of the most highly regarded of all the professions, with a trust rating of 91 per cent, compared with politicians, journalists and estate agents who each score less than 20 per cent.[66] We have a strong tendency to go along with them, right or wrong. One study by Charles K. Hofling showed that twenty-one out of twenty-two nurses were prepared to administer what they knew to be a fatal dose of medicine if they were told to do so by a doctor. What's more, in Hofling's research, the instruction came from a doctor the nurse didn't even know. It was just someone claiming to be a doctor on the phone. The pressure to simply nod along is immense. It's all very tricky, particularly when we are talking about our loved ones.

I should make clear at this point: I'm not taking a position either way on these issues of euthanasia, assisted dying or whatever you want to call it. I genuinely am not sure what I feel about all this. I certainly do not have a fixed view. Like most people, my opinions swing depending on the context. These are hideously complicated dilemmas in which we would all feel conflicted. But isn't that the point? It is precisely in cases of such conflict that we should keep the language clean. When we are dealing with dilemmas as complex as these, the last thing we want is dissonant voices muddling our thinking, inexorably persuading us to follow a path that could be wrong and from which there could be no turning back.

The term 'permanent vegetative state' is fundamentally misleading. There may not be anything permanent about the condition. Nor is there anything vegetative about a human being. Even Bryan Jennett, the man who originally coined the phrase, conceded the phrase should be dropped.[67] The Australian National Health and Medical Research Council are also now campaigning for the term to be withdrawn. Many of the doctors I spoke to also argued it should go, saying it was inappropriate and needlessly upsetting for relatives.

Nevertheless, its use is increasing. Hansard records just one single use of the term 'vegetative' in parliamentary debates in the nineteenth century, twenty-three uses in the twentieth century and now, just eighteen years into the twenty-first century, it's already been mentioned sixty-seven times. As issues of assisted dying are being debated, such language could prove instrumental. The word 'vegetative' has a great power.

In 2011, Kurt Gray, T. Anne Knickman and Daniel M. Wegner of the University of Maryland and Harvard University explored the impact of the vegetative metaphor. They found its power was profound and led to a quite topsy-turvy turnaround in people's perceptions. They revealed that we attribute to people who are dead more of the attributes associated with being alive than we do to people who are in a vegetative state. Yes, you read that right. People consider dead people are more alive than people in a vegetative state.[68] That's ludicrous. It's surreal. That is the power of metaphor.

I wanted to go deeper. I wanted to check the impact of using the term 'semi-vegetative state' specifically in the case of Alfie Evans. One of my researchers stood outside Finsbury Park in the first week of April 2018 and surveyed 200 people asking if they agreed that Alfie's life support machine be turned off. She asked the first 100 people using the straight medical terminology which was used to describe Alfie's condition in the hearing, i.e. that Alfie had an 'unknown degenerative neurological disorder'. The second 100 people were asked using the metaphor, referencing the term 'semi-vegetative state'. These were two descriptors used by clinicians to describe the same child yet the difference the metaphor had on the results was extraordinary.

QUESTION 1

Alder Hey Children's Hospital in Liverpool is about to turn off the life support machine of Alfie Evans. Alfie Evans is a 23-month-old boy who has spent most of his life in a coma. Doctors have said Alfie has an unknown degenerative neurological condition. Do you think it is right that his life support machine is turned off?

Agree: 23
Don't know: 34
Disagree: 43

QUESTION 2

Alder Hey Children's Hospital in Liverpool is about to turn off the life support machine of Alfie Evans. Alfie Evans is a 23-month-old boy who has spent most of his life in a coma. Doctors have said Alfie is in a semi-vegetative state. Do you think it is right that his life support machine is turned off?

Agree: 47
Don't know: 19
Disagree: 34

This is an astonishing swing. Using the term 'semi-vegetative' more than doubled the amount of people who agreed Alfie should be allowed to die. In terms of opinion polling and attitudinal change, from 2:1 against to 3:2 in favour is pretty extraordinary. That is the power of metaphor.

So the fact that all of the press was reporting Alfie was in a 'semi-vegetative state' should be very concerning. It made a huge difference to how people felt about this case.

But there was one person who wasn't going to accept the verdict. After Mr Justice Hayden delivered his judgment, Tom Evans delivered a defiant and impromptu speech to reporters outside the High Court.

'Can you believe that my son has just been sentenced to a death penalty? ... This isn't over. This is just the start. I am going to take this absolute NHS down.'

The fight metaphor was clearly uppermost in Tom's mind. I analysed all of Tom's posts to the Facebook page and found that, over a total of 8,000 words, he used a war or conflict metaphor on 129 separate occasions, which is once every fifty-seven words. War is a powerful metaphor which is frequently used to rally people – a war on crime, a war on drugs, a war on litter – and, using social media, Tom was able to amass incredible support and phenomenal sympathy for Alfie's plight. The Alfie's Army Facebook page attracted almost a million members and 600,000 people signed a petition demanding Alfie's reprieve.

We saw earlier how patients dislike the war metaphor because it makes them feel under attack. In the Alfie Evans case, it was the other way around. It was the doctors who didn't like it. They felt intimidated and under attack from Alfie's Army.

Merseyside Police deployed dozens of officers to the hospital. There were genuine concerns about public order. The chairman and chief executive of Alder Hey, Sir David Henshaw and Louise Shepherd, issued a joint statement:

> We have endured attacks upon our motivation, our professionalism and our ethics. It has been a very difficult time… Our staff have received in person, via phone calls, email and through social media channels a barrage of highly abusive and threatening language and behaviour that has shocked us all.

Tom pursued every last legal option available to him. US Vice-President Mike Pence offered him his support. So too did Pope Francis. The Italian ambassador to the UK granted Alfie Italian citizenship and offered him safe passage to Rome.

Nevertheless, on 23 April 2018, after numerous appeals and hearings, Alfie's life support was removed. Doctors had told the court that they expected Alfie to die in minutes. In fact, he did not die until five days later. Tom Evans finally announced his death on Facebook on 28 April 2018, saying, 'My gladiator lay down his shield and gained his wings … absolutely heartbroken.'

Mr Justice Hayden had said that one of his main concerns in this case was to ensure that Alfie had dignity. Dignity was not something that was always afforded to anyone who came out in favour of Alfie Evans. Some of his online supporters were depicted as 'trolls'. The protestors outside were labelled a 'circus'. Members of the family were called 'scum'. The judge described the father's grief as 'almost primal'.[69] And, of course, what started it all off in the first place, Alfie was described as 'semi-vegetative', or as Tom heard it, 'semi-vegetable'.

The first principle of the NHS is based upon respecting everyone's human rights. It's hard to see how anyone's human rights can be respected when we don't even respect their right to be perceived as human.

SCUM

On the morning of 14 June 2017, the whole world woke to the most horrific news. A fire was raging through a 24-storey council block in north Kensington, London. The fire had started just after midnight when a fridge-freezer exploded on the fourth floor. Fire had engulfed the building in minutes, making the inferno instantly visible across the capital. Locals gathered around the base of the tower, many were streaming live videos to Facebook, YouTube and other social media. They screamed up to their friends and neighbours to flee. Some residents tied together sheets, creating makeshift ropes to climb down.

When Theresa May became Prime Minister eleven months earlier, she had pledged to 'fight the burning injustice that if you're born poor you will die nine years earlier than others'. On that morning, smoke still billowing out over London, her metaphorical quest lay in literal ashes. Questions were already being asked. How had the fire spread so quickly? Was the building's exterior cladding, which had only recently been applied, flammable? If so, how had it been signed off? Why had the fire service been instructing residents to 'stay put' in their flats? What was the council's role in all this? Had residents really been warning them that the building was a fire hazard? Rumours spread rapidly. Anger was palpable. People demanded answers.

I know Grenfell Tower well. I grew up in a council estate very nearby and have always lived in that area of London. When you say you come from Kensington, people instantly assume you're posh. It's not true. Kensington is a tale of two cities. You can cross from one side of Ladbroke Grove to the other and find that the life expectancy for residents falls by twenty years. Kensington is deeply divided. There is a rich side and there is a poor side. People on the rich side are pre-occupied with doing everything they can to keep the poor side out – spending huge sums of money on big gates, chauffeur-driven cars and security cameras. People on the poor side are desperate to make it up into the rich side. As a young boy, I used to walk past the houses of local stars like Freddie Mercury, Frankie Howerd and John Cleese, looking up in awe. We'll explore the enticing allure of the star metaphor later, but suffice to say it carries a particular appeal for those perceived to be at the bottom of society: as Oscar Wilde famously wrote, 'We are all in the gutter, but some of us are looking at the stars.'

When I was ten years old, with help from the Royal National Children's Foundation (then the Royal Wanstead Trust), I was scooped out of my council estate and placed in a private boarding school in Hampshire. This was a great break for me, giving me some amazing friends as well as a love of music and language which will remain with me for life. But I can't deny it was weird, coming out of a council estate to live alongside kids who apparently had everything: massive stereo systems, heaps of cash and dads who drove Bentleys. When I heard the kids who lived in local council houses being called 'troggs', I decided to keep my own background quiet. I remember one time, when I was about twelve or thirteen, being dropped off in London by the school minibus after a choir trip to Suffolk. I asked the teacher to drop me a mile away from home because I didn't want anyone to see the estate where I lived. I can't even remember what I was so ashamed of now. My estate was perfectly clean and the residents were good people, but I just didn't want anyone to see it.

In the end, I was expelled from school when I was sixteen. I will never forget getting the train back from Hampshire and walking down the long corridors on my estate: it was the ultimate walk of shame. I was expelled on Thursday and started work the following Monday. I was ambitious and worked hard. I did a range of casual jobs: playing piano in a French restaurant, doing telesales for a number of companies: double glazing, insurance, fundraising – frequently doing a number of jobs at once. This was the age of the 'yuppie' – the young upwardly mobile professional. There were bright Porsches all around that provided an incentive to hard work. I was desperate to move up in the world.

That notion of upward mobility and moving up is a metaphor that is common to all of us. Up is good, down is bad. Like many conceptual metaphors, this is one that starts in infancy and arises from that feeling of looking up to our parents and recognising that height brings power. But it also relates back to the Great Chain of Being. As human beings, the metaphorical story of our life is that we emerge from the soil (the word 'human' comes from the Latin *humus*, meaning soil) and end up higher, closer to God. This is what made living in high-rise towers like Grenfell so attractive. For once, people will look up to you and you can look down on people. The notion of height relates directly to our understanding of our social status.

These connections have never been better presented than in that fabulous '60s sketch from *That Was The Week That Was*.

John Cleese – 'I look down on him because I'm upper class.'
Ronnie Barker – 'I look up to him because he's upper class. But I look down on him because he's working class. I am middle class.'
Ronnie Corbett – 'I know my place.'

My first big chance to move up in the world came when I got an interview to become an executive officer in the civil service. I had already done some casual administrative work in Whitehall but, as I headed for the Civil Service Commission down Whitehall for my interview, I was terrified. I had always been fascinated by politics – *Yes Minister* was my favourite TV programme growing up – and I couldn't believe I was just a few doors down from the office of the real Prime Minister. The interview panel comprised three people: two very precisely spoken tall thin men and a big smiley lady. They were all wearing suits. I didn't even own a suit. I wore a nice burgundy wool jacket I'd bought in Camden and a pair of chinos which seemed to me to be the pinnacle of style. My heart was thumping, I was so keen to make a good impression. I blundered and blustered through a few questions then, halfway through, I totally lost it.

They asked me some question about policy: how would you advise ministers to deal with the issue of joy riders, i.e. young car thieves (an issue that was controversial in the press at the time)? I blurted out some garbage about 'kids today', the importance of discipline, sending a clear message... I stopped and listened to myself. It was like a different person speaking, like I was having an out-of-body experience. I stopped, drew a deep breath and reached for a glass of water. As I did so, I was horrified to see my hands were shaking violently. I looked up at the three panel members, half expecting them to declare me an imposter, point to the door and ask me to leave. Instead, the kindly-looking lady smiled and nodded slowly. She told me to relax and take my time. I drew a deep breath, just about managed to take a sip of water without splashing it all over myself, and the interview proceeded. Ten minutes later, I walked out of the room into a posh Whitehall corridor and promptly burst into tears.

When I received the letter two weeks later telling me I'd passed the interview and was being posted to my first choice department of the Department for Trade and Industry, I assumed they'd either felt sorry for me or made a terrible mistake. Whatever the case, I didn't challenge the decision; within months, I started work at the DTI, and soon bought my first flat at the age of twenty-one: a one-bedroom Victorian conversion in Kensington Olympia for what seemed to be a massive sum: £41,000.

The civil service seemed great too and definitely offered me the chance to move up in the world. Promotions seemed to come every couple of years as long as you worked hard. The organograms that were prepared within the civil service even looked a bit similar to Valades's Great Chain of Being. This sense that grade related to godliness was even embedded in an old civil service joke, as you were rewarded with honours at different stages of your career. It was said about these honours that CMG stood for Call Me God, KCMG stood for Kindly Call Me God and GCMG stood for God Calls Me God.

I won a place on the fast stream programme and then, landed my dream job as a minister's private secretary (like Bernard Woolley's job on *Yes Minister*), working on the top floor of 1 Victoria Street. I felt like I'd gone up in the world. The Private Office Directorate was even called TLO – Top Level Office. I was delighted to get the job and particularly thrilled when I met the minister that I was going to work for on and off during the next ten years: Alan Johnson.

Alan came from the same part of London as me, left school at sixteen like me and played music like me. He wore flash suits, greased his hair back and spoke in a cockney twang. He also liked a laugh, shared my obsession with the Beatles and believed there was much more to life than politics. When people asked if he had ambitions to be Prime Minister, he replied that his only remaining ambition was to have a number one hit record. I can't overstate the difference he made to my life, showing me by example how you can move up in the world. His approach was that of a mod. As the Who's first manager, Peter Meaden, put it: 'Clean living under difficult circumstances.'

I worked with Alan in a number of government departments including DTI, Health and Education. His political focus for much of this time was 'improving social mobility', which basically means giving kids from poor homes the same chances as kids from rich homes. This was a thrilling programme to work on, particularly with Alan. Every week there was some new exciting initiative. Free books were sent to families across the country. Kids in care were given money to buy musical instruments. Public schools were forced to open their playing fields to kids from state schools. As a result of these interventions and massive extra investment, the gap in education closed over these years and so too did the gap in life expectancy. These were huge national achievements. I also made some progress myself. I learnt a bit about some of the things that had held me back in life, particularly in my education. I resolved to put them right so, whilst I was at the Department for Education, I went back to school and gained an MA in Mass Communications. Onward and upward.

But one of the things that struck me during my time in Whitehall was how pejorative the everyday language was in talking about people from poorer backgrounds. This was a Labour government, but much of the talk from the top concerned people living on 'sink estates', going to 'bog-standard' schools, or speaking about bad schools as 'dumping grounds'. And this was not a language that was used in private, but very openly. Such terms came up regularly in conversations and usually, it had to be said, by people who had probably never been anywhere near a council estate in their whole lives. The message was clear. Low-life. The dregs. The underclass. I was particularly conscious of this use of language because one of my main roles as speechwriter was to mediate linguistically between the department and the public, striking a balance between what the department wanted to say and what the public wanted to hear. There was frequently a very large gap.

I found that working-class people were openly described using dehumanising metaphors in a way that would never have occurred had they been black, or gay, or Jewish. It seemed like a curious blind-spot. Indeed, the last piece of legislation put through by the last Labour government was the Equality Act of 2010, which outlawed discrimination on all sorts of grounds – sex, race, disability, religion, belief, height, sexual orientation and age – but which completely failed to deal with the issue of class. This seemed like a whopping omission, particularly given the dominance of old Etonians in high society at that time – with the Conservative leader, a Mayor of London, an Archbishop of Canterbury and Princes William and Harry all having attended a single school.

I couldn't help wondering: why was class discrimination the one issue of discrimination no one wanted to touch? Why did no politician want to go near it? I think that metaphor plays a role. Politicians who want to move up in the world do not believe they will get there by associating themselves with people who are at the bottom. We all understand the metaphorical frame that poor means dirt. What ambitious politician wants to be tarnished with that? Most aspiring politicians want to be associated with virtue, moral purity and cleanliness. You won't get that dealing with the complex and often entrenched problems of long-term poverty, which is why this is something politicians only tend to do when their political careers are over: John Profumo being a case in point.

But where did this link between poor people and dirt arise? In the past, the connection between poverty and dirt was simply a matter of fact. In Renaissance London, it was a huge challenge for someone to make it through the poorer streets 'unbepissed', i.e. without getting splashed by someone's slops being thrown from a window... Edward Bulwer-Lytton famously described the poor as 'the great unwashed' and, when he said this, there is every chance he was speaking literally.

But then, in the nineteenth century, a number of great reformers came along, investing huge amounts of money in public baths and sanitation programmes. Many of these old public baths are still visible. The idea that poor people are dirty no longer has any basis in fact. Friends who work for consumer goods companies tell me that people from poor homes today actually devote more time to their personal hygiene than people from richer homes. But still, mud sticks. Whilst the experience of poverty has changed beyond recognition, those tired, tarnished associations remain and are evident from our everyday language. That estate is a *toilet*. He lives in a *dump*. It's a *shit-hole*.

Shit is a mighty powerful metaphor. It speaks straight to our instinctive brain. Even rodents know to keep their shit well away from where they eat. We feel so strongly repelled by it, that even the mere suggestion of it can fill us with disgust.

Paul Rozin, Professor of Psychology at the University of Pennsylvania, did an experiment with a group of four- and five-year-old children. He offered them chocolate fudge ice cream – that's bound to go down well, you think – but he had curled the ice cream up into the unmistakeable shape of a dog turd. When the children saw the ice cream, they showed every sign of physical disgust as if they had actually come into contact with a bit of real poo. Their eyes thinned, lips curled and noses contracted. As Charles Darwin noted in *The Expression of the Emotions in Man and Animals*,[70] these are powerful instinctive physical reactions designed to protect us – closing our passages and keeping the toxic matter out. But they were reacting like this to ice cream! Just the mere suggestion of poo had made them respond like this. So imagine the effect these associations could have on people too.[71]

Open a newspaper and find a photo of someone. Stare at that photo and repeatedly, 'Shitface. Shitface. Shitface.' Within literally just a few seconds, those words will gather meaning. With each repetition, your conviction will grow. Before long, your face will start manifesting signs of disgust.

And this is what we have done for years with some of our most vulnerable communities. For years we've heard this talk about bog standard schools and sink estates. These estates are toilets or shit-holes. Mud sticks. And this is what we saw with Grenfell Tower. For all the subsequent rhetoric about the community standing united, the truth is that before the fire many of the people who lived in the leafier parts of Kensington regarded Grenfell Tower and the surrounding estates as a no-go area.

Such instinctive fears may still have been lingering after the fire. I found it extraordinary that a whole prime ministerial visit was organised without anyone thinking it would be a good idea for the Prime Minister to meet local residents. Her office claimed it was because of security concerns, but it's hard to imagine those security concerns would not have been immediately overruled if this fire had taken place in the Tory shires. Someone would have found a way around. May's apparent diffidence seemed to confirm for some the very class problems which had led to the fire in the first place and anger flared up in the community.

Ishmahil Blagrove became a national celebrity after an interview he gave to Sky News went viral.

> We have a Conservative borough that has neglected … this community, that does not see this community … that looks down on working-class people in this community … These are the most vulnerable and marginalised people. The council doesn't hear these people. They don't even see them. That's why they went and spent ten million on the façade of a building rather than putting in sprinklers and fire alarms… They're much more concerned about the aesthetics of the exterior of a building … This isn't a race thing. It isn't black or white. It's a class thing… The voiceless people are not heard … Do not give me this bullshit about 'lessons will be learnt'. Do not treat this community like some ignorant low-IQ community. We are not going to be dismissed by hollow platitudes … People should be in jail for this.

Was it true that the council did not hear this community? There was worrying evidence that residents had previously raised concerns about fire safety issues in Grenfell to the Kensington and Chelsea Tenant Management Organisation.

Seven months before the fire, a member of the Grenfell Action group wrote an eerily prophetic blog titled '*KCTMO* – Playing with fire!'

> It is a truly terrifying thought but the Grenfell Action Group firmly believe that only a catastrophic event will expose the ineptitude and incompetence of our landlord, the KCTMO, and bring an end to the dangerous living conditions and neglect of health and safety legislation that they inflict upon their tenants and leaseholders… It is our conviction that a serious fire in a tower block or similar density residential property is the most likely reason that those who wield power at the KCTMO will be found out and brought to justice! … We have blogged many times on the subject of fire safety at Grenfell Tower and we believe that these investigations will become part of damning evidence of the poor safety record of the KCTMO should a fire affect any other of their properties and cause the loss of life that we are predicting.[72]

The council wrote to the author of this blog warning him his comments were 'unfounded', 'defamatory' and constituted 'harassment'.[73] It's not clear, however, if they took any action to address the fundamental points he was making about fire safety.

Blagrove attacked the council for their failings but he also attacked the media for complicity. Addressing the journalist from Sky News directly, he said:

It's you, the media. You are the ones who facilitate this. You are the people that make this possible … You are the ones who validate it. You are just as culpable as the government. You're all in it together. Since Thatcher and Reagan, you've monopolised and capitalised this country … I say fuck the media. Fuck the mainstream. You don't deserve to be there … For two years you've hounded and demonised Jeremy Corbyn. And you said, 'He's unelectable: there's no possibility of this man getting elected.' And you created that narrative and people actually believed that bullshit for a while. But what this election has shown is the people are immune – we're in bulletproof vests – to you and all the billionaire sort of media owners: Rupert Murdoch and all the other motherfuckers.

There was a false media narrative against Jeremy Corbyn. I wrote an article for *Total Politics* in September 2015 pointing it out, arguing media predictions of his failure were 'nothing more than tribal prejudice masquerading as analysis'. Real-time analysis of reporting in the 2017 general election by Loughborough University's Centre for Research in Communication and Culture showed the media was measurably more hostile to Jeremy Corbyn. The day before the election, *The Sun* pictured Jeremy Corbyn's head popping out from a metal bin with the headline, 'Don't chuck Britain in the Cor-Bin'. Trash.

It's ironic that the newspaper that claims to represent the working class persistently condemns them. *The Sun* even turned on the Tory Party after they elected their first working-class leader: John Major. *The Sun*'s editor, Kelvin MacKenzie, displayed an utter contempt towards him. Famously, Major telephoned MacKenzie on the afternoon of Black Wednesday, on 16 September 1992, asking how *The Sun* was going to report the currency crisis. MacKenzie replied, 'Prime Minister, I have on my desk in front of me a very large bucket of shit which I am just about to pour all over you.' Major laughed. 'Kelvin! You're such a wag!'[74] But this is a pretty accurate depiction of what *The Sun* has done to poorer people for many years. In particular, it was *The Sun* that actively took steps to propagate this idea that poor people are scum.

'Scum' was an old-fashioned word, with origins in the early fourteenth century when a scummer, or shallow ladle, was used for removing unwanted debris that had risen to the top of the pot. It was first deployed as a metaphor against the poor in 1580 but was in wide use amongst aristocrats and the governing classes by the nineteenth century. The Duke of Wellington wrote a letter in 1813 to one of his aristocratic friends, describing his army as 'scum of the earth'.[75] As Marxism grew support, sympathisers were regularly described as 'socialist scum'.

The connotations of scum are arguably even worse than dirt or faeces. This is not just talking about people as 'men of the soil'. Scum goes one level further. Scum is dirt which has risen above water. So not only are you dirty, you've risen above your rightful place. If water is the symbol of moral purity connected with hard work, then scum has risen above the hard-working people. This is the opposite of cream rising to the top. The message is clear. You're a cheat, you're dirty and you're subverting the natural order. Get back in your place.

It was under Kelvin MacKenzie's editorship of *The Sun*

that the word came into mainstream use. MacKenzie fought so hard to get the word in use that he inadvertently provoked one of the biggest industrial disputes in the history of Britain. It started in late 1983: the height of the miners' strikes, with tensions running high and miners fighting the police and vice versa. *The Sun* wanted to condemn the miners in the strongest possible terms. Kelvin MacKenzie drafted an editorial which said, 'Miners were rightly once called the salt of the earth. No longer. Too many of them have become the scum of the earth.'[76]

The paper went out for production but, when the printers read the copy, they downed tools and withdrew labour: refusing to print the edition. They were furious to see their union comrades denigrated in such a foul manner. To the 'inkies', the printers who worked on the newspapers, 'scum' was seen as the ultimate swearword, worse even than 'cunt'. They demanded the offending word be removed. MacKenzie, backed by Rupert Murdoch, remained absolutely defiant. The paper was not produced for four days. MacKenzie walked around the printing presses later, laughing and jeering at the inkies, telling them they had 'fucked themselves over'. Four months later, they discovered what he meant. Printing was moved to a new site in Wapping, and the workers lost their jobs. Never again would the printers be able to raise an issue about the word 'scum' or anything else that appeared in the paper for that matter. And, once the word had been normalised in *The Sun*, it came to appear with a startling regularity, not just in the tabloid press, but the mid-markets as well.

Richard Littlejohn is the scum-hating writer extraordinaire. Characteristic of his style is an article he wrote for the *Daily Mail* called 'Welcome to Britain, land of the rising scum' in which he described seeing a family in Blackpool, dressed in matching shell-suits and baseball caps. 'They could just have been scum… I'm going with scum… My guess, though, is that they're both living on benefits in some scruffy council garret, halfway up a burned-out tower block, surrounded by raggedy children… We're now on to second- and third-generation scum…'[77]

Read it. Read it again. Are your eyes thinning? Lips curling? There's a reason why articles like this produce such a strong reaction. FMRI and behavioural studies show that reading about scum produces the same response in the brain as if we had really come into contact with scum. It's called simulation theory. So, if you read about a disgusting smell, the part of your brain that deals with smell is activated.[78]

Now, imagine three million people, all reading this article on a train in the morning, all experiencing the same powerful sensations. This is 'othering'. It's not dissimilar to what Orwell described in the hate sessions of *1984*: a 'hideous ecstasy of fear and vindictiveness, a desire to kill, to torture, to smash faces in with a sledgehammer [that] seemed to flow through the whole group of people like an electric current, turning even one against one's will into a grimacing screaming lunatic'.

It's not just about the way poor people are depicted in the press, it's also about how they're depicted on screen. The 2008 paper 'Chav Mum Scum Mum' by Imogen Tylor at Lancaster University explored how contemporary depictions of the white working class on television were designed to arouse disgust. Owen Jones also covered this in his 2011 book

Chavs: The Demonization of the Working Class, which shone a spotlight on the class prejudice evident in shows like *Little Britain*, which featured extremely wealthy privileged men prancing around mocking extremely vulnerable poor single mums. The problem has got a lot worse since then, though.

Benefits Street first aired on Channel Four in 2014. It was supposedly a docudrama, following the lives of residents in a deprived area of Birmingham but it was actually little more than poverty porn. As former Cabinet minister Clare Short, who grew up in the area featured in the programme, said, all it did was give people the chance to 'judge and sneer' at those less fortunate than themselves.[79] If the intention of the producers was to stir up hate against society's most vulnerable people, it worked. These were some of the reactions on Twitter when the first episode aired.

I want to walk down #BenefitsStreet with a baseball bat and brain a few of these scum bags

#BenefitsStreet They should all be spayed and neutered. Procreation amongst these people just leads to the next generation of pathetic scum.

Why aren't these fucking scumbag was of spaces [*sic*] being hug [*sic*] up and shot. Filming them steel? [*sic*] Just get rid of them. #BenefitsStreet

The residents who took part in the programme complained that they'd been misled. They said the programme makers had made out they were making a show about the power of local community but instead 'we've been made to look complete scum'.[80] One resident attempted suicide.

The programme almost certainly exercised a degree of dramatic licence, but this would not necessarily have been understood by viewers, particularly those with no personal experience of poverty themselves. The then Prime Minister, David Cameron, actually mentioned the programme in the House of Commons in support of his welfare cuts as if he was citing some serious research.[81]

Love Productions, which makes *Benefits Street*, also makes programmes such as *The Baby Borrowers*, *Britain's Youngest Grannies* and *Underage and Having Sex*.[82] These programmes all have at their heart a desire to make audiences feel superior. That's why people watch. There are countless other ventures in the genre, such as *Jamie Oliver's School Dinners*. This showed Oliver visiting the homes of, as he put it, 'white trash' trying to get them off 'junk food'. 'White trash' was a phrase that emerged in the United States in the nineteenth century and it's been central to the debate of class on the other side of the Atlantic, but it is becoming increasingly common in Britain. When Oliver went on Jonathan Ross's programme to promote his show, Ross said, 'Perhaps we should put something in the water to stop some people having children in future.' The audience loudly cheered.[83]

The metaphorical frame here is powerful. When we're talking about sink estates, toilets, shitholes, scum, we demand solutions, even though they are just metaphors. But this is where the metaphor can have a surreal effect, because the metaphorical perception of the problem can prove more powerful than the literal. In the '80s, Thatcher in London and Giuliani in New York both combined anti-litter campaigns with anti-poverty campaigns. Since then, we've had much talk about social cleansing. But, in one more recent episode, the metaphorical frame appeared even more determinative.

In 2011, riots broke out across all of the major cities in the UK, following the police shooting of a young man in London, Mark Duggan. According to the LSE, many of those arrested were white and from deprived backgrounds.[84] It didn't take long for the newspapers to decide which metaphorical framework they'd use to depict these people. The *Daily Express* headline of 10 August 2011 was 'Sweep Scum Off Our Streets'.[85] Similar language was used in a number of other reports. So how do we respond to this? When we see scum in the bath-tub, what do we do? We get the shower and jet-spray it off. This may explain why the Metropolitan Police and the then Mayor of London, Boris Johnson, both felt so strongly compelled to respond to the riots by calling for water cannons. The cannons were eventually purchased at a cost of £320,000.[86] The fact that they were impractical, irrational and also probably illegal seemed to be neither here nor there. At least it satisfied the urge for a 'clean-up'.

Similar responses can be played out at a far more personal level. A homeless man, Russell Allen, fell asleep outside Debenhams in Portsmouth on Christmas night 2016. When he woke up, his socks, trousers and bedding were wet. He looked up and saw a store security guard pointing a hose at him, laughing. 'Enjoy your water bed,' he said.[87] How could anyone act so cruelly? Research shows that when people see beggars, the part of the brain that deals with empathy effectively shuts down. There is reduced activity in the medial prefrontal cortex and higher activity in the amygdala and insula, the areas associated with fear and disgust. So, our capacity for compassion is effectively disabled and instead we feel a strong wish for them to be gone.[88]

I speak to Alex, who has spent time homeless himself, but who is now working as a research officer for The Wallich, a Cardiff-based charity committed to helping the homeless. He tells me ambivalence is actually the least of the problems you encounter living on the street. You regularly encounter frequent verbal and physical abuse, and you never know when that might occur. Even when you are sleeping, he tells me it's not unusual to wake up and find someone urinating on you. *Toilet. Shit-hole. Dump.*

The metaphor is not just instrumental in how society views people in poverty; perhaps the most pernicious aspect of it is the effect it has on poor people themselves. If you spend years seeing, reading and hearing yourself depicted as rubbish, what effect is that going to have on your self-perception, self-image and self-esteem? How are you going to feel when you wake up every morning? What will you see when you look in the mirror? If you believe you're rubbish, why shouldn't you treat yourself like rubbish? Why shouldn't you eat junk food? Why shouldn't you act like trash? Why shouldn't you become a junkie? Is it any wonder rates of obesity and drug addiction are highest in areas of greatest deptivation?

Sarah Wilson was one of the young victims of the Rotherham child abuse scandal. Her autobiography, *Violated*, shows how metaphors dominated perceptions towards her throughout her life. From her first day at school, the other kids mocked her. They told her she looked like 'shit'. Other kids were told, 'Don't play with Sarah! She's got the lurgy! You'll catch her germs!'

She was bullied, and started hanging around with some local Asian men. She was raped for the first time when she was eleven years old. 'They kept telling me it was all my fault. I was a little slag, they said, I was white trash. I'd brought it all upon myself so this was what I deserved: to lie on a dirty, lumpy mattress, awaiting a never-ending queue of men, all old enough to be my dad … Scores of horrible men abused me like I was a piece of rubbish.'

She quickly came to the attention of social services and the police. They scarcely viewed her any more favourably. 'The police saw us as dirty little prostitutes.' Her social workers 'treated us all with utter contempt'. One of her keyworkers, Rita, 'used to look at me as if I was a piece of dog shit she'd dragged in off her shoe'.

Today, Sarah is beginning to get her life back together. However, the same will sadly never be true for her sister, Laura.

Laura, like Sarah, also got involved with local Asian men. When she was fifteen, she fell in love with a slightly older boy called Ashtiaq Ashgar. Their relationship collapsed when she found out he'd been sleeping with other girls. To get him back, she had a brief fling with one of his friends: an older, married man called Ishaq 'Zac' Hussein. Laura became pregnant. Filled with remorse, and desperate to win Ashgar back, she went to his house in the middle of the night. They had a huge stand-up row in the street. He threatened to kill her and hurled abuse at her. 'White trash'. 'Filthy scum'. Ashgar's mother hit her with a shoe and called Laura 'a dirty white bitch'.[89]

The following week, Laura went missing. A big police hunt ensued. Eventually, Laura's corpse was recovered from the local canal. She had been stabbed several times. Hussein and Ashgar were both charged and prosecuted with her murder. Hussein was cleared but Ashgar was found guilty. In summing up the case, Lord Justice Davis said to Ashgar that Hussein 'seems to have regarded girls, white girls, simply as sexual targets. He does not treat them as human beings at all. You got into that mind-set yourself.'[90] He commented that Laura was tossed in the dirty water 'like a piece of rubbish'.[91]

Lord Justice Davis hit the nail on the head. Isn't that the danger? If people are spoken about as rubbish and depicted as rubbish, then surely there is a risk they will be treated as such.

VERMIN

When Luciana Berger, the 34-year-old MP for Liverpool Wavertree, sat down upon the green leather benches of the House of Commons on 3 December 2015, she knew she faced one of the most critical political decisions of her career since becoming an MP five years previously. The House of Commons was debating whether to extend bombing raids from Iraq into Syria. She had to decide whether she was going to vote in favour of those bombings or against. This meant either siding with the leader of the Conservative Party, David Cameron, or with the leader of her own party, Jeremy Corbyn. This was an incredibly controversial issue and Berger had been subjected to intense pressure from both sides. Her constituents had taken to Twitter vehemently demanding she vote against the action in Syria. However, many of her closest political colleagues and natural allies on the Labour benches were voting in favour. Now, as she took her seat in the Chamber, it was for her alone to decide what was the right thing to do.

The atmosphere in the House of Commons for debates like this is different to any other time – and rightfully so, for there can be no more serious question than whether to send armed forces into combat. Such actions frequently reverberate in ways that are never anticipated when the original decision is taken. Wars spill over borders, alliances shift, multilateral institutions come under challenge. The House feels a particular pressure to consider all the ramifications. Relatively new backbenchers like Luciana Berger tend to play a limited role in these debates – attention is mostly focused on the parliamentary grandees whose speeches invariably invoke the ghosts of parliaments past: Churchill, Thatcher, Benn – but their votes are nonetheless critical.

This was not the first time Luciana Berger had been required to vote on Syria. The last time had been in August 2013. On that occasion, David Cameron had sought approval to use military force against Syrian President Bashar al-Assad to deter the use of chemical weapons.

Cameron had taken a measured approach to that debate. His rhetorical style was sober and statesmanlike, almost as if he was deliberately trying to distance himself from the hyperbolic, almost hysterical Tony Blair, who had led Parliament to support the fateful invasion of Iraq back in 2003. Indeed, Cameron referenced that debate, acknowledging it had 'poisoned the well of public opinion'. He continually underlined the differences between the position Blair took then and the stance he was taking now, stressing, 'This is not about invading, it is not about regime change.'

He maintained this measured and moderate position throughout the debate and, for his troubles, he wound up being defeated – 285 votes against to 272 votes for – the first time that a Prime Minister had been refused by the House of Commons on a request to take the country to war in the whole of British history.[92] On that occasion, Luciana Berger voted against the action in Syria, voting alongside her then leader, Ed Miliband.

This time, the context was very different: in Syria, and in British Politics. The Conservative Party was resurgent after an unexpected general election win in 2015, whilst Jeremy Corbyn had recently been elected leader of the Labour Party with a whopping majority, but the majority of the Parliamentary Party were appalled at his victory. Corbyn had spent much of his career attacking Tony Blair and Gordon Brown, and most members of the Parliamentary Party were Blair or Brown loyalists, many of them owing their positions to one of the former Prime Ministers. They wanted him out.

The issue of Syria became a focal point for tensions. Jeremy Corbyn had a long history as fiercely anti-war – he had been one of the few Labour politicians to speak out against Blair in 2003, leading the Stop the War coalition against the invasion of Iraq – and this debate caused all those old memories to resurface. Feelings in the party were running very high. And the higher up you were, the deeper those differences in opinion became. Nowhere was the disagreement more pronounced than between the positions of the leader of the Labour Party, Jeremy Corbyn, who was opposed to the bombing, and his Shadow Foreign Secretary, Hilary Benn, who was in favour.

In the Labour Party's crisis, Cameron saw an opportunity. He calculated that, if he could pull those wavering

backbenchers over behind Hilary Benn – the likes of Luciana Berger – the same ones who had voted against him in
2013, this was a vote he would be able to win – finally making
amends for his previous humiliating defeat. He wasn't going
to take any chances with his strategy this time, though. Out
went the mild, measured Cameron of 2013. In came a new
furious and feverish Cameron: it was Blair 2003 with bells
on.

He explicitly sought to connect recent terrorist attacks in
Europe with Assad's regime in Syria.

[We] have had a full briefing from the Chair of the independent Joint Intelligence Committee. Obviously, I cannot
share all the classified material, but I can say this: Paris…
showed the extent of terror planning from Daesh in Syria
and the approach of sending people back from Syria to
Europe. This was, if you like, the head of the snake in
Raqqa in action. So it's not surprising that the judgement
of the Chair of the Joint Intelligence Committee and the
judgement of the Director General of the Security Service
is that the risk of a similar attack in the UK is real.

So… 'The head of the snake'? Powerful stuff. Words like this
do not slip in to Prime Minister's speeches by accident. Cameron's speech would have been seen in draft form by literally
hundreds of people throughout Whitehall, including senior
officials at No. 10, the Cabinet Office, the Foreign Office,
the Ministry of the Defence and the Treasury. So why was
he talking about snakes? There was no problem with literal
snakes in Raqqa. Where had this idea come from?

I'm a big believer in life imitating art. I can't help wondering if perhaps he got the idea from the US espionage thriller, *Homeland,* that he was watching at the time – he said as much in an interview with Steve Wright.[93] The opening credits of that series featured an audio sample of Hillary Clinton making a speech about Islamist extremism in Pakistan in which she said, 'You can't keep snakes in your backyard and expect them only to bite your neighbours.'[94] It's not much of a leap for him to then see the same metaphor in the context of British intelligence. And it's certainly preferable to think he was inspired by that television drama than by any other source.

For, from his earliest speeches, Hitler referred to the Jews as snakes. In a speech made on 12 April 1922, he said:

> My feeling as a Christian points me to my Lord and Saviour as a fighter ... The Lord at last in his might rose and seized the scourge to drive out of the Temple the brood of vipers and adders ... As a Man I have the duty to see to it that human society does not suffer the same catastrophic collapse as did the civilisation of the ancient world some two thousand years ago – a civilisation which was driven to its ruin through this same Jewish people.

There are multiple other vermin references throughout Hitler's early speeches. He talked about how the Jews 'wormed their way into the families of the upper classes', how they 'spread as a pestilence spreads' and how Germany became a 'refuge where this vermin can enrich himself without restraint'.[95] Andreas Musolff at the University of East Anglia has found many more examples of dehumanisation across Nazi literature, including depictions of the Jews as maggots, bloodsuckers and parasites.[96]

These speeches were critical to Hitler's ascent. As he gained power, and particularly as he gained control over the media, he was able to pump out this insidious imagery at every opportunity: in propaganda posters, public information films and even in schoolbooks.

The infamous Der Stürmer publishing house put out a book of stories for children. One of these was a special Nazi version of Aesop's fable 'The Farmer and the Viper', in which a farmer takes a sick snake into his house and is surprised when the snake recovers and turns on him.

The moral of the tale is saved until the end:

There are poisonous snakes not only among the animals, but also among people. They are the Jews. As long as the poisonous snakes do not sense a victim, they behave like the most peaceful and harmless animals. Only when a victim nears do they show their true face … Just as the snake's bite poisons the blood of its victims, the Jews poison the blood of their host peoples … Just as the danger of poisonous snakes is eliminated only when one has completely eradicated poisonous snakes, the Jewish question will only be solved when Jewry is destroyed. [97]

Snakes occupy an incredibly powerful place in the popular imagination and have the capacity to simultaneously invoke disgust and fear. They are often small, yet they are phenomenally powerful, and can suffocate, squeeze and even swallow us. They are often depicted as a source of terror in popular culture, from *Indiana Jones* to *Harry Potter*.

The snake metaphor is very different to the others we've looked at. Where demons create fear, vegetables provoke ambivalence and dirt demands cleansing, vipers and vermin present an immediate threat – and one that demands nothing less than a complete and utter extermination. As John T. MacCurdy put it in his 1917 essay, 'The Psychology of War', 'We have sympathy for a dog, an animal useful to us, but we will kill snakes and insects without any revulsion or feeling for the act.'[98] And it's a metaphor that has long been used in connection with the Jews.

All of the main religions have depicted Jews as snakes, including, in fact, within Judaism itself. Hitler's own story about the Jews being driven from the Temple comes from the Gospel according to Matthew, the first book of the New Testament, written in 80–90 AD. In that, the Jews are castigated by Christ: 'You snakes! You brood of vipers! How will you escape being condemned to hell?'[99] In Islam, the thirteenth-century Muslim writer Al-Jaubari characterised the Jewish people as snakes in *The Chosen One's Unmasking of Divine Mysteries*.

Why snakes in particular? It may be connected with the blood libel. The blood libel is a recurring anti-Semitic trope based upon false stories that Jews feed on the blood of Christians. It is said that the blood of Christian children is needed to make matzah, bread for Passover. This story has existed and circulated in various forms for hundreds of years. It first appears to have emerged after the murder of twelve-year-old William of Norwich in the twelfth century, when it was alleged he had been murdered by Jews for his blood. That allegation led to the expulsion of the Jews from Britain in 1290 – what Jonathan Sachs has described as the first wave of anti-Semitism in Britain.

You can see how the idea of the blood libel would readily lead to parasitic or snake metaphors and this is imagery that has persisted for many centuries now. Martin Luther, the German Reformation leader, wrote a vicious 65,000-word anti-Semitic diatribe in 1543 called *On the Jews and Their Lies*. The opening pages alone are stuffed full of snake metaphors, referring to 'these poisonous envenomed worms' who should be drafted into forced labour or expelled for all time. This deeply religious man also used the metaphor to justify killing: 'We are not at fault for slaying them.' Luther's text proved immensely influential on Hitler and he used the snake metaphor, not only to depict the Jews as deceptive, murderous, greedy – feeding off the blood of the German body politic, but critically, to legitimise their extermination.

It was in this way that Hitler was able to make the Holocaust seem like a reasonable course of action. As Aldous Huxley put it in a speech at the Albert Hall in 1936:

> Most people would hesitate to torture or kill a human being like themselves. But when that human being is spoken of as though he were not a human being... we lose our scruples. All political and nationalist propaganda aims at only one thing; to persuade one set of people that another set of people are not really human and that it is therefore legitimate to rob, swindle, bully and even murder them.[100]

The snake metaphor was, to use the German word, *Lebens lüge*: a lie that enables people to live with a clear conscience. Viewed as subhuman, Jews could legitimately be abused and beaten, their synagogues burnt down. The perpetrators could tell themselves they were acting in a noble cause. Nobody wants to believe they're a bad person, so people learnt to justify their own behaviour.

Nazi medic Dr August Hirt reminded his colleagues in the Nazweiler-Struthof concentration camp: 'Remember! The prisoners here are animals before all else.'[101] The SS officer and commandant of the Sobibór and Treblinka concentration camps, Franz Stangl said: 'Before dying the victim must be degraded, so that the murderer will be less burdened by guilt.'[102] '[We had] to condition those who actually had to carry out the policies, to make it possible for them to do what they did.'[103] As Telford Taylor, chief prosecutor in the Nuremberg Trials put it in his opening statement, 'To their murderers, these wretched people were not individuals at all. They came in wholesale lots and were treated worse than animals.'[104]

The metaphors of the Holocaust conditioned not just the fact of the killing, but the manner of the killing. When Josef Mengele, the so-called Angel of Death and chief physician at Auschwitz, was preparing the gas chambers, the poison gas he used to kill his victims was Zyklon B, a cyanide-based pesticide.

We all know that the Nazis dehumanised the Jews. But what is perhaps less well known is that the Allied powers have also dehumanised their enemies in pursuit of military objectives.

The dropping of the atomic bombs on Hiroshima and Nagasaki in 1945 represented the deadliest bombing ever carried out in the history of the planet. The United States knew they had to prepare attitudes before unleashing this mighty and unprecedented power. So, in March 1945, the same month that the United States adopted a policy of low-level incendiary bombing upon Japanese cities, they began cranking up the propaganda. The US Marines' in-house magazine *Leatherneck* featured a picture of a grotesque caterpillar-like animal with a Japanese face.[105] It was described as *'Louseous Japanicas'*. The accompanying text had a semi-satirical tone:

> The first serious outbreak of this lice epidemic was officially noted on December 7, 1941, at Honolulu. To the Marine Corps, especially trained in combating this type of pestilence, was assigned the gigantic task of extermination … Flame throwers, mortars, grenades and bayonets have proven to be an effective remedy. But before a complete cure may be effected the origin of the plague, the breeding grounds around the Tokyo area, must be completely annihilated.[106]

So it was that the metaphorical and conceptual frame for genocide was set. Admiral Halsey, commander of the Pacific fleet, called for 'the almost total elimination of the Japanese as a race'. Elliott Roosevelt, the president's son and confidant, told Henry Wallace in 1945 that the United States should continue bombing Japan 'until we have destroyed about half the Japanese civilian population'.[107] An internal memo at the British Embassy in Washington confirmed that the Americans saw the Japanese as a 'nameless mass of vermin'.[108]

Following the Potsdam Conference, the Allies warned the Japanese that they faced 'prompt and utter destruction' if they didn't surrender. The Japanese ignored this warning and so, on 6 August, a 'Little Boy' uranium gun-type bomb was dropped on Hiroshima, followed swiftly by a 'Fat Man' plutonium bomb which was dropped on Nagasaki on 9 August. These two bombs between them killed well over 100,000 people, most of them civilians.

When the Second World War concluded, with sixty million left dead, most people said 'never again'. In some quarters, however, there were concerns that the killings had not been high enough.

Lieutenant Colonel Dave Grossman was a training officer in the US Army for many years. He has written a number of books on the psychology of killing – what he calls 'killology'. He explains how, at the end of the Second World War, senior officers were concerned that the firing rate – the best measure of a soldier's efficacy – was too low. At the end of the Second World War, it was only 15 per cent. That means that, for every 100 soldiers who got a clear shot at the enemy, only fifteen actually fired. As Grossman puts it, 'That is like a 15 per cent literacy rate among librarians.'

The main problem is that killing is incredibly hard, even for a trained soldier. We are taught from the earliest age that killing is wrong – it is a central tenet for every single religion and culture in the world. We are all brought up to develop the most powerful moral resistance to killing. Overcoming that resistance is not easy, and the associated traumas can be overwhelming.

Chief US Army combat historian S. L. A. Marshall

explained in *Men Against Fire: The Problem of Battle Command*, 'The man who can endure the mental and physical stresses of combat ... still has such an inner and usually unrealized resistance towards killing a fellow man that he will not of his own volition take life if it is possible to turn away from that responsibility. Though it is improbable that they may ever analyse his own feelings so searchingly as to know what is stopping his own hand, his hand is nonetheless stopped. At the vital point, he becomes a conscientious objector.'[109]

Those objections manifest in a multitude of ways amongst even the most hardened killers. Soldiers, gangsters and contract killers can find they flee, lose control of their bowels or go into utter panic at the actual point of killing. I remember in my younger, wilder days being warned by a friend that the person who won every fight was not necessarily the strongest person; it was the one with least scruples. It was the person who would not stop, even when the person they were attacking was pleading, begging for mercy, suffering extreme pain. These are the people that can look at someone else glass-eyed, without any empathy, feeling or compassion. They are the people who can look someone else in the eye and think, *you are not human.*

It's the same with soldiers. In order to overcome the first rule of humanity, first they must believe that they're not dealing with humanity. Seeing the enemy as vermin turns killing from an act of evil into an act of social good; an act of sanitation, rather than extermination. In this way, a group of decent, well-brought-up young men can be turned into efficient and effective killers.

And so, the better the US Army got at dehumanisation,

the more successful they became at killing. The firing rate went up from 15 per cent in the Second World War to 55 per cent by the Korean War and, by the time of Vietnam, it was 95 per cent. At that point, killing had ceased to be a source of dread and was becoming, as Grossman put it, 'a source of entertainment: vicarious pleasure rather than revulsion. We are learning to kill and we are learning to like it.'

One soldier who served in Vietnam admitted as much.

> I enjoyed the shooting and the killing. I was literally turned on when I saw a gook get shot. When a GI got shot, it would bother me even if I didn't know him. A GI was real. But if a gook got killed, it was like me going out here and stepping on a roach.[110]

This imagery of the Vietnamese as vermin came down from the very top. President Lyndon B. Johnson called Vietnam 'a piddling, piss-ant little country'. It was trickle-down killonomics. And within that insidious imagery, US soldiers found permission to commit all manner of atrocities.

Probably the most brutal episode in the history of the Vietnam War came on Saturday 16 March 1968 when 100 soldiers from Charlie Company descended in Black Hawk helicopters upon Mỹ Lai, a small hamlet in the Quảng Ngãi province of Vietnam. They were told the area was 'infested' with booby traps and enemy soldiers and it was their job to destroy everything in their sight.

They arrived at 7.30 a.m. Ronald Haeberle, a photographer who was embedded within the US Army, described what happened next.

There were some South Vietnamese people, maybe fifteen of them, women and children included, walking on a dirt road maybe 100 yards away. All of a sudden, the GIs just opened up with M16s. Beside the M16 fire, they were shooting at the people with M79 grenade launchers ... I couldn't believe what I was seeing.[111]

This little civilian village was subjected to the full might of the US military, which showed no ounce of humanity. Mothers with babies were shot straight through the chest with machine guns. Huts were set on fire and the fleeing inhabitants shot. Women were raped, their bodies mutilated. Two dozen women and children tried to seek sanctuary at a local temple where they fell to their knees, praying and begging for their lives. A soldier walked behind each one, shooting them straight in the back of the head. Mothers held their babies tight to their chests pleading 'No VC [Viet Cong]! No VC!' They were machine-gunned down.[112] As many as 500 people were killed in Mỹ Lai in less than two hours. Not a single bullet was fired back in self-defence.

Harry Stanley was one of the soldiers there that day. He was just twenty years old. When his commanding officer, Lieutenant William L. Calley Jr, ordered him to shoot and kill a group of women and children, Stanley refused.[113] Even when Calley pointed his .45 pistol at Stanley and threatened him with a court martial, he remained defiant. Today, every year on 17 October, Berkeley, California, celebrates 'Harry Stanley Day', where they recognise this extraordinary man's ability to maintain his humanity when all around others were losing theirs.[114] Such people are few and far between. Most people will just follow orders. However, as Stanley explained afterwards, 'Being trained to kill is one thing but murder is something else ... Murder was totally against my nature. You can't order me to do this. It's craziness.'

The dehumanisation had served its purpose, though. As the attack on Mỹ Lai demonstrated, the US Army would not have much problem getting its soldiers to kill in future, notwithstanding the exceptional Harry Stanley. But there was a price to pay. The more the US increased its firing rate, the higher the rates of PTSD and suicide rose amongst veterans.[115]

Hundreds of thousands of soldiers returned to America from Vietnam, their perception of reality forever distorted. The inner conflict for many was insufferable as they contemplated the gap between the illusions of stamping on cockroaches and the reality of committing brutal murders. Grossman recalled meeting veterans who had what he called 'haunted, thousand-yard stares'. He told how two of these veterans remembered finding family photos in their victim's pockets after they had killed them. They both described staring at these photos, seeing the wives they'd turned into widows, the children they'd deprived of fathers. The veterans could not forget these photos. They reminded them that the people they had killed were not vermin but humans, just like them.[116]

Many Vietnam veterans were determined that future generations of soldiers would not suffer the same fate they had. In the build up to the Iraq conflict, one veteran, Stan Goff, wrote an open letter to the soldiers due to go out there and fight.

We had to dehumanise our victims before we did the things we did ... [They] never surrendered [their] humanity. I did. We did. That's the thing you might not get until it's too late. When you take away the humanity of another, you kill your own humanity. You attack your own soul because it is standing in the way.[117]

It was a heartfelt letter, but it didn't make much difference. The pictures that emerged from Abu Ghraib prison shortly after the Iraq War began showed that dehumanisation remained a central plank in the US strategy. In particular, there was widespread horror at the unforgettable image of Lynndie England, a US Army reservist, dragging a prisoner along the floor by a leash, as if he were a dog. England, who had a history of mental illness, was sentenced to three years in prison for torture and prisoner abuse. But was she really the only one who was most culpable?

Philip Zimbardo, author of *The Lucifer Effect: Understanding How Good People Turn Evil*, said what happened at Abu Ghraib wasn't a case of a few rotten apples; he argued that it was the whole barrel that was rotten. The culture of prisoner abuse was established throughout the prison and it came down from the top. Major General Geoffrey D. Miller had told the commander of Abu Ghraib prison, 'They are like dogs and if you allow them to believe at any point that they are more than a dog then you have lost control of them.'[118] Lynndie England had simply taken Major General Miller at his word.

It wasn't just at Abu Ghraib that atrocities were committed. Chemical weapons were also deployed in Iraq, with multiple reports of their use in Fallujah. The soldiers referred to white phosphorus as 'Shake and Bake', a reference to the Kraft Foods breadcrumbs you can sprinkle on pork or chicken before cooking.[119] For those who don't know, white phosphorus burns right through the skin, melting the bones, bringing about an unimaginably torturous death.

One embedded journalist spoke to a soldier who was blasting rounds of white phosphorus into the city. He asked him how he felt about what he was doing. He admitted he didn't even know what the charges hit. He couldn't see if anyone was being killed. He was firing the white phosphorus in from outside of the city limits. He said, 'I just don't want to come home and have someone calling me a baby killer. That would piss me off.'[120]

This is one of the features that makes the wars of the present so different from the conflicts of the past. In traditional combat, men genuinely had to look one another in the eye as they battled to the death. This made it much harder to lose humanity.

Now, killers can be based literally thousands of miles away, never seeing whose lives they are taking. And much also now takes place on computer screens, where targets are frequently reduced to little more than blurry specks. This heightens the sense of dehumanisation and makes it even easier for soldiers to pull triggers and drop bombs.

The 2015 Helen Mirren movie *Eye in the Sky* depicted military personnel agonising for days over whether or not to blow up a house in Nairobi in which terrorists were hiding when there was a child nearby, considering all of the moral and ethical questions. This film is a fiction. Predator drone operators who are responsible for operations simply do not get this morally engaged. They habitually describe killings as 'bug splats'. That's how insignificant human life looks on a grainy video screen. It is like an insect hitting your car window whilst you drive down the motorway. To challenge this inhumanity and to try to restore a sense of humanity amongst their attackers, an artist collective has installed a massive portrait of a child in the heavily bombed Khyber Pakhtunkhwa region of Pakistan. Now, when a drone operator looks down, they see not an anonymous little dot, but the face of an innocent little girl.[121]

It's not just soldiers whose perspective must be distorted to legitimise mass killings in wars. Conflicts, such as those in Syria and Iraq, are also dependent on support from the public. This is where the role of the mass media can prove instrumental.

Erin Streuter and Deborah Wills of Mount Allison University, Canada, carried out an extensive study of media reporting in the UK, US, Australia and Canada after 9/11. They found that the dominant metaphor for depicting Islamist extremists across the whole of the Western press was vermin. Headlines ranged from 'Raid Zaps Iraqi Rat' to 'Canadian Soldiers mop up Taliban rat's nest' and 'Iraq War breeding terrorists'. The imagery is ubiquitous. Our soldiers 'hunt', 'capture' and 'ensnare' whilst the enemy 'scurries', 'slithers' and 'wiggles'.

Remember how Gaddafi was caught like a 'rat in a drain'?[122] Or how Saddam Hussein was captured in 'a spider-hole'? Remember, too, how Bin Laden was said to be 'hiding in caves' and need to be smoked out?[123] The language is often discreet – as so often with metaphors, its power comes from its ability to land straight in our unconscious brains, bypassing rational scrutiny – but the message of the metaphor was clear. These were not people, but vermin and that is exactly how Gaddafi, Saddam and Bin Laden were all executed. No Nuremberg trials for these people. They were not human.

Many people would say that the depiction of Islamist extremists was apt. These are brutal killers who do not behave like humans and they therefore should not be treated like humans. Such a view is understandable as an emotional response, but it's a slippery slope. There are very real dangers in depicting Islamist extremists as vermin. Metaphors cannot be tightly controlled. Metaphors do not live in tightly encircled boundaries. We cannot assume that people who hear this metaphor will perceive a distinction between 'Islamist extremists are vermin' and 'Muslims are vermin'. This can prove a particularly pernicious unintended consequence of the dehumanisation: people fleeing violence can be depicted as the same as those who are causing it.

In a now infamous article for *The Sun* dated 17 April 2015, columnist Katie Hopkins wrote of the hundreds of refugees who were drowning as ships sank in the Mediterranean: 'No, I don't care. Show me pictures of coffins, show me bodies floating in water, play violins and show me skinny people looking sad. I still don't care… They are like cockroaches…' She was using a simile, not a metaphor, but it was a potent image nonetheless. Prime Minister David Cameron used the same imagery again a couple of months later when he spoke of refugees as 'a swarm of people coming across the Mediterranean'.

Donald Trump, predictably, took this one step further.

One of his regular party pieces to his core supporters on the campaign trail was to read out a lyrical version of Aesop's fable 'The Farmer and the Viper' (yep, the same one which featured in *Der Stürmer*). He read it again in his speech marking his 100 days in office (dedicating it to US immigration officials)[124] and again in April 2018 in a speech at the Conservative Political Action conference.

He spat out the punch-line: '"Oh shut up, silly woman," said the reptile with a grin. "You knew damn well I was a snake before you let me in."'

The crowd roared with applause and gave him a standing ovation that lasted a full twenty seconds. Just in case the meaning of his metaphor was not crystal clear, he spelled it out. 'You have to think of this in terms of immigration.'

We should be extremely careful when this kind of language is directed against minority groups in any country. We all know where this might lead in future, because of where it has led in the past.

Rwanda was a relatively peaceful nation of farmers until a series of incendiary radio broadcasts on RTLM radio in 1994 led to the murder of 800,000 people. The Tutsi minority had been declared to be 'cockroaches' by the Hutu majority. Neighbours turned on neighbours, friends on friends. Many of the killings were carried out using everyday farming tools, such as machetes.[125]

The French journalist Jean Hatzfeld interviewed some of the Hutu killers to find out what happened. Their testimonies are contained in his book *Machete Season: The Killers in Rwanda Speak*. These people were mainly farmers for whom hunting and killing animals was a way of life. It is striking how frequently animal metaphors occur across all of the killers' testimonies.

Ignace Rukiramacumu: We called them 'cockroaches', an insect that chews up clothing and nests in it, so you have to squash them hard to get rid of them. We didn't want any more Tutsis on the land. We imagined an existence without them.

Pancrace Hakizamungili: The radios were yammering at us since 1992 to kill all the Tutsi. The intimidators shouted, 'Just look at these cockroaches – we told you so!' And we yelled, 'Right, let's go hunting!' We weren't that angry; more than anything else, we were relieved.

Elie Mizinge: We had to work fast, and we got no time off, especially not Sundays – we had to finish up. We cancelled all ceremonies. Everyone was hired at the same level for a single job – to crush all cockroaches.

Adalbert Munzigura: The radios exaggerated to get us all fired up. 'Cockroaches! Snakes!' It was the radios that taught us those words. The evil-mindedness of the radios was too well calculated for us to oppose it.

Elie Mizinge: In the end, a man is like an animal: you give him a whack on the head or the neck and down he goes. In the first days, someone who had already slaughtered chickens – and especially goats – had an advantage, understandably. Later, everybody grew accustomed to the new activity, and the laggards caught up.

Pio Mutungirehe: I had killed chickens but never an animal the stoutness of a man, like a goat or a cow. The first person, I finished him off in a rush, not thinking anything of it, even though he was a neighbour, quite close on my hill.

Adalbert Munzigura: When we spotted a small group of runaways trying to escape by creeping through the mud, we called them snakes. Before the killings, we usually called them cockroaches. But during, it was more suitable to call them snakes, because of their attitude, or zeros, or dogs, because in our country we don't like dogs; in any case, they were less than nothings.

Léopord Tawgurayezu: We no longer considered the Tutsi as humans or even as creatures of God. We had stopped seeing the world as it is, I mean as an expression of God's will. That is why it was easy for us to wipe them out.[126]

The incitement took place through the vermin metaphor of cockroaches (*inyenzi*). But curiously, as it came to the actual act of killing, so the metaphor changed and the killers, accustomed to slaughtering their own animals, began to view their victims as livestock.

It's extraordinary that almost all of the killers who Jean Hatzfeld interviewed used this animal imagery as they recalled their killings: right up to the barbaric description by a man who sneaked up and shot two young children in the back: he described them sitting as 'quiet as mice'. In April 2016, Léon Mugesera, a senior politician in Rwanda's ruling party, was sentenced to life imprisonment for public incitement to commit genocide, based upon a speech he made at a rally in the town of Kabaya in 1992, calling the Tutsi cockroaches.[127] Maybe twenty-four years from now, someone will be convicted for some of the rhetoric we're hearing today.

Politicians are all aware of how dehumanising language has been used in the past. That is why I was so surprised when David Cameron, a politician I had long admired (check out my glowing remarks about him in my last two books if you don't believe me), used this language in the House of Commons during the debate on Syria. But what surprised me most was that no one called him out about it. In fact, the only person who even began to interrogate the metaphor was Cameron's arch-nemesis and former leadership rival, David Davis. His objection was not that the language was genocidal, but more that it was misleading as to the nature of the conflict. He quoted an American ex-Special Forces general who said, 'We should never believe that we can cut off the head of the snake in this kind of war, because it always regenerates and reorganises. He said that that was the wrong metaphor for this kind of warfare and that it would not work on any level.'

Everyone else simply nodded along. And, having planted the idea of a snake at the beginning of the debate, so that image continued to develop in the ten-and-a-half-hour debate which followed. I counted twenty-seven references to snakes, monsters and barbarians in various forms. This was not a war in the Middle East. It was nothing to do with civilians and cities. This was about the world of ancient mythology, of Dungeons and Dragons, a story of an intrepid hero looking up and seeing a massive serpent looming right over him, poised and ready to strike... and the only question was, what did he do?

When Philip Hammond, the Secretary of State for Defence, closed the debate, he provided the resolution to the narrative that everyone craved. He explicitly reminded everyone of the imagery that Cameron had started off, bringing the narrative journey absolutely full circle, and he invited them all to do the only thing they could reasonably be expected to do to bring this awful matter to an appropriate conclusion.

'We are not debating tonight … whether or not to "go to war" … The simple question that we are deciding tonight is whether to extend those operations to tackle ISIL in their heartland in Syria – targeting the head of the snake.'

This was different to 2013. This time the House of Commons did approve the bombing. Cameron won his vote by a whopping 397 to 223 in favour. The motion was carried.

The day after the debate, the press merrily reported Cameron's metaphor: 'Take fight against ISIS to head of the snake, Obama is urged' (*The Times*). 'We must crush the IS snake's head and hit Raqqa' (*The Sun*). 'David Cameron targets "snake's head" in Syria' (*Daily Mail*). 'Britain must strike the head of the ISIS snake to destroy terrorists' (*Evening Standard*). 'Fight against ISIS: Time to "tighten noose around head of the snake in Syria" says Fallon' (*Daily Express*).

So it was that the bombing commenced. Today, Raqqa is flattened. Look at the drone footage on YouTube. There's nothing left. It is like Hiroshima, Mỹ Lai or Ground Zero. And yet there is no evidence the head of any snake was killed in this operation. This was primarily a civilian city. We do, however, have evidence that many hundreds of civilians were killed.[128]

Luciana Berger voted in favour of the bombing in the end. She found herself singled out and targeted, subjected to some particularly ferocious online abuse for her decision.

'Nice one for betraying your constituents, you snake.'

'Once a snake, always a snake...'

'It's incredible how many of these snakes voted in favour of bombing Syria.'

Luciana Berger is Jewish, and many of the attacks on her character were connected to that. In April 2018, she described some of the abuse she'd been receiving from people online. 'They have said that I am Tel Aviv's servant and called me a paid-up Israeli operative. This is Anti-Semitism of the worst kind, suggesting that I am a traitor to our country. They have called me Judas, a Zionazi and an absolute parasite.'

A number of far-right activists have received custodial sentences for anti-Semitic abuse of Berger. This must have been terrifying for her, particularly following the brutal killing of fellow Labour MP Jo Cox at the hands of a far-right activist in 2016.

Sadly, it is clear that anti-Semitism is on the rise in Britain today, and it is growing in a number of different places, including on the left. In March 2018, hundreds of people gathered in Parliament Square, protesting against Labour's inability to get to grips with the problem. Berger addressed the rally. She said that anti-Semitism within the Labour Party was now 'more conspicuous, more commonplace and more corrosive' than ever. Jeremy Corbyn has repeatedly made clear that anti-Semitism has no place in the Labour Party, but his critics are not impressed. It was widely reported in July 2018 that veteran Labour MP Margaret Hodge, who is Jewish, had confronted Corbyn in the House of Commons and called him a 'fucking anti-Semite and a racist'.

It's not only on the left that anti-Semitism is rising, it's also on the increase amongst some Muslim communities. The idea that Jews are snakes regularly appears in anti-Israel propaganda across the Middle East, including in textbooks, as well as in posters, speeches and political films.[129]

Anti-Semitism is equally growing amongst conspiracy theorists. People who feel angry or alienated from mainstream society often seek out counter-narratives they can believe in, narratives which explain why they do not feel like they belong.

David Icke has popularised the idea that the world is controlled by Rothschild Zionist lizards. This may seem like a pretty roundabout way of surfacing the old metaphorical idea that Jews are snakes – but Icke actually claims that, when he speaks about lizards, he's not using metaphor but speaking literally. He means real lizards. It might sound absurd, but it's gaining traction.

A Public Policy Polling report carried out in the US in 2012 showed that 4 per cent of respondents believe that 'shape-shifting reptilian people control our world by taking on human form and gaining political power to manipulate our societies'.[130] A further 7 per cent were not sure. If this were extrapolated to the whole population that means twelve million Americans have fallen for this conspiracy. We should beware the power of the conspiracy theory: lest we forget, America just elected a President who thinks climate change is a conspiracy invented by the Chinese to destroy US industry.

The web provides an easy forum for the circulation of conspiracy theories, as well as a free and frequently febrile space for the spread of anti-Semitic material. Many websites actively celebrate Hitler and Nazi Germany. Hitler's original propaganda videos are available for all to see on YouTube and they attract horrifyingly favourable comments. Unbelievably, there is even a US website called the Daily Stormer, which openly celebrates the Nazi tabloid *Der Stürmer*. The material on there looks worryingly familiar. The site contains multiple references to 'Jew Snakes'.[131] NBC's Duane Pohlman, businesswoman Audrey Russo and journalist Josh Gerstein have all been characterised as 'Jew Snakes' on the site. British businessman Philip Green was described as a 'fat python', who must be very fat indeed, 'for he has just swallowed a very big employee pension pot...'[132]

Many websites target particular Jewish individuals in this highly personalised way. In October 2017, PewDiePie – a Swedish vlogger who is said to earn more than $10 million a year from advertising and appearances – uploaded a video titled 'Mark Zuckerberg is Not Human'. This showed Zuckerberg, the Jewish CEO and founder of Facebook, with snake eyes. PewDiePie talked about Zuckerberg hissing, digging himself into a hole and shedding his skin. The video already has almost 7 million views and this is increasing by about a million more every month.[133]

Luciana Berger has also been targeted for particular abuse. A US far-right website started a #filthyjewbitch campaign which led to Berger receiving over 2,500 violent, pornographic and extreme anti-Semitic messages over a three-day period. By calling Berger a #filthyjewbitch, they were highlighting not just her religious and cultural roots, they were also highlighting her gender. Let's move on to that subject next.

BITCH

Let me tell you what 'Like a Virgin' is about... It's a metaphor for big dicks... It's all about this cooze who's a regular fuck machine ... One day she meets this John Holmes motherfucker ... Now, she's getting some serious dick action and she's feeling something she ain't felt since forever. Pain ... It hurts. It hurts her. It shouldn't hurt her. You know, her pussy should be Bubble Gum by now, but when this cat fucks her it hurts. It hurts like the first time. The pain is reminding a fuck machine what it once was like to be a virgin. Hence, 'Like a Virgin'.

So began *Reservoir Dogs*. It's one of the most gripping film openings in movie history, featuring some of the shortest, sharpest, snappiest screenwriting, delivered by dead cool gun-toting gangsters and, what's more, they are even talking about metaphor. Talk about attention grabbing. I can still remember watching this film for the first time. I'd never seen anything like it before. *Empire* magazine heralds *Reservoir*

Dogs as the greatest independent movie ever made, and of course this was the film which launched Quentin Tarantino upon the world, courtesy of Harvey Weinstein's company, Miramax.

Today, as millions of women around the world have joined the #MeToo movement, and Harvey Weinstein is facing multiple allegations of rape and assault, it is perhaps worth looking again at the cultural significance of those early films which gave him his power. *Reservoir Dogs* was undoubtedly ground-breaking, but nowhere was it more ground-breaking than in its unprecedented levels of violence and explicitly sexual swearing.

Reservoir Dogs featured an eye-watering 421 curse words. Around half of these were 'fucks' and 'bitches'. No film had come close to these levels beforehand. During a screening at Sitges Film Festival, fifteen people walked out. Even horror film director Wes Craven and special makeup effects artist Rick Baker couldn't stomach it.[134] It's easy to forget now just how shocking it was. Tarantino said at the time, 'It happens at every single screening. For some people the violence, or the rudeness of the language, is a mountain they can't climb. That's ok. I'm not their cup of tea.'[135]

Not that the criticism served as a deterrent. With accolades galore, the pair returned soon after with their follow-up: *Pulp Fiction*. Where *Reservoir Dogs* had not featured a single woman with a speaking part, much of the marketing of *Pulp Fiction* revolved around the super-sexy image of Uma Thurman playing Mia Wallace, a gangster's wife. One of that film's most memorable moments shows Jules (played by Samuel L. Jackson) talking with Vincent (played by John Travolta) about whether or not he should take Mia out, given Marsellus Wallace's psychopathic tendencies. Jules warns off Vincent, reminding him of a previous occasion when Wallace had left someone disabled just for giving Mia a foot massage. They start arguing about whether or not a foot massage constitutes infidelity.

> Eating a bitch out and giving a bitch a foot massage ain't even the same fucking thing… Now look, maybe your method of massage differs from mine but, you know, touching his wife's feet and sticking your tongue in the holiest of holies ain't the same fuckin' ballpark. It ain't the same league. It ain't even the same fuckin' sport. Look, foot massages don't mean shit.

There's so much talk today about 'fuckin' bitches' and 'bitches fuckin'' that this excerpt doesn't even appear surprising any more. It's easy to forget that there was ever a time such language was not socially acceptable. In 1785 Francis Grose described the term 'bitch' in *A Classical Dictionary of a Vulgar Tongue* as 'the most offensive appellation that can be given to an English woman'.[136] To call someone a bitch was worse even than to call them a whore. In Victorian times, it had been eliminated from the language to the extent that it no longer even appeared in the dictionary.

But it has come back into fashion in a very big way in the intervening years. What's striking is that whenever feminism has moved forward, this has been matched with a concurrent increase in the use of the word 'bitch'. And this increase has largely been spurred on by the overwhelmingly male-dominated creative industries: from publishing to music and the movies.

The first wave of feminism came immediately after the First World War, after women won the vote in Britain and the States. Between 1915 (when women did not have the vote) and 1930 (when women got the vote), the use of the word 'bitch' in print almost doubled.

The second wave of feminism occurred in the late 1960s and early '70s, when women gained employment and sexual rights. In the '60s, it was very rare to hear a song containing the word 'bitch'. It doesn't feature at all in the whole of the Beatles' back catalogue. Then, in the early 1970s, in the years between the introduction of the Equal Pay Act in 1970 and the Sex Discrimination Act in 1975, practically every major English act of the time released a song which had the word 'bitch' in the title: the Rolling Stones released 'Bitch' in 1971, David Bowie released 'Queen Bitch' in 1971 and Elton John released 'The Bitch Is Back' in 1974.

Then, the third wave of feminism occurred in the 1990s. This was when new laws were introduced to tackle domestic assault, female genital mutilation and sexual harassment. This was the time of the release of *Reservoir Dogs* and *Pulp Fiction*. Following that the use of the term 'bitch' trebled on TV between 1997 and 2008.[137]

Today, its use is widespread. Listen to music now and clock up the bitch references. The use of the word 'bitch' in rap music has trebled over the last thirty years whilst the word 'fuck' has doubled.[138]

It was 'Smack My Bitch Up' by the Prodigy in 1997 that represented the watershed moment. The release of that song set a new standard. Despite being condemned at the time by many feminist groups as misogynist, it nonetheless went on to become one of the most popular dance tracks of all time.

Today, songs like 'Me & My Bitch' by the Notorious B.I.G. and 'I Love My Bitch' by Busta Rhymes make the term seem almost like a term of endearment. When Kanye West wrote 'Perfect Bitch' for Kim Kardashian in 2012, she was reported to be honoured by the tribute.[139] Kanye was surprised when people suggested there might be something weird about calling his loved one a bitch. 'I usually never tweet questions but I struggle with this so here goes... Is the word BITCH acceptable?' He was quickly advised it was not acceptable. He then asked 'Is it ok to use bitch as long as we put BAD in front of it? Like you a BAD BITCH?'

The pattern we have seen throughout history is that, as the legislature has sought to dignify, so the cultural industries have sought to demean. Of course, it's not just men in creative and cultural industries who have promoted the use of the word bitch, women have too. For instance, in the '60s, Jo Freeman wrote *The BITCH Manifesto*. In the 1990s, the all-female band Fifth Column released a song called 'All Women Are Bitches' and Elizabeth Wurtzel wrote the book, *Bitch: In Praise of Difficult Women*. Today, I'm reading *Bitch Doctrine: Essays for Dissenting Adults* by feminist writer Laurie Penny.

There is an argument for reclaiming the word, as black people have with the N-word or gay people with 'queer', but 'bitch' has a very clear status in the hierarchy of nature. Can it ever be turned into a positive? We all have a very precise understanding of the position of the dog in relationship to mankind. Yes, dogs can potentially be man's best friend, but only with training, and we know very well that they can never, ever, become master.

This is why the term 'bitch' is fundamentally associated with domination. This is true whether it is used by a man against a man, a woman against a man, a woman against a woman or, as is usually the case, men against women. Today, the word can even appear to have a fashionable aura. People might joke about their bitches. In some communities, it can seem little different to calling someone 'mate'. Some groups of men might regard it as hip prison talk. Such talk can even sound cool and contemporary, which is kind of ironic – because the idea of women as bitches is one of the oldest metaphorical frames imaginable.

The satirists, poets and storytellers of ancient Greece and ancient Rome, the creative industries of their time, were using the term almost three thousand years ago. In the seventh century BC, Semonides of Amorgos, an ancient Greek satirist, wrote a poem, depicting various types of women through the prism of different animal metaphors. Amongst these, he described:

> A bitch ... wants to hear everything and know everything. She peers everywhere and strays everywhere, always yapping ... A man cannot stop her by threatening, nor by losing his temper or by knocking out her teeth with a stone ... not even if she is sitting with friends, but ceaselessly she keeps up a barking you can do nothing with...

The idea of women as bitches was prevalent in ancient Rome; indeed, it plays an integral role in the story of Rome's founding. Romulus and Remus were born in Alba Longa – an ancient city near what is now Rome. They were born to Rhea Silvia, a royal Vestal Virgin, and their father was said to be the god Mars. Given their regal and godly status, the reigning King Amulius regarded them as a threat. He ordered Romulus and Remus be chased out of town and killed. They hid on the River Tiber, where they were looked after and nursed by a she-wolf (a lupa), in a cave now known as the Lupercal. The boys eventually decided to build a city of their own. That city was Rome.

The image of Romulus and Remus suckling on the she-wolf was ubiquitous across Rome, then as now. The city had a bronze statue of the she-wolf which Cicero referred to in one of his speeches and it remains a major tourist attraction in Rome today, displayed with great prominence in the Capitoline Museum (well worth a visit, incidentally!). Mussolini was also fond of the image, and he ensured it featured frequently in fascist architecture and design. It remains the symbol of the city today, as well as the logo of A. S. Roma, one of the city's two main soccer teams.

The she-wolf may be a benign image of nurturing motherhood, but it also has other connotations. Ancient Rome called their brothels *lupanaria*, which meant wolf dens. *Lupanaria* were all over the place in ancient Rome, and legend has it that there was one for every fifty men.

So the wolf imagery ubiquitous in ancient Rome sent the message that women were only good for one of two things: feeding or fucking – not so different to today's rap music, which often celebrates women as either 'mamas' or 'bitches'. In ancient Rome, such imagery was a covert way to surreptitiously smuggle in dehumanising messages, enforcing the patriarchy and keeping women in their place. We're now 2,000 years on, but have things really changed?

If you google 'Hillary Clinton' and 'bitch' you get a staggering 9 million results. This is more than if you google 'Hillary Clinton' and terms like 'climate change', 'foreign policy' and the 'Oval Office'; things that you might arguably consider more important, given that she has just recently stood for the greatest political office in the world.

The idea that Hillary Clinton was a bitch featured with a startling regularity throughout her campaign. This was, of course, partly due to the character and campaign of her principal opponent. Trump rallies were stuffed full of misogynistic merchandise including caps, T-shirts and car stickers declaring 'Jail the bitch', 'Trump that bitch' and 'Ditch the bitch'.[140] Badges and bumper stickers were sold saying: 'Life's a bitch: Don't vote for one.' This language spread like wildfire amongst those who attended his rallies. At one rally in Ashburn, Virginia, in August 2016, a ten-year-old boy was filmed sitting atop his mother's shoulders shouting, 'Take the bitch down.' When reporters later challenged the mum about her son's language, she laughed it off. 'Children are children...'[141]

Hillary Clinton was not the first female leader to be subjected to such demeaning abuse on her climb to the top. When Margaret Thatcher won the Tory leadership election, the first reaction of the then vice-chairman of the Conservative Party was to declare, 'My God, the bitch won.'[142] Britain's top political cartoonist, Gerald Scarfe, marked the occasion by drawing his first ever cartoon of her: he depicted her as a dog on the top podium at Crufts, with large stabbing nose, drooping eyes, fangs and a dog's body, squatting above a steaming dog turd. The podium said, 'Top Bitch'.[143]When Thatcher entered the Commons for the first time after winning the leadership, male Labour MPs on the opposite benches chanted 'Ditch the bitch'. Still, to this day, there are many people whose first word on hearing Margaret Thatcher's name is simply to utter 'bitch'.[144]

Margaret Thatcher, faced throughout her career with this dehumanisation, chose not to address or acknowledge it. Instead, she developed her own metaphorical mantle, one which continues to define perceptions of her to this day. It was the Russian newspaper *Pravda* who first dubbed her the 'Iron Lady'. This was an image she was very happy to accept. In a speech in her constituency on 31 January 1976, with cameras present, she said:

> I stand before you tonight in my Red Star chiffon evening gown (Laughter, applause), my face softly made up, my fair hair gently waved (Laughter). The Iron Lady of the Western world. Well, am I any of those things? (No!) …Yes. I am an iron lady. After all, it wasn't a bad thing to be an iron duke.* Yes, if that's how they want to interpret my defence of values and freedoms fundamental to our way of life.[145]

So it was that the legend of the Iron Lady was created. The metaphor was vital to the public's perception of her, and her success. Professor Jonathan Charteris-Black at the University of the West of England has argued that the metaphor of

---

* A reference to the Duke of Wellington, the hero of Waterloo and vanquisher of Napoleon.

iron was a powerful weapon in establishing her identity as a woman in a man's world because of its hardness, its inflexibility and its unlikeliness ever to have been touched by the milk of human kindness.[146]

Hugo Young shared this view, writing in his biography of Thatcher:

> It established her importance: for nobody important would be worth the Russians' while to attack. It gave her an identity as an international, and not merely a domestic, politician. It also neutralised the danger still seen to lurk in the fact that she was a woman, completely unversed in the male world of high diplomacy. Nobody could be too disturbingly feminine who was now presented as being made of iron.[147]

Hillary had no such image on her side. On the contrary, she was at a disadvantage in terms of the metaphors which were established to define her. As Hillary's adviser, Mark J. Penn, advised her in her ultimately doomed attempt to be the Democratic candidate for President in 2008, the American people saw the President of the United States as father of the nation. This was the first time a woman from a major party had stood for that post* and he advised that they were not prepared to see the role of father of the nation changed to mother. In a careful nuance, he advised that they would be prepared to see a woman play the role of father of the nation. He went on to say that the best example of a woman successfully playing the role of father in the nation in the West was Margaret Thatcher.

---

* The first was Victoria Woodhull, who ran in 1872 for the Equal Rights Party.

Hillary never really developed a strong metaphorical narrative to match Trump's 'draining the swamp' or to beat the story of the Iron Lady. Instead, it was the idea of 'Hillary the bitch' that seemed to dominate the discourse, even amongst her own supporters. Tina Fey and Amy Poehler went on *Saturday Night Live* and said Clinton WAS a bitch – and that everyone should deal with it. 'You know what, bitches get stuff done.'[148] In 2016, Tina Brown, former editor of the *New Yorker* and *Vanity Fair*, argued in an interview with Mishal Husain on the *Today* programme that Hillary Clinton must 'own her inner bitch'.[149] Andi Zeisler wrote a piece for the *New York Times*, 'The Bitch America Needs'.[150]

They were trying to reclaim the word. As many have argued previously, sometimes you want to say it before it's said to you. Whether Hillary's strategy worked or not is a moot point – she did win more votes than Trump in the end – but ultimately it is her rival who is sitting in the Oval Office today and not her.

As we explored earlier, metaphors give us the ability to understand people's perspective on the world. Trump's everyday language clearly shows he instinctively associates women with bitches. The connection comes quickly and naturally to him. It is clearly a central part of his perceptual framework. In 2006, he said of the then Secretary of State, Condoleezza Rice, 'I think she's a bitch. She goes around to other countries and other nations, negotiates with their leaders, comes back and nothing ever happens.' In 2011, when *New York Times* columnist Gail Collins wrote an article calling him a 'financially embattled thousandaire' and suggested he was going bankrupt,[151] Donald Trump returned a copy of the column to her: he'd drawn a ring around her face and scribbled 'The

Face of a Dog!' on it. In 2012, he tweeted, 'Robert Pattinson should not take back Kristen Stewart. She cheated on him like a dog and will do it again – just watch. He can do much better.' In 2015, he called Arianna Huffington, journalist and founder of the *Huffington Post*, a dog.[152] In the midst of the 2016 election, he even appeared to call Hillary Clinton a bitch during one of the televised debates when he thought he was off-camera.[153]

I've not found any examples of Trump calling men bitches. He will, if he is angry with a man, call him a 'son of a bitch'. He has done this on a number of occasions since becoming President. With reference to the NFL protests alone, he urged NFL owners to fire players who were kneeling: 'Get that son of a bitch off the field.' He also called *Meet the Press* presenter, Chuck Todd, 'a sleeping son of a bitch'. So, in Trump's world, even when a man has wronged, it's the woman who must be condemned.

Trump clearly likes using the word, but perhaps his most controversial use came in what he thought was a private conversation with Hollywood reporter Billy Bush on board the *Access Hollywood* bus as they headed to the *Days of Our Lives* soap opera studio to record a clip about a cameo he had made on the show some years previously. As he and Bush talked and joked on the bus, Trump was relaxed and off-guard, and seemingly unaware that he had a microphone attached to his lapel.

> I moved on her like a bitch … You know, I'm automatically attracted to beautiful – I just start kissing them. It's like a magnet. Just kiss. I don't even wait. And when you're a star, they let you do it. You can do anything … Grab 'em by the pussy. You can do anything.[154]

He's then introduced to Arianne Zucker, one of the stars of *Days of Our Lives*. When she explains to him that she's been on the show for eight years, Trump says to her, 'You're the vixen.' This was presumably Trump's attempt at charm: calling her a female fox. When played the tape later, Zucker said, 'It feels very surreal.'[155] Indeed. By combining her with a fox, this could almost have been a work by Magritte.

Michelle Obama condemned Trump for these remarks in a speech in New Hampshire. 'Last week, we saw this candidate actually bragging about sexually assaulting women. And I can't believe that I'm saying that a candidate for President of the United States has bragged about sexually assaulting women.' She told a story about a six-year-old son of a friend who had concluded that Trump could not possibly win the election. 'Because [he] called someone a piggy and', he said, 'you cannot be President if you call someone a piggy.'[156]

Trump tried to brush it all off. He described it as 'locker room banter, a private conversation that took place many years ago'. He then went on to say, 'Bill Clinton has said far worse to me on the golf course – not even close. I apologise if anyone was offended …We're electing a leader to the free world, we're not choosing a Sunday school teacher … No one has more respect for women than me.'

What is interesting is the line of logic between Trump's 'I moved on her like a bitch…' and 'Grab 'em … You can do anything'. As we've already explored, the way someone speaks affects how they perceive the world around them, and ultimately, their behaviour. When we are looking specifically at calling women bitches, the consequences can be very alarming indeed.

In 2011, Laurie A. Rudman and Kris Mescher of Rutgers University investigated the links between the dehumanisation of women and sexual aggression. They showed that men who automatically associate women with animals are more likely to sexually harass women, more likely to report negative attitudes towards rape victims and more likely to be sympathetic to those who are accused of rape. And they are more likely to rape.[157]

This is where the consequences of this seemingly innocuous, increasingly ubiquitous term become more sinister. There is a clear connection between seeing women as bitches and treating them violently. Not that we should be surprised. A number of old proverbs also highlight this connection. 'A Spaniel, a woman and a walnut tree, the more they're beaten the better they be'; and 'Women are like dogs: the more you beat them, the more they'll love you.'[158] Shakespeare also often preceded violence with a reference to a bitch, as in *King Lear* when the Earl of Kent beats Oswald after calling him 'the son and heir of a mongrel bitch; one whom I will beat into clamorous whining' or in *Troilus and Cressida*, when Ajax beats Thersites, calling him a 'bitch-wolf's son'.

Louise du Toit of Stellenbosch University in South Africa has taken this line of enquiry further, exploring how rapists often used verbal abuse to justify their actions.[159] She cites the account of Nancy Venable Raine, who described being raped in her book, *After Silence: Rape and My Journey Back*. She was standing at her kitchen sink one sunny day, washing a pan, when suddenly she was attacked from behind. She heard the voice behind her, 'Shut up shut the fuck up you bitch you dirty bitch you fucking cunt shut up do you hear me you fucking dirty bitch I'm going to kill you if you don't shut up you bitch I'm going to kill you.'[160]

The repetition of the word 'bitch' is a double-edged sword in this instance: not only does it intensify the attack upon the victim, it reinforces the attacker's sense that what he's doing is OK. He is superior. He is dominant. She is not human. Looking back at #MeToo, we've seen similar language as this in some of the age-old stories about misogyny and domestic abuse in Hollywood. In 2010, Mel Gibson shouted at his then girlfriend, Oksana Grigorieva, 'You look like a fucking bitch on heat', before punching her teeth out. O. J. Simpson said to mediators, 'I'll kill that bitch' about his wife before famously not killing her.

This is wholly pernicious language, but crucially, it is also completely ubiquitous. A study of misogynistic language on Twitter by Brandwatch found more than half of the abuse was based around animal metaphors.[161] Such imagery regularly appears in the press too, with talk about 'bitches' in the red-tops and 'vixens' in the mid-markets. There are also references in the broadsheets, albeit more discreet. During the 2017 UK general election, I analysed the front-page stories of the British press, identifying different patterns in metaphor use. *The Guardian* reported May had been 'barking instructions at civil servants', the *Sunday Times* talked about how few politicians had the power to stick to a line 'as doggedly as the prime minister' and the *Financial Times* talked about how her policy proposals have 'gone down like a pile of dog poo'.

It's quite absurd. Since 2015, *The Times* has carried 'Pet Announcements'. They are, by their own admission, 'pioneering anthropomorphic journalism'. So one of Britain's oldest and most authoritative papers of record is reducing Prime Ministers to the status of dogs whilst elevating dogs to the status of human beings. It's a topsy-turvy world. Is it down to sexism? It's hard to say for sure, but during my study, I did not see a single instance of Jeremy Corbyn, her male opponent, being referred to as a dog.

What can be done about it? Should the term be embraced, reclaimed and owned? Or should we attempt to reduce its use? Sheryl Sandberg, Facebook's COO and author of *Lean In*, announced in 2014 that she was starting a campaign to ban the b-word. It turned out that the word she had in mind was 'bossy', not 'bitch'.

In 2007, Councilwoman Darlene Mealy of New York Council did try to get the word 'bitch' banned in New York City, citing in particular its use in rap music. She said the word created 'a paradigm of shame and indignity' for all women, describing it as 'a vile attack on our womanhood'. Her mission did not succeed; indeed, from my experience on past trips to New York, banning the word 'bitch' there would be like banning the letter 'a'. But nineteen of the fifty-one council members did sign up to the measure. Had it gone through, she would have wound up criminalising one of New York's most famous and successful residents.

Madonna definitely believes in reclaiming the word 'bitch'. In 2015, her song 'Bitch I'm Madonna' was released with a video shot from the rooftops of New York. That year, Madonna set off on her 2015/2016 Rebel Heart Tour. In Brisbane, she called on stage a seventeen-year-old member of the audience, Josephine Georgiou. 'Josephine! The new unapologetic bitch of 2016! Oh yeah! [everyone laughs]… She's the kind of girl that you just want to slap on the ass.' Madonna then tugged on Josephine's top and, before an audience of 14,000 people, she exposed Josephine's breast and nipple. The audience gasped. 'Oh shit. Sexual harassment,' said Madonna, in a dead-pan voice.

After the event, a number of lawyers stepped forward, suggesting Josephine should sue Madonna for sexual assault. Josephine laughed it off. 'Why would I sue Madonna for the best moment of my life?'[162] Her response wasn't surprising: not many minors do sue stars for sexual assault. This is something we'll explore in the next chapter.

GROOMING

'What are we? Humans? Or animals? Or savages?' asks Piggy in *Lord of the Flies*. A staple of the school curriculum for decades, the book tells the story of a group of schoolchildren who set off on a choir trip but, after a plane crash, wind up stranded on a desert island, where they end up descending into tribalism, murder and savagery. Piggy's question provides the central focus of the whole book. It seems all the more poignant because his character serves as a symbol of humanity throughout. So when he is later savagely killed, his question appears to have been answered beyond a doubt. They are not human.

This was not the first book to explore the relationship between children and animals. It has been a recurring theme in literature from Romulus and Remus through to Tarzan and *The Jungle Book*. But why is it that *Lord of the Flies* is the one we all study at school? Is it because it's such a thumping good read? Or is it because it provides a unique teacher's perspective on the true nature of children?

William Golding was a teacher at Bishop Wordsworth's School in Salisbury when he wrote *Lord of the Flies*. Golding was regarded by colleagues and pupils alike as a bit weird. His nickname was 'Scruff'. He used to carry out experiments on the children – behavioural science was just taking off at the time and *Candid Camera* was big on TV. On one occasion, he divided the children into gangs. He told one group that they were attacking a prehistoric camp whilst the other group was told to defend it. It was watching these experiments that provided inspiration for the characters in *Lord of the Flies*, and formed the basis of the story.[163]

Funnily enough, I know Bishop Wordsworth's School. I used to sing with their school choir at Salisbury Cathedral when I was younger, under the tutelage of Alan Harwood, a great organist. We never had any experiments carried out on us – not that I'm aware of, anyway – and I have some happy memories of these occasions. The teachers who came with us on these choir trips were the very best: the kind who turned a blind eye when you nipped off for a cigarette and who wouldn't cause a problem if they saw you in the pub. In fact, they'd probably discreetly pass you a half of cider.

Teachers have an incredibly difficult job. I go into schools occasionally to give talks on rhetoric now, and there are few audiences more intimidating than a group of excited and excitable young children. When Golding had Piggy ask if children were humans, animals or savages, it was probably because this was a question that he himself pondered several times a day as he looked out on his class.

Talking about children as animals seems to most of us to be wholly and entirely natural. If they're playing up, we might say that they're 'cheeky monkeys', 'rug rats' or 'laughing hyenas'. If they're being adorable, they could be a 'baby bear', 'a cute little kitten' or 'a little pup'. If they're being stupid, they could be 'bird-brained', 'a jack-ass' or 'a dodo'. And what about being 'a pig' or 'a monster' or 'wallowing around' if they're being disgusting? Such images lie so deep in our cultural conception of children, or 'kids', that we use such language without thought.

Most of us, for instance, would never have thought that the very word 'kids' is based on the idea of children as baby goats. This was a term that first originated in the 1200s, was extended into slang in the 1500s, and then came into informal use in Victorian times.[164] The underlying idea still remains today. George Bernard Shaw famously described schools as 'child-farms'. In June 2012, when the then Education Secretary Michael Gove was asked about a two-tier education system, his reply was that he wanted 'no separation of sheep and goats'. Michael Gove is now the Secretary of State for Farming. I wonder if he's noticed he's in a different department.

Peter Wanless, the CEO of the NSPCC, tells me he is concerned about how animal metaphors are used to justify the treatment of children. He says it relates to an increasingly strong sense he has that the British people are happier to give money to support animals than children. He mentions a study carried out in 2015 by the Harrison's Fund, the charity for children with Duchenne muscular dystrophy. The fund put out two different adverts online asking the same question: 'Would you give £5 to save Harrison from a slow painful death?' One advert showed a picture of an eight-year-old boy who really suffers from Duchenne. The other included a picture of a dog taken from the internet. The advert that featured the dog attracted twice as many click-throughs as the advert showing the child.[165]

Our willingness to help out dogs over children may be shocking, but it has a long history. The RSPCA actually preceded the NSPCC by sixty years. When the NSPCC was formed, the explicit aim of the founder, Benjamin Waugh, was to 'place the child of the savage on the same level as the dog'. Nevertheless, even after forming the charity, he still remarked, 'It is not the dogs but the children to whom fall the crumbs from the table.'[166] Peter Wanless sums up the absurdity of the anomaly, which persists today. 'Not only do we do children down by comparing them to animals, we then feel guilty about it and offer our charity to assist the poor animals!'

In Finland, where children are famously regarded as more equal – schools in particular are less hierarchical, with teachers usually called by their first names – such animalistic language is used far less frequently. In fact, the only real animal term that is used for children is the term *pentu* – 'little cub' – but even that is seen as old-fashioned, and is generally only used when a child has been naughty.

In the UK, the discourse is very different. Children are dehumanised literally from the moment of conception. From that point on, every step of their growth is marked almost week by week in reference to a different point on the Great Chain of Being. Most parents are familiar with the idea of comparing a baby in the womb to a fruit or vegetable during the different stages of pregnancy. At four weeks, your baby is the size of a poppy seed. At fourteen weeks, your baby is the size of a lemon. At twenty-eight weeks, your baby is the size of an aubergine, and so on.[167]

Then, when the child is born, the baby ceases to be a vegetable and becomes a little animal. The nineteenth-century biologist Romanes catalogued an infant's development through references to different animals. At ten weeks, he said, they are instinctive like insects. At eight months, they can use simple language, like birds. At twelve months, they can use tools, like monkeys. At fifteen months, they are capable of understanding basic concepts of morality, like a dog.

And it goes on throughout their lives until at some magical moment their parents might decide they are full human beings. But their nature is constantly being revised, constantly being assessed and they are well aware that they can slip up and down the Great Chain of Being depending on what they do. Sometimes they can be little angels or stars; sometimes they can be little devils.

Some parents choose to run with continuous metaphor, which acts as a label. You see on parenting websites some people continually referring to their children with monikers such as 'the beast' or 'the monster'. It's hard to imagine that, although all of these names almost certainly start off jocularly or even affectionately, the continuous repetition of this idea does not have at least some effect on perceptions and behaviours. What's particularly striking is how parents will typically resort to animal imagery when they are seeking power and control.

One incredibly successful parenting book is *Toddler Taming* by Dr Christopher Green. It has sold millions of copies and gets rave reviews. The two-word title neatly summarises the whole of the book as it is set out: the first part establishes 'the toddler' effectively as a different species, introducing notions such as 'the terrible twos', as if children all of a sudden become terrorists on their second birthday; the second part of the book is based on techniques for 'taming' the toddler, many of which come straight from the world of animal training.

Green recommends various 'behavioural modification techniques'. This comprises a number of parenting methods which make little sense outside of the mind-bending parameters of the book. For instance:

> Occasional appearances of the [wooden] spoon usually act like a magic wand, producing an instant Lourdes-like cure … You can debate all day with a defiant 2+-year-old. You can explain about the finer points of love, example and character building and even your evangelical views against corporal punishment, but the chances are that words may miss the mark, while a gentle gesture of a smack may land centre bull's-eye, right on target.

The psychologist Albert Bandura, who carried out the 'these people are animals' research on dehumanisation we looked at earlier, has led experiments that show the harm smacking has on children. He's demonstrated that the main lesson most children take from witnessing aggression is that the best way to resolve problems is through violence.

One of the other techniques Green recommends is 'controlled crying', also known as 'sleep training'. This is a technique where you leave your baby to cry themselves to sleep at night, rather than cuddling them off. The technique is pretty controversial, with arguments for and against. Those in favour say it's vital to teach the children to put themselves to sleep. Those against say it is inherently stressful and constitutes child cruelty. Both arguments probably have some truth to them. But what is striking is how metaphor is often used to distort the debate on the issue on both sides, creating a smoke-and-mirrors scenario in which unreasonable actions can be made to appear reasonable.

Martin Daubney wrote an article for the *Daily Mail* explaining why he backed controlled crying:

> We listened whilst our precious boy Sonny flung himself round the room like a whirling dervish, and screamed like a caged animal behind his bolted door. But despite the heartbreaking sounds of his distress, I turned away and led Diana by the hand downstairs. If someone had told me before my son was born that I would find myself bolting him in his room at night, let alone issuing an ultimatum to my partner that I would move out if she didn't agree, I never would have believed them. I would have found it abhorrent.[168]

Leaving a distressed toddler behind a bolted door could well be considered negligence. Locking an out-of-control animal behind a bolted door is common sense and a necessary act of self-defence. But thinking about this in terms of parenting, the only breakthrough Martin has made is his creation of a fictitious narrative about who or what he's parenting, which enables him to get a good night's sleep with a clear conscience. Within this world where the child is a wild animal, the parent is granted complete power to take whatever steps they need to restrain and control him.

Some parents who read the article vehemently rejected Daubney's depiction. They were trying to smash down his fictitious world and bring him back to reality. 'Holly' wrote a blog piece in response entitled 'How to get away with child abuse'. As she wrote:

> I am struggling to find a point in the day where this poor boy enjoys quality time with loving parents. Babies who have gotten off to a shaky start in life, who have not necess-arily formed a secure attachment to at least one parent, often exhibit insecurities as toddlers. This poor boy was desperate to get out of his room, to be not on his own.

Holly was speaking up on Sonny's behalf. She was giving voice to the voiceless. I suspect that, had Sonny able to ar-ticulate the overwhelming complex emotions he must have been feeling, no doubt he would have said something similar.

It's so easy to forget how confusing the world can appear from a child's eyes. A young child has little comprehension of the difference between metaphorical and literal commu-nication. What must they think when they hear their parent speak about them as an animal? They would be entitled to conclude that their parent's perception is fundamentally flawed. They might also conclude they were being subjected to a deep injustice. Nor would they necessarily understand that phrases like 'I'll wring your neck', 'I'll thrash you to within an inch of your life' or 'I'll have your guts for garters' are just 'figures of speech'. Such phrases may well be terrifying, particularly coming from a big, towering adult who clearly perceives you as little more than an animal. And yet language like this is very common in discipline, whether it's parents talking about children as 'little monsters' or teachers talking about children as 'feral'.

I went to a school where being caned or hit with a slipper was not at all unusual – or at least it wasn't for me. I probably deserved it. But once, I literally pissed myself a bit as I stood, aged eleven years old, in my housemaster's office, waiting for him to strike me with the cane. I had a number of instances like this. I was kicked in the balls by a maths teacher and thrown over a desk by a PE teacher. There was nothing I could do about it. I had no right of recourse. This was the early 1980s. At that point, corporal punishment was still completely above board in schools in Britain. In that respect, we were several decades behind the rest of the world.

In a House of Commons debate on corporal punishment in 1947, Peter Freeman, the then MP for Newport, called for a ban. He pointed out that, even then, corporal punishment had already been banned in countries like Argentina, Belgium, Brazil, Bulgaria, China, Czechoslovakia, Egypt, Estonia, Finland, France, Greece, Ireland, Italy, Mexico, the Netherlands, Norway, Peru, Poland, Portugal, Romania, Switzerland, Turkey, Russia and most of the United States.

He shared a number of stories of terrifying child abuse in British schools. He spoke of a boy who came home with his face covered in blood; a teacher who beat a boy with a whip handle; a seven-year-old orphan who was caned so badly he had to go to the police seeking protection.

Freeman rejected any idea that corporal punishment might have a valid place in education, quoting Bernard Shaw:

> Any callous fool with a cane in his or her hand can terrorise a child into learning the alphabet and the multiplication table; and that process does all the mischief. Are we prepared to say that it is better to leave a child unschooled than intimidated physically? I am. Fear compels children to learn, but also to hate learning.

The Labour Education Minister who replied to Freeman largely agreed with his view, saying, 'No reputable educationist … can defend its continued use.' But the problem was that the teaching unions were not prepared to let it go: they regarded it as an essential defence against unruly children.[169] It was in the teeth of opposition from the teaching unions when the government did finally ban corporal punishment in the 1980s. There was also substantial opposition in Parliament, not least from those MPs who were themselves former teachers, like Mr Harry Greenway, who had been a schoolteacher for twenty-three years before becoming an MP. He pointed out in a House of Commons debate in 1986:

> There are schools not far from this House where there is little or no discipline. Children of all ages, primary and secondary, trot about like packs of hounds, doing what they like, totally out of control, cheeking teachers … What does the Bible say? In Proverbs we read: 'He who spares the rod hates his son, but he who loves him is diligent to discipline him.'[170]

The reference to religion was adroit. It's hard to argue with God, and governments in particular will do everything they can to avoid a public row with the Church. In 2005, several headmasters from private schools sought to get corporal punishment reintroduced, arguing the ban was a breach of their religious freedom. They were roundly sent packing, but there is still a significant body of teachers who would welcome its return. A *Times Educational Supplement* (*TES*) survey in 2008 showed that 22 per cent of secondary school teachers supported bringing back corporal punishment, along with 16 per cent of teachers in primary schools.[171] Even though corporal punishment has now been banned, the language lingers on. Many schools still record pupils' misdemeanours as 'strikes', a testament to the days when they were literally beaten.

Of course, it's not just adults who dehumanise children to legitimise violence. Children dehumanise children too, as William Golding demonstrated. This dehumanisation can start as young as five and six.[172] Children perceive their friends as human and those who are not their friends as less than human. This is the beginning of the in-group/out-group dynamic. The more distant a particular child is within the out-group, the more harsh are the behaviours to which they can be subjected. New technologies have led to all manner of new forms of cyber-bullying, and catfishing is one such example: where people are innocently lured into forming intense personal online relationships with fake identities. They are charmed, flattered, understood and feel as if they are in love. They will often share all sorts of intimate information, exposing their deepest insecurities and being induced to send compromising photos. Then, sometimes after months or even years, they discover that the identity they have been corresponding with was fake. At this point, their messages, their photos and videos are revealed and shared. The victim is left not only dejected but humiliated – the innocent butt of a sick joke. The consequences can be catastrophic.

Katelyn Davis, a schoolgirl from Georgia, was catfished by someone known as 'Ben' for seven months. When she found out she had been catfished, she uploaded a video saying, 'He catfished me. So that killed me. Badly.'[173] Katelyn Davis lived out her life on social media. She was desperate to be a You-Tube star (a concept we will explore later). On 30 December 2016 – streaming live on Live.me – she went out into her backyard, hung a rope around a tree and hanged herself live in front of her followers. Katelyn was just twelve years old.

Another craze is 'bitch slapping' or 'happy slapping' – where the bully hits an unsuspecting child whilst being videoed by their friends. There are countless videos of this on YouTube. A shocking number of these attacks have left children in comas, severely disabled for life.

But possibly the strangest term to have emerged in the past few years is the notion of grooming. The term 'grooming' first appeared in the context of child abuse in an article for the *Chicago Tribune* dated 28 May 1985. The article explored how paedophiles justify their own behaviour to themselves. 'These "friendly molesters" become acquainted with their targeted victim and the victim's parents, gaining their trust while secretly grooming the child as a sexual partner. Some youngsters are seduced so skillfully, they do not initially sense anything unnatural or wrong about engaging in sex.'[174]

'Grooming' is a strange term to use to talk about child abuse. It starts from the precept that the child is an animal, and that the process is natural and loving, yet there's clearly nothing natural or loving about it. There is, however, a connection between animal abuse and child abuse.

In 88 per cent of cases of child abuse where there are pets in the home, the pets have also been abused.[175] That's why the National Society for the Prevention of Cruelty to Children advises professionals investigating signs of child abuse to look at how the pets in the home are being treated.[176] One study showed that 43 per cent of the shooters in the recent spate of schoolyard killings had committed animal cruelty beforehand and usually with an animal frequently kept as a pet – and viewed as a member of the family – such as a cat or a dog.[177] Many countries in the world are now linking up animal abuse charities with those that work on domestic abuse.

In many cases of domestic abuse, the relationship between the perpetrator and animals in the house serves as a metaphor for the relationship between the perpetrator and their victims. Pets are invariably seen as part of the family. If the pet is being abused, a message is sent to the child: 'I can do this to our pets; I can do this to you too.'

Donna Ferrato is a photojournalist who has spent years investigating domestic abuse. Her enquiries first began in the late 1970s when she was photographing a celebrity couple. 'One night, I witnessed a horrific scene: Garth attacked Lisa and beat her mercilessly as she cowered in the master bathroom. That night changed me forever.' She noted that Garth kept 'a pet boa constrictor and a pet ferret in adjacent glass boxes in the same bathroom where he had beaten Lisa. The ferret was forced to live in a state of constant anxiety next to the eye of the ever-hungry snake.'[178]

The animals sent a message through metaphor: 'This is the nature of our relationship. I am powerful. You are weak. This is our natural order. I can kill you any time I like. You are mine.'

When I read about Ferrato's work, I remembered a story about Michael Jackson. Peter Guber, who ran Sony for much of the 1980s, once told how Jackson invited him to his house in the early 1990s to talk about his career. Jackson was, at that time, riding high on the success of *Dangerous*, but he'd decided he wanted to make a shift into the movies. Guber was sceptical. But what do you know about drama, Michael?

Jackson took Guber upstairs to the hallway outside his bedroom and showed him a huge glass terrarium housing his boa constrictor, Muscles. Muscles was coiled around a tree branch, tracking a little white mouse that was trembling in the wood shavings below. Jackson explained that they had to feed Muscles live mice because otherwise he wouldn't eat. The dead ones just didn't get his attention. Jackson explained Muscles's modus operandi. 'First he uses fear to get the mouse's attention, then he waits, building tension. Finally, when the mouse is so terrified it can't move, Muscles will close in. That's drama!'[179]

Jackson was using his boa constrictor to make a point. But can you imagine how terrified a child would have been to see this huge boa constrictor tracking a live mouse as they headed into the King of Pop's bedroom for one of his pyjama parties? What kind of point would that make? What if Michael Jackson had made a similar point to the child to the one he made to Guber? How would that child have felt?

Michael Jackson kept a whole menagerie of dangerous animals on his Neverland estate, including tigers and alligators, whom he would feed chickens. He once described inviting Jane Fonda to his house, saying he got the tiger out and was 'fooling around with him' and everyone got scared.[180] Likewise, he'd often remove Muscles from the glass terrarium and stroke him, removing his dead layers of skin.

To Guber's point, Jackson clearly did understand the art of drama. He knew that drama was all about fear and control. Remember how he dangled his baby over a hotel balcony in Berlin? Themes of fear ran right through his main albums – from *Thriller* to *Bad* and *Dangerous*. The cover of *Thriller* featured Michael Jackson with a tiger on his lap. The original artwork for *Dangerous* includes an array of animal and angels, like a perverted version of the Great Chain of Being, with symbols of evolutionary progress at the bottom, and Michael Jackson and his chimpanzee, Bubbles, at the top.

When Michael Jackson was investigated for child abuse in 2003, his home was raided. He was eventually exonerated of all the charges against him, but an extensive collection of pornography and homoerotic literature was found. This included naked pictures of the child actors from the set of the 1963 film of *Lord of the Flies*. It was also revealed in 2016 that multiple pictures of animal torture, sadomasochism and child pornography were found in a triple-locked closet in his bedroom. Radar Online quoted insiders from the investigation who said, 'The documents exposed Jackson as a manipulative, drug-and-sex-crazed predator who used blood, gore, sexually explicit images of animal sacrifice and perverse adult sex acts to bend children to his will.'[181]

Whether this insider's conclusions are right or wrong, we may never know. But certainly, there were not the same numbers of accusers rushing out to condemn Michael Jackson as there were who came out after the death of Jimmy Savile. Savile has been posthumously exposed as one of Britain's most prolific paedophiles. He was, however, never charged with any crime during his life. The one time that he was interviewed by police on suspicion of child abuse – in January 2009 by officers from Surrey Police – Savile used a series of dehumanising metaphors to 'other' his accusers.

Early on in the interview he said:

In my business … people are looking for a bit of blackmail … It started in the 1950s and it's always either someone looking for a few quid … I grew up in a charity type family … The reward for helping people is sometimes you get, like a situation like this for instance, when you are very nice, cos you can see the friendly way that I am, and all of a sudden, somebody turns round and bites your leg.

So, children are dogs…

Towards the end of the interview, he again referred to the people who were making allegations against him as animals: 'My business there's women looking for a few quid, we always get something like this coming up for Christmas, because we want a few quid for Christmas, right, and normally you can brush them away like midges.'[182]

He was also asked questions about allegations of sex abuse at Duncroft, a state school for intelligent but emotionally disturbed teenage girls. He described it as a 'lock-up', emphasising that the children there were like animals, kept under lock and key.

In 2012, the former headmistress of Duncroft joined Savile in dismissing some of the allegations by former pupils. She agreed with Savile that some were motivated by money. She also dehumanised the accusers, using her own animal imagery: 'They come out of the woodwork for money. I do object to my school being targeted … wild allegations by well-known delinquents.'[183]

Sadly, there are many people in positions of responsibility over children who see children as little more than animals. It's what makes the educational establishment's obsession with *Lord of the Flies* particularly concerning. It seems more of an indictment of the whole system than the children they are supposed to be protecting.

After William Golding's death, his private diaries came to light. These provided further insight into his own perspective on children.[184] In his journals he recorded an occasion in his first year at university when he took a fifteen-year-old girl called Dora for a walk on Marlborough Common. He described how he 'tried unhandily to rape her'. He wrote that she was 'depraved by nature' and 'already as sexy as an ape'.[185] Angry with himself because he 'made such a bad hand at rape', he cried that she was a 'silly little bitch', at which point she began to 'howl' and he let her go.[186]

Maybe when he crafted the quote for Piggy that opened this chapter, what Golding was considering was not the savagery of children. Maybe the real question he was contemplating was his own savagery?

GORILLA

In the teaching of ethics, there is a famous thought experiment known as 'the trolley problem'. It usually goes something like this. A trolley is rolling very fast down some railway tracks towards five people who are tied to the tracks. They will all be killed on impact. You have in your hand a lever. If you pull it, the trolley will divert to a different track, where it will kill a fat man who is tied to the other track. What do you do?

This problem raises all sorts of moral questions and introduces ethical theories such as utilitarianism (how you can do the most good for the most people) and deontology (how you can do as much good as possible, although your actions are more important than the consequences). It's an intriguing moral quandary and it can leave people merrily arguing for hours. It comes up frequently in popular culture. Season 5, Episode 8 of *Orange Is the New Black*, titled 'Tied to the Tracks', explored some of the issues involved. It's tricky.

Thankfully, most of us will never wind up in a position

like that. But many of us do drive, and driving also requires quick life-or-death decisions.

So, let's imagine a different scenario. Say you're driving along a road in northern France at 80 kph and you see a concrete block in the middle of the road ahead of you. Two people are walking on the pavement to the left. One person is walking on the pavement to the right. What do you do? Do you:

1. Continue forward, heading straight into the concrete block, leading almost certainly to your own death?
2. Turn the car left, into the two people on the pavement, who you will probably kill, but who will cushion your blow enough to save your own life?
3. Turn the car right, into the person on his own, who you will also probably kill, but again saving your own life?

This is a moral quandary that can keep people happily arguing for weeks. Now let's complicate the matter further. The two people to your left have a different skin colour to yours whilst the person to your right is your mother. Does that make a difference?

If you don't feel comfortable sorting out these kinds of dilemmas, then you probably don't have what it takes to be a police officer. Every day, police officers are regularly thrown into all sorts of dangerous situations – terrorist attacks, robberies, fights – where they have to make split-second life-or-death decisions, the consequences of which could live with them for ever.

Take Blane Salamoni from the Baton Rouge Police

Department in Louisiana. On 5 July 2016, he was called out to the parking lot of a Triple S Food Mart following reports there was a black man outside the store, selling CDs and waving a handgun.

When Salamoni arrived at the scene with his partner Howie Lake, they were confronted by a large African-American man who stood 5 feet 11 inches tall and weighed over 200 pounds. They moved in to arrest him. Salamoni put a gun to his head and forced him over the hood of a nearby sedan. 'Put your hands on the car or I'm going shoot you in your fucking head! You understand me?' They administered a Taser, then rugby tackled him to the ground, pinning him to the floor. Salamoni noticed the suspect had a gun and called out to Lake, 'He's got a gun! Gun!' Lake warned the suspect, 'If you fucking move, I swear to God!' The suspect moved. Salamoni cried, 'Lake, he's going for the gun!' Six bullets were fired. The suspect died on the scene from multiple gunshot wounds to chest and back.

The man they killed was Alton Sterling. Sterling was a 37-year-old African American with an extensive criminal record, including a history of sexual and violent offences. The post-mortem revealed he had cocaine, opiates, amphetamines, methamphetamines and several forms of THC in his bloodstream at the time of the killing, as well as alcohol and caffeine. Officers also retrieved a loaded .38 calibre revolver from his front pocket.

So... what do you think? Do you think the officers took the correct action? If you do, your views are sharply at odds with those of the local community. Videos of the killing were posted on social media immediately after the attack, prompting hundreds of demonstrators to come out and protest at the Triple S Food Mart. Chanting 'No justice, no peace,' they lit candles and left flowers. Someone painted a mural of Sterling across the side of the store. As time passed, anger grew, the protests spread and tensions between the African-American community and the local police grew.

Two days later, at another protest in Dallas, Texas, a former soldier called Micah Xavier Johnson opened fire, killing five police officers and wounding eleven others. It was the deadliest incident for US law enforcement since 9/11. Then, on 17 July, in a separate incident, another former soldier, Gavin Eugene Long, shot and killed three police officers in Baton Rouge before being shot himself by a SWAT officer. Eight police officers murdered in a fortnight – all provoked at least partly by the split-second decisions of Salamoni on the night of 5 July 2016. But do you think he did the right thing?

The Baton Rouge Police Department didn't think so. Before that night, Salamoni had been a highly commended officer and came from a long line of public safety officers. His mother, Melissa Salamoni, had been Baton Rouge Police's first female chief of staff, whilst his father, Captain Noel Salamoni, had led the city police union.[187] He ended up getting sacked by the Baton Rouge Police Department for violating use-of-force policies.

Tricky, isn't it? Let's take another officer in a different situation.

Timothy Loehmann was a 26-year-old officer with the Cleveland Police Department. On 22 November 2014, he was on patrol with his partner, 46-year-old Frank Garmback, when they received a report of a black male outside the

Cudell Recreation Centre who 'keeps pulling a gun out of his pants and pointing it at people'. As the officers drove into the parking lot of the recreation centre, they saw the suspect putting the gun into his waistband. Loehmann told the suspect to put his hands up. The suspect reached for his waistband. Loehmann instantly fired two shots from a distance of less than ten feet and the suspect fell immediately to the ground.

The suspect in this case, Tamir Rice, was just twelve years old. The gun he had in his waistband was not a real gun but a toy. It was capable only of shooting little plastic pellets. Rice's injuries were clearly devastating, yet neither of the officers present gave him first aid. And when Tamir's fourteen-year-old sister ran forward to comfort her wounded brother, Loehmann forced her down to the ground, handcuffed her, put her in the back of the patrol car and told her she would be arrested unless she calmed down.

The whole situation unfolded in less than two seconds, from Loehmann's arrival to Tamir's shooting. You can see it on YouTube. That's how long Loehmann had to think about his response when he saw Rice reach for his waistband... The police car had not even stopped properly at the time that Tamir was shot.

The county prosecutor, Tim McGinty, absolved Loehmann of any responsibility. He described it as a perfect storm of human error and miscommunication. Tamir's mother rejected his verdict. She said McGinty had acted 'like the police officers' defence attorney'. She filed a suit for wrongful death against Loehmann, Garmback and the City of Cleveland. The case was settled in 2016 for $6 million.[188]

These are incredibly difficult dilemmas. It's hard to decide what's right or wrong, even when we have lots of time to consider the facts calmly and rationally. But here's the thing: in situations like this, there is no time for calm, rational contemplation. Our hearts are pounding. Our minds are racing. We are dependent wholly on instinct. But can we necessarily trust our instincts?

Jennifer Eberhardt at Stanford University thinks not. Her life's work has been the study of instinctive bias against African Americans. In her paper 'Not Yet Human: Implicit Knowledge, Historical Dehumanization and Contemporary Consequences', she carried out one experiment which seems particularly pertinent.

She gathered together 115 white male undergraduates and split them into two groups. She showed both groups a two-minute video clip of police officers violently subduing a suspect of undeterminable race. The first group was told the suspect was black. The second group was told the suspect was white. When asked if they thought the violence was justified, both groups replied yes/no in approximately the same proportions. So, no racial bias was evident at that stage.

Then she repeated the experiment. This time, she flashed words such as 'chimp', 'gorilla' and 'orangutan' on the screen. The words did not appear long enough for the rational brain to notice, just long enough for the instinctive brain to see. This time around, when the participants were asked if they thought the violence was justified, there was a marked difference. In the case of those who were told the suspect was white, the subliminal words made no difference. In the case of those who were told the suspect was black, they were more likely to believe that the violence was justified.[189]

Eberhardt argues that this shows we have lying with us a strong association between black people and apes, which needs only the gentlest prompt to tease out and it will provoke the most violent reaction. Just the slightest suggestion of an ape – imperceptible even to the conscious brain – is enough to provoke a change in the appropriateness of the punishment which is meted out.

So it seems particularly significant that, earlier on in the evening of the infamous Rodney King beating which sparked the LA riots, Laurence Powell, the notorious 28-year-old officer who administered most of the strikes against King, had used racist language in a message he sent on the squad car when describing a case of domestic violence he'd attended earlier that evening involving a mixed-race couple. 'It was right out of *Gorillas in the Mist*,' he said.

The violence Powell meted out to King that night was unimaginably brutal: King was left with nine separate skull fractures, a shattered eye socket and cheekbone, a broken leg, concussion, injuries to both knees, a partially paralysed face and brain damage.[190] What provoked King's attack? Maybe it takes us back to Eberhardt's experiment. Maybe, somewhere deep in Powell's subconscious, he didn't quite perceive he was face-to-face with a human, but with someone whom he likely saw as a 'gorilla', given his previous comment. It seems possible that his otherwise inexplicable motives in carrying out such a brutal attack were due to how he viewed black people in general. His first reaction when he saw the video of the attack was to say, 'Is that even me?' He may have been acting on autopilot, but where did these ideas come from originally?

The idea of black people as apes dates back hundreds of

years. As Winthrop D. Jordan wrote in his book, *White Over Black: American Attitudes Toward the Negro, 1550–1812*, the dehumanisation of black people was an essential strategy for colonialists and slave traders who wanted to justify their wicked subhuman treatment. If you want to put people in chains, cages and beat them to within an inch of their lives, it's much easier if you perceive them as less than human.[191]

To be regarded as an ape is different to the other animals we have looked at: they are not easily stamped upon, like vermin; nor are they easily controllable, like dogs or pets; instead, apes need a very special care – because whilst in some ways an ape is subhuman, in others it is superhuman: extraordinarily strong, powerful and exceptionally aggressive. Maybe this explains the exceptional punishment which is often meted out to black people today? Certainly, it was used to justify the inhumane treatment that was dispensed by the colonialists.

But this myth that black people were like apes was not just perpetuated by those with a commercial interest in colonialism; it was supported by leading scientists of the day. Samuel Thomas von Sömmerring and Charles White produced numerous texts comparing black people with apes.

When the Swedish botanist and zoologist Carl Linnaeus produced his *Systema Naturæ* in the eighteenth century, the most advanced and detailed analysis of the Great Chain of Being ever, categorising 4,400 animals and 7,700 plants into a hierarchy, and he explicitly placed black people close to apes. And, whilst *Homo Europæus* was described as 'gentle mannered, acute in judgement', *Homo Afer* was portrayed as 'crafty' and 'indolent'.

Josiah C. Nott and George R. Gliddon's 1854 *Types of Mankind* contained illustrations that explicitly compared black people to apes: and this was not a text that had been produced by the far right; this was the leading and supposedly objective American scientific text on racial differences at the time.[192] Such attitudes prevailed right up until the twentieth century, when French Nobel Prize-winning physiologist Charles Richet wrote an essay entitled 'La Sélection humaine', which argued that black people were intellectually like children and physically like apes.[193]

To illustrate the genetic similarities between apes and black people, in 1906, a man from the Congo named Ota Benga was placed in a cage with a gorilla and an orangutan at the Bronx Zoo. Benga was given a bow and arrow and the cage had also been thoughtfully littered with bones for his amusement. Forty thousand people came to visit him in the zoo. Most visitors were amused but not everyone was so impressed.

Reverend Gordon, a local black minister, wrote to the *New York Times*: 'Our race, we think, is depressed enough without exhibiting one of us with the apes. We think we are worthy of being considered human beings.' The *New York Times* responded instantly and in no uncertain terms: 'The Reverend colored brother should be told that evolution ... is now taught in the textbooks of all the schools, and that it is no more debatable than the multiplication table.'[194] Well, that put him in his place. You can't argue with science.

This was a long time ago, but still these pernicious perceptions and attitudes linger on. At football games around the world, you can still hear thousands of fans making monkey noises when a black footballer gets the ball. Sometimes, bananas are thrown on to the pitch. When neo-Nazi group National Action marched on Parliament Square in 2014, they put a banana into the hand of the Nelson Mandela statue.

Black people, particularly those in positions of power, continue to be derided as apes. In the past year alone, Michelle Obama, Diane Abbott and Gina Miller (the British-Guyanese lawyer who is challenging Brexit) have been described respectively as an 'ape in heels', an 'ape in lipstick' and 'a primate [who] should be hunted down and killed'.[195]

During the Plebgate inquiry into the conduct of police officers working in Downing Street, it was revealed that one had sent a text message during the London riots saying, 'These little black cunts are really fucking me off. If they want to act like monkeys why don't they fuck off back to the jungle.'[196]

These metaphorical frames can affect black people in all sorts of everyday ways throughout their lives. It starts from the minute they arrive at school, and sometimes even as early as preschool. Studies show that black children are perceived as more apelike than white children. They are perceived as four or five years older than their white counterparts. This inevitably affects how they are treated. They are almost four times as likely to be suspended from school.[197] And it's not just white teachers who treat black pupils unfairly: teachers of all races are likely to treat black kids unfairly. Even black teachers have a dim view of their black pupils.[198]

When you follow this trend through to the criminal justice system, the problem becomes even more pronounced. Black children are eighteen times more likely than their

white counterparts to be sentenced to adult correctional facilities as opposed to juvenile facilities. And children who
are sentenced as adults are twice as likely to be assaulted by
a correctional officer, five times as likely to be sexually assaulted and eight times as likely to commit suicide.[199] It even
affects the literal life-or-death issue of capital punishment.

Jennifer Eberhardt examined 153 cases in the Philadelphia
area in which a defendant was found guilty and statutes
allowed for the application of the death penalty. Reports of
those cases in the *Philadelphia Inquirer* showed that black
men were much more likely to be described in apelike terms
than whites. More worryingly, the number of ape-related
metaphors used in relation to the defendant predicted the
likelihood that they would be sentenced to death.[200] So terms
like 'aping a victim's screams' and 'urban jungle' might sound
relatively innocent but, make no mistake: potentially these
are words that kill.

This is where insidious images and frames of reference
can be activated wholly outside of our conscious awareness.
If someone intervened at a dinner party and said, 'Well,
these black people are monkeys!' then they would rightly be
instantly condemned. But they could almost certainly talk
about an urban jungle without any censure. Is there really any
difference? Isn't this ultimately just the same kind of imagery?
Doesn't it have precisely the same effect? If this is so, then we
are almost certainly all guilty, particularly over the last few
years, because we've all been talking about the Calais Jungle.

By locking dehumanising imagery into the name of this
refugee camp, it's become impossible even to speak about it
without conjuring up the image that the occupants are not

human. How can any compassionate conversation take place about the occupants when it starts from that point?

According to the book *Voices from the 'Jungle'*, it was the French media who first coined the phrase *la jungle de Calais*.[201] When you google 'Calais and Jungle', you get 70 million results. Googling 'Calais and croissant' garners only 500,000 results. Today, the phrase is universally understood across Europe.

But why was it called the Calais Jungle? Why not the Calais Enclosure, the Calais Dungeon or the Calais Internment Camp? The 'Jungle' implies scary, unknown animals – and of course the majority of the people living there were people of colour. Descriptions of the people in the camp invariably added to this imagery, with descriptions of the inhabitants usually characterising them as wild, ferocious, beastly.

This certainly seems to have affected the way they were perceived and treated. A report by Human Rights Watch reported police were interrupting the delivery of vital aid to the camp, including food, water, clothing and blankets.[202] Ninety-seven per cent of children surveyed said they had experienced police violence.[203] And of course, when the jungle was removed, with young children tear-gassed and their homes set on fire, no one much objected. It's not often we burn down people's homes, but this is considered (just about) OK to do with a jungle. In fact, for many thousands of years we have understood that demolishing jungles clears the path for civilisation.

It wasn't just the police who saw the refugees as subhuman; many members of the public did too. Lorry drivers along the A16 road near Calais have been frequently uploading videos to YouTube showing themselves deliberately driving into and shouting abuse at the refugees who walk along these roads. These videos are attracting millions of views; many of the commentators celebrate the drivers, describing the refugees as wild animals and savages.[204] This is not just a game they're playing. Dozens of refugees have now been killed along this stretch.[205]

On 10 October 2016, the MailOnline reported that a refugee from Eritrea had been killed along this road. The story was related under the headline 'Migrant thugs attacked British driver after he ran over and killed an Eritrean at Calais when he stopped and tried to save his life'. The dead man was not even given the dignity of a name in the story. In researching this book, I have searched everywhere to try to find out this man's name. I even offered a prize on Twitter to any followers who could identify him. It is extraordinary that in an age when the media has made sure everyone knows the names of 'Harambe the gorilla' and 'Cecil the lion', a real human being who was killed by a motorist should be left nameless.

To date, 1,618 people have commented on the MailOnline's article. Just three commentators showed sympathy for the dead man. Most condemned the migrants, describing them as 'savages', 'violent animals' and 'beasts'. Many sympathised with the driver: 'My thoughts are with the driver and his family.' One commentator simply said, 'Hope the car's paintwork wasn't scratched too badly.'

So, returning to the trolley problem we started with, this commentator's main concern would not have been the people tied to the track; if they had been black, he'd probably be more concerned by what happened to the trolley.

SPIN

John Ayrton Paris was the Brian Cox of his day. Throughout the early nineteenth century, he travelled the capital cities of Europe demonstrating science to children using an ingenious selection of little toys he'd invented especially for that purpose. One of the most enchanting of these toys was the thaumatrope.

Today, thaumatropes are rarely to be found outside of animation museums, but we have bought a few of them, which we keep at home. The thaumatrope is a circular disc with a hole on either side with a piece of string connecting the two holes. You draw a picture of one thing on one side, a picture of something else on the other and then, when you spin the disc around using the string, the two pictures blur into one. So, for instance, you can draw a bird on one side and a cage on the other: spin the disc quickly and, hey presto, it looks like the bird is in the cage. Or you draw flowers on one side and a vase on the other and it looks like the flowers are in the vase. And so on. You get the idea.

Paris invented the thaumatrope to demonstrate 'persistence

of vision', which is the way our brain retains an image long after it's gone. It was Aristotle who first wrote about 'persistence of vision', after observing how long the vision of the sun remained in the mind long after one had stopped looking at it. Thaumatropes demonstrate this point in a delightful way. In the film *Sleepy Hollow*, Johnny Depp's character, Ichabod Crane, spins a thaumatrope to a young girl called Katrina. Katrina cries gleefully, 'It is magic!' Crane replies, 'It is not magic. It is what we call optics. Separate pictures which become one on the spinning. It is truth. But truth is not always appearance.'

The thaumatrope sums up to me what we mean when we talk about spin: in the context of political spin, the art of spin and spin doctors. You spin two images together, repeatedly and rapidly. Eventually, the two images become blurred and inextricably interconnected. That's what advertising, branding and political communication is fundamentally about: establishing connections between what a company is selling and what a customer needs. Dolce & Gabbana = style. Ferrari = machismo. ASDA = a sense of belonging.

Advertising works very much like a thaumatrope. On one side, you have your literal product; on the other, you have your customer's dreams. On one side of the disc, you have what is real; on the other side, you have something surreal. Spin them together and you've created a new truth: something that far surpasses your real offer, enabling you to sell something which is much more desirable and valuable.

Take Jack Daniel's. The literal reality is a drink, and a very successful one at that: it is the bestselling whiskey in Britain and the bestselling American whiskey in the world.[206] But how many people actually buy it because of the taste? Do you remember the first time you tried whiskey? People usually wince and grimace on a first taste. We have to force ourselves to like it, trying it over and over again until eventually we can regard it as bearable.

Why do we do this to ourselves? Why do we put ourselves through this? Why must we seek to overcome that natural resistance? It's because we are not seeking whiskey: our deepest desire is to escape. We want transportation somewhere different. We want to go to that timeless place that only Jack Daniel's promises: that land of 'well-rounded hills, untroubled skies, elm shaded lanes and long shadowed cattle astandin' in the corners of meadows ... Old families and flowered front porches ... Sunlight slanting on weathered barns. Cowbells that are rung when it's time for dinner and fresh baked pies simmering in the kitchen.'

The creative director who worked on the original brief for Jack Daniel's back in the 1950s knew what they were doing. 'We're not selling a bottle of booze, we're selling a place.'[207] The notion of Jack Daniel's country has barely changed in the sixty years since. So, when we're sat in our living room on a Friday night knocking back a glass of Jack Daniel's, we're probably doing it not because we crave that drink so much as we crave escapism. That promise of transportation lies deep in our subconscious minds because we've seen it so many times throughout our lives, in imagery on adverts, bottles and bars, every time we go shopping, flick through a magazine or glance at the bottles in a bar.

David Ogilvy, the godfather of advertising, once scoffed at the idea people might actually buy Jack Daniel's because of the taste.

Why do some people choose Jack Daniel's, while others choose Grand Dad or Taylor? Have they tried all three and compared the taste? Don't make me laugh. The reality is that these three brands have different images which appeal to different kinds of people. It isn't the whiskey they choose, it's the image. The brand image is 90 per cent of what the distiller has to sell.[208]

The Jack Daniel's campaign is one of the most successful branding campaigns in the history of advertising. On one side of the thaumatrope, you have the real product, which is whiskey; on the other side, you have the surreal image of Jack Daniel's country. Spin them together, you have a best-selling product. That's branding.

But what we've been looking at through this book is like a branding campaign as well. The thaumatrope provides the perfect metaphor for what's going on. On one side of the disc we have the little Alfie Evans his parents saw, which you can still see in videos on YouTube: his eyes open, yawning and stretching, responsive to touch; on the other side, we have a vegetable, inanimate matter, best off underground. On one side of the disc, we have Luciana Berger, a hard-working MP trying to do the best for her constituents and her country; on the other, we have a snake. On one side of the disc, we have an Eritrean refugee; on the other, a powerful, vicious animal. On one side is realism; on the other, surrealism. On one side, truth; on the other, lies. Spin the two together and they combine to create our perception of truth.

And, just as those conceptions of Jack Daniel's are deeply embedded in our mind, so too are the conceptions of what different social groups represent: of what it means to be black, to be a woman or to be a child. They are deeply ingrained in our consciousness. The words and images by which we dehumanise different groups have been slowly coming at us, repeatedly, over and over, since the day we were born.

There is a glorious innocence in the child who does not yet understand the world of metaphor. I have watched with wonder as my daughters have at first rejected, then become confused by and finally accepted the various metaphorical concepts we all live by. It doesn't take long. By the age of three, children have heard between 3 million and 11 million words.[209] Assuming we hear a metaphor once every sixteen words, that means a child has already heard at least 200,000 metaphors by the time they've started school. How long before they stick? The Leitner system says that we need to hear a word five times before its meaning sticks. That's not much. If you spend three minutes listening to 'Is That Yo' Bitch?' by Jay-Z feat. Twista and Missy Elliott, you've heard the word 'bitch' no fewer than forty times. That's more than enough to get the idea that women are bitches in less time than it takes to boil an egg.

This is how we learn things. Learning is all about establishing connections in our brain. We have billions of neurons in our minds and, when connections are forged between these neurons, we've learnt something. The more these connections are repeated, the stronger the links grow, until eventually we create synapses. From then on, such associations can be activated instantly and immediately with a minimum of effort.

If you are walking through a shopping centre and someone shouts out 'Bitch!', what is your first instinct? Would you assume they were talking about a dog or a woman? Such associations are deeply embedded, and it is from that grounding that our conception of social hierarchy has grown. This is how we learn our place in the world and our relationship with others. The notion that all people must be treated equally is an idea that is written down in the texts of pretty much every religion or constitution on the planet, but it has no basis in reality: it is a myth. Different societal groups are readily ascribed their own status, and these are positions that we all learn and understand from not long after we're born.

A 2015 study by psychologists at MIT and Harvard University asked a cross-section of 201 American subjects to rate different societal groups against the famous *March of Progress* with 100 being 'most evolved' and 0 being 'least evolved'. Americans scored themselves 91.5 but placed Mexican immigrants at 83.7, Arabs at 80.9 and Muslims at just 77.6.[210] This was not a sophisticated test to tease out implicit bias; this was a simple question to ask people to admit they perceived some societal groups as less than human, which they readily agreed to do.

So that's conscious bias. It gets even more complicated when you start looking at instinctive bias. Harvard has developed an online test to check out your own prejudices which anyone can access at understandingprejudice.org. The test is impossible to cheat. It works through what is called 'affective priming'. It shows you pictures of white faces or black faces, followed quickly by words that are either positive or negative, e.g. good words might be flower, sunshine, warmth; bad words might be devil, cockroach, cancer. You have to quickly categorise the words as good or bad. If you perceive the image you have just seen as positive, you will quickly be able to categorise a positive word. If you perceive the image you just saw as negative, you will hesitate. That hesitation may only last a millisecond but, by identifying patterns in the pace you are categorising words as good and bad, the programme can quickly identify if you have positive or negative associations with different skin colours. It can identify instinctive biases which you might not even be aware of yourself.

I grew up in a multicultural part of London, travel all around the world and think of myself as a pretty OK human being. I was horrified to see I have a 'strong preference for white people'. Moreover, this is apparently the result for 48 per cent of people who take this test (and remember, too, that it is probably only people who are concerned about prejudice who will take the test, which makes you wonder about the rest). Many black people also take this test. They too are frequently horrified to discover that they have a 'strong preference for white people'.

These preferences lie very deep. And such instinctive feelings are impossible to shake off. Even people with chronic short-term memory loss can still remember if someone is an 'insider' or an 'outsider' with 89 per cent accuracy.[211]

Such cultural frames of reference become even more insidious when you look at their role in big powerful institutions like the NHS, the police and government. These are the institutions which determine more than any other how fair our society is. If you are a nurse in a hospital and you hear a respected doctor talking about the poor homeless people who come in for treatment as 'rubbish' or 'the dregs', how long before you repeat that idea? If you are a young police recruit, and you hear a senior officer who guards the Prime Minister's residence talking about black people as 'monkeys' who should 'fuck off back to the jungle', how long before you start thinking that way yourself? If you are a young soldier who is instructed by a major general to treat prisoners like 'dogs', then why shouldn't you put someone on a leash?

We are bound to comply. With a few very rare exceptions, like Harry Stanley in Mỹ Lai or the one nurse out of twenty-two who refused to administer the fatal drug when instructed, it's human nature to comply with authority. But these are people who hold in their hands the power of life and death. You can see the problems that might arise: when doctors are deciding which patients to give priority to on a Saturday night in A&E; when police are deciding how to respond in a volatile situation; when local authorities are deciding where to target resources.

It's like the parachute test. A plane carrying five people is about to crash. A lawyer, a mother, a scientist, a nurse and an engineer are on board – but there's only one parachute. Who gets it? Whose life do you save? But let's think of it another way. The engineer is black. The lawyer is disabled. The mother comes from a council estate. The scientist is Muslim. The nurse is a refugee. Whose life do you save now? None of us can be blind to the prejudices that exist within ourselves. They are inescapable.

Many of the linguistic and perceptual metaphorical frames we have been exploring in this book have been around for thousands of years. George Orwell famously warned we should never use a metaphor we are used to seeing in print.

With all due deference to the great man, this is bollocks. On the evidence of this book, there's just a small handful of metaphors which been repeated over and over for many thousands of years. Their power is evident when you look at the distribution of wealth, health and power around the world. And they continue to be perpetuated every day, across all sorts of forums, media and channels.

Just look at the newspaper stands on any particular day. I analysed all of the front-page stories across the whole of the British press in the six weeks leading up to the 2017 general election. More than 70 per cent of those front-page stories included one or other of the metaphors examined in this book. Such repetition is bound to affect our language, thought and perception. It's the same as the phenomenon of 'persistence of vision'. The images remain in our mind's eye long after we've ceased to look at them. It's like the little blots we see in our minds after staring at the sun.

Which brings me to my next point. So far in this book, we have looked at how something beautiful – a human life – can be spun into something disgusting. Well, just as you can spin something attractive into something grotesque, so you can spin something grotesque into something attractive.

The Sun newspaper is, as Kelvin MacKenzie once put it, a newspaper for the bloke 'in the pub, a right old fascist, wants to send the wogs back, buy his poxy council house, he's afraid of the unions, afraid of the Russians, hates the queers and the weirdoes and drug dealers'.[212] Yet when we talk about the sun, this instantly activates associations of light, warmth and happiness. Maybe it's even godlike. Certainly, we look up to it. We can't help but activate these positive associations.

The neural connections are too deep to avoid. And, make no mistake, *The Sun* actively uses these abiding images to maintain its power and escape accountability.

After the Leveson Inquiry recommended that the press be subjected to regulation, Trevor Kavanagh wrote an article in *The Sun*'s defence: 'Sunlight is the best disinfectant – and the press shines a light on our public figures and services and holds them to account.'[213] He's actively using the sun metaphor to maintain the newspaper's power and authority. As Malcolm X put it, 'If you're not careful, the newspapers will have you hating the people who are being oppressed, and loving the people who are doing the oppressing.' It doesn't have to be that way. In Liverpool, of course, many people still call it 'The Scum', after Kelvin MacKenzie wrote in an article titled 'The Truth' that fans at Hillsborough had behaved like animals. And one of the first reviews of *The Sun* after Rupert Murdoch took control said it was 'more like a paraffin lamp in a brothel than a sun'. Touché.[214]

But *The Sun* is not the real problem here. The power of the press is diminishing by the day. We need to look at who has power in today's world. The first part of this book explored metaphors of dehumanisation, exploring the subhuman layers in Valades's image. Now we are going to start looking further up that picture, exploring how metaphor can be used to bring things to life and endow people with superhuman, celestial and even godlike status. Step on up. We're on the stairway to heaven.

ALEXA

Last Christmas, I spent several days with close family and friends, lounging around in a gorgeous Georgian rectory in Devon, enjoying log fires, boozy meals, slow games, food, chocolate and, of course, presents. Last year, as every year, the present that grabbed the most attention came from Harry. Harry has a reputation for wowing us all at Christmas with something flash, invariably the latest gizmo. This year was no exception. He produced this small, circular, white device and placed it in the middle of the coffee table. He smiled proudly. Then, after a brief dramatic pause, he said, 'Alexa, what's the weather today in Bideford?' A voice came out of the little white device, 'The weather today in Bideford is 7 degrees centigrade.'

I've known Harry for fifteen years. He's retired now. I'm not sure exactly what kind of work he did but I know it was something high-security that involved a lot of overseas travel to glamorous places. He never much wanted to talk about it. Whenever I tried to find out more, he'd gently nudge the topic on to something different. He also has this amazing knack for disappearing whenever a family photo is being taken; and if, God forbid, he is still there just whilst the photographer is snapping, his face will invariably disappear just behind someone's shoulder at the crucial moment. He is a fascinating chap. He is like James Bond with issues. Yet, unless my eyes deceived me, here he was, willingly installing a listening device: a device that was capable of hearing every single thing he did, not just from dawn until dusk, but right around the clock.

I couldn't help noticing over the next few days that Harry was becoming increasingly fond of Alexa. He addressed her with an almost affectionate tone. This was very strange. I started winding him up about it. I tried to make him jealous. 'Alexa, would you go out on a date with me?' I asked this little contraption. 'I like you as a friend,' she replied. 'Are you sure?' I asked. 'I'm sorry,' she said.

Now, Alexa is obviously not the first product to be present-ed as a person. Just rustling around my kitchen cupboards, I can find Cap'n Crunch, Uncle Ben and the Jolly Green Giant. We've got Mr Muscle beside the sink, and everybody's fa-vourite vacuum cleaner, Henry, under the stairs. But Alexa seems to have a special power. Lottie, my nine-year-old daughter, came back from school the other day. She told me that one of the girls in year six had told her that Alexa was her best friend. 'Can we get her, Daddy?' Lottie asked. 'Pleeease?!' Thanks, Harry.

Researchers at Cornell University have explored how people perceive, relate and respond to Alexa. In their recent study, '"Alexa Is My New BFF": Social Roles, User

Satisfaction, and Personification of the Amazon Echo', they examined user reviews for Amazon Echo (the product that contains Alexa) and found that more than half of the reviews used the personified name Alexa at least once. They also found a clear correlation between the level of personification and the level of customer satisfaction. So the more we look upon this listening device as a person, the more favourably we respond to it.[215]

Amazon is something of a master of the art of personification. 'Alexa' was given a name, a gender, a personality and a sense of humour. This played a critical role in the marketing of the product. She was actively presented as the ideal woman. The very first advert for Alexa showed a father alone with his daughter – no wife, parents or friends anywhere to be seen – but no matter, Alexa was there to help him cook dinner, put music on for him and even read a bedtime story to his daughter so that he could put his feet up, watch telly and enjoy a nice glass of wine. Brilliant! Wouldn't we all like someone like that in our lives?[216]

Amazon's 2017 Christmas ad campaign was equally enchanting. Whilst thousands of real stores in the UK shut their doors last year for the last time (5,855 stores closed in the UK in 2017, the highest figure since 2010), Amazon's adverts depicted lots of smiling little boxes charmingly bouncing around a massive warehouse, merrily boarding motorbikes, trains and planes, before finally leaping into our hands at our front doors, all accompanied by the soundtrack of Supertramp's 'Give a little bit of my love to you'.[217]

So we're left with the paradox that whilst we can feel ambivalent when another news report comes on the television of redundancies at Mothercare or Toys R Us, we can't help but grin when we see the Amazon adverts with these irresistibly cute and bouncy little boxes. But is Amazon really smiling at us? I don't know, but in Christmas 2017, Jeff Bezos, Amazon's CEO and founder, overtook Bill Gates to become literally the richest man who has ever lived in the history of humanity. His fortune today is estimated at $105.1 billion.[218] I don't think he's smiling at us. I think he's laughing his head off.

Personification is a long-established way of making something strange and new appear attractive. That's because, as human beings, we are fundamentally social creatures and we are instinctively attracted towards other humans. The human face is the most enticing symbol on earth. To find yourself drawn towards a smiling human face is as unconscious and natural an impulse as to recoil from a raging fire. So when you are selling something that people are fearful of – like a new technology – there's an easy way to overcome this. Just stick a whopping big smiling face on it.

Take the car. When cars first appeared on the streets, people were profoundly suspicious and scared of them. These new things were making the most incredible noise, releasing disgusting toxic fumes into the air, and they were self-evidently dangerous. Back then, with few rules or regulations governing what people did on the road, accidents and deaths were occurring all over the place. People were terrified! Cars were perceived, described and regarded as demons. This was probably not surprising given their early appearance: the first models of car, like the Flocken Elektrowagen, looked like some strange spooky apparition. People called them the 'horseless carriage', a description which emphasised their life-lessness, unfamiliarity and lack of soul.[219]

The big leap forward in design and perception came in 1908 with the introduction of Henry Ford's classic Ford Model T. Ford wanted his car to appeal to the widest possible market so not only was it the first mass-produced and readily affordable car, it was also the first car to be designed to look like a human face. It was instantly recognisable as such. The engine was a nose, the lights were the eyes and the front axle represented a smile. The design clearly had the intended effect on people's perception, because no one ever talked about the Model T as a horseless carriage. They instantly got that this was a person. So the Model T came to be known as the 'Tin Lizzie' or the 'Leaping Lena'.

Henry Ford set the standard. And, once Ford had come up with the idea of giving cars faces, they've been built into pretty much every car built ever since. FMRI studies have shown that, when we look at cars, the fusiform face area in the brain – the part that deals with facial recognition – is activated. For people who work in sales and marketing, this part of the brain represents the jackpot. It's quite bizarre: we can come to believe that cars have more personality than people.

This paradox was highlighted in an advert that Magritte produced by commission for Alfa Romeo in 1924. His painting emphasised the facial features of the car, whilst characteristically completely removing entirely the faces from the two women who were standing beside it.[220] Ever the subversive, Magritte was, I think, highlighting that juxtaposition. The personification of products is so powerful it can make a product more attention grabbing even than a human.

And it's remarkable just how easy it is to achieve this effect: just type out a colon, dash and closed bracket and you'll see what I mean. But of course designers can go much further than this, ever so slightly tweaking the design of that face in order to project different personalities and emotions that speak straight to our instincts. We can create faces that make people fearful. Faces that make people protective. If we produce a smiling face, the chances are it will make people smile as well.[221] This is how emotional connections are established.

But superimposing faces on to products can produce surprising behavioural changes as well. One piece of research showed that doing nothing more than sticking a pair of eyes on a dustbin made people more likely to put their rubbish in the bin.[222] Presumably this has the effect of making us subconsciously imagine that there is someone watching us, which guides us to behave more responsibly. I'm sure that after reading this my wife will discreetly draw a human face in our shower to remind me to use the squeegee. And I'll most likely start doing it, too. Smart woman, my wife.

Our minds are always on the lookout for human faces anyway. We actively seek them out. Do you ever look up at the clouds and see a face appear? When my daughters were babies, they would stare at my watch for minutes on end, pressing the glass face in wonder. I wondered why they were doing it. They were instinctively drawn to it because they could see the face.[223] With clock faces, it's easy to perceive a face, which is why we call them that. It's a trick of the trade for sellers to try to heighten this sense of facial perception by setting the hands at 10.10, thereby matching the approximate position of two eyes. A recent check of the top 100 bestselling men's dress watches on Amazon showed that all but three were set at 10.10. Susanne Hurni, head of advertising and marketing at Ulysse Nardin, one of the finest Swiss watch manufacturers in the world, confirms this is standard practice. 'It has the aesthetic of the smiley face, so we try whenever possible to opt for that.'[224]

Sometimes, the personality of a product can feel so strong that we will see it, perceive it and talk about it as if it's a member of the family. We've got a camper van. Her name is Poppy. We're very proud of her. And, let me be clear: she's *definitely* a 'her'. One time a man from the AA came on a call-out. When he arrived, he admired her, patted her on the bonnet and then said, 'What's his name?' I was flabbergasted. I told him firmly – and not a little indignantly – that she was a her, and her name was Poppy, and that I would be grateful if he showed her a little more respect. We laughed about it, obviously, but I did genuinely feel protective of her. She's our baby.

Volkswagen has always been great at personification. The company was conceived by Hitler in a deliberate attempt to emulate Ford's success in America.[225] Volkswagen's first big product was the VW Beetle, designed by Ferdinand Porsche: fun and friendly, the Beetle was an instant success on its release in 1938 and wound up becoming one of the longest-running cars ever made. In the '60s, Disney took the personification of the Beetle even further with the *Herbie* movies. VW's next release – the VW ID due to come out in 2020 – appears even more personified than Herbie. Its features are less angular and more rounded. It reminds me a little of Lightning McQueen in Disney/Pixar's *Cars* movie. I half-expect the car's mouth to open and say, 'Speed. I am speed.'

It's appropriate we turn to Disney at this point, because no one was better at bringing things to life than Walt Disney himself. Of course, animation is all about bringing things to life. The very word 'animation' derives from the Latin *animare*, to give life. This is what animators do. The Disney guide to creating art, passed down from generation to generation of Disney animators, is actually called *Disney Animation: The Illusion of Life*.

Disney's belief was that every object or product had an integral personality. He argued that it was the responsibility of the animator to identify and understand that personality and then bring it to life on screen. He demonstrated how to do that beautifully in one of his earliest films, *Steamboat Willie*. Disney projected Steamboat Willie not just as a steamboat, but as something living: with motivations, feeling and personality. It is hard-working, a bit clumsy, maybe even a little bit tired as well, but ultimately, cheerily getting on with its job, as we all must do. As we watch the cartoon, we can instantly and instinctively interpret and understand these different emotional and behavioural traits.

Frank Thomas and Ollie Johnston were two of Disney's nine old men, the original animators who worked on those classic early films like *Snow White*. They explained how it works in *Disney Animation: The Illusion of Life*.

Most of the machines in [our] lives have personalities that are clearly apparent: the elevator that works only when it wants to (and goes particularly slow when its occupant is in a hurry); the car that will not start (or seems to sulk when not treated just right); the door that always sticks when it can cause most trouble – we are surrounded by objects that do seem to have minds of their own. To find the face in the design of these objects, and one that expresses the feelings that we already have sensed is the problem for the artist.

The ability of the great Disney animators to create life is extraordinary. With nothing more than a paintbrush and a blob of paint, they can take a boring old wardrobe, slap on some big saucer eyes, dilated pupils, flush in a little rosiness to the cheeks and, hey presto, they create within us exactly the same feelings as if we were looking at a newborn baby. They're co-opting our most powerful human instincts.

Walt Disney understood very well the commercial power of personification. Like Magritte, he mastered his craft in advertising. His first job was at Gray Advertising Company at the Pesmen-Rubin Art Studio in Kansas City, producing advertisements and posters for agricultural supply companies. There aren't many people who would see the scope for creating deep bonds of affection in the literally mucky world of agricultural supply, but Disney quickly began putting together posters which made those animals lovable, giving them personalities, feelings and humanlike traits. It was in these anthropomorphic doodles that the seeds of the Disney Corporation were planted.

It's a peculiar world where depicting humans as vermin can legitimise murder whilst turning a mouse into a human can create one of the most successful movie characters, franchises and businesses the world has ever seen. Mickey Mouse's films have won ten Oscar nominations and he even has his own star on the Hollywood Walk of Fame. But arguably Walt Disney's greatest achievement of all was the Disney Corporation: an enterprise that has far outlived him, yet which remains imbued with all his characteristics, ambitions and values. And what a company Disney is too: for many years, it was the most successful animation studio in the world; that was, until someone else came along and created one that was even better.

Steve Jobs could be described as many things – a visionary, a genius, a designer, an artist, a salesman – but crucially, first and foremost, he too was an animator. His power was his ability to create and breathe life into anything: a company, an idea, an argument, a vision or a product. And, as Henry Ford brought the car to life, and Walt Disney brought Mickey Mouse to life, so Steve Jobs brought the computer to life.

Steve Jobs knew the Macintosh computer had a great spec from the word go – with its graphical interface and its inbuilt mouse – but he also knew it would take more than that to win people's hearts. He recruited the best designers from around the world to help. They created what was called the Snow White design language – a tribute to Disney's genius – which was embedded in all the early protocols. There was one element of Mac's design which was particularly important to Jobs. As Walter Isaacson related in his definitive biography:

Jobs kept insisting that the machine should look friendly. As a result, it evolved to resemble a human face. With the disk drive built in below the screen, the unit was taller and narrower than most computers, suggesting a head. The recess near the base evoked a gentle chin, and Jobs narrowed the strip of plastic at the top so that it avoided the Neanderthal forehead that made the Lisa [one of the predecessors to the Mac] subtly unattractive.[226]

The personification was evident not just in Mac's design, but also in the Mac attributes they decided to highlight in the launch.[227] Steve Jobs was adamant that Mac had to be able to speak in the launch – something Danny Boyle depicted in his film *Steve Jobs*, showing Jobs berating his staff for not having completed the voice feature in time. 'You had three weeks. The universe was created in a third of that time,' shouts Jobs. 'Well, someday you'll have to tell us how you did it,' replies a developer.

In the event, they got it all sorted out in time for the launch so that Steve Jobs was able to say, 'We've done a lot of talking about Macintosh recently. But today, for the first time ever, I'd like to let Macintosh speak for itself.'

And Macintosh spoke.

'Hello. I'm Macintosh. It sure is great to get out of that bag.'

The crowd shrieked. Mac spoke! Wow! What else could he do? Mac continued: 'Unaccustomed as I am to public speaking, I'd like to share with you a maxim I thought of the first time I met an IBM mainframe. NEVER TRUST A COMPUTER YOU CAN'T LIFT!'

A joke! So Mac was funny and irreverent too. What other treats awaited…?

'Obviously, I can talk, but right now I'd like to sit back and listen. So it is with considerable pride I introduce a man who has been like a father to me: Steve Jobs.'[228]

So Mac was humble, courteous and family-oriented as

well. The audience rose to its feet and applauded for a full minute. Steve Jobs beamed, looking at his newborn with what appeared to be genuine heartfelt affection but was almost certainly combined with profound relief. He had just launched the most successful brand of computers in the history of computing. He also critically established the status of the computer as an intimate family friend. And, as Henry Ford set the prototype for transport technology design which has endured for over a hundred years, so Steve Jobs has set the prototype for computer design which will probably endure for the next hundred years. And it's all based on personification.

Personification doesn't just affect the way we see our computers; it affects the way we think about them, relate to them and speak about them. We put our computer to sleep. We wake it up. We bring it back to life. When they lose our files, we'll shout at them, scream at them and curse them. Sometimes we'll even threaten violence… But, as personification enabled Ford to smash the old canard of the horseless carriage that tormented us, so Jobs smashed the old canard of technologies that enslaved us, instead presenting to us the Mac, our comrade-in-arms in the technological revolution, with Steve Jobs leading the way.

The Macintosh launch did mark the beginning of the technological revolution, but ironically, at the same time there was also an uprising within the company. A year after launching the Macintosh, Steve Jobs was forced out of Apple – the company he created – after an internal power struggle. This did not stop his ambitions. Following his curiosity and intuition, he simply took the opportunity to explore his anthropomorphic and artistic talents even further. In February 1986, he bought the nascent computer graphics company Pixar from George Lucas for $5 million, investing a further $5 million as capital. At Pixar, Jobs was united with a young and brilliant former Disney animator called John Lasseter, with whom he shared a deep fascination in the power of anthropomorphism. Each found within the other a kindred spirit, and they established an incredibly fruitful partnership that was to last until Steve Jobs's death. It didn't take long before they made their first big impact on the world. In August 1986, they launched the first ever fully computer-generated animation: a two-minute film called *Luxo Jr*.

Luxo Jr depicted two anglepoise lamps. Both of the lamps had clearly identifiable and understandable personalities: Luxo Sr was stiff and serious, Luxo Jr was fun-loving and impudent. The film provides two minutes of sheer joy as the two lamps respond in their own unique ways to a bouncy ball, thereby demonstrating their different emotions and characters. It's an extraordinary film: utterly charming and with great humour. When it was first premiered at SIG-GRAPH, the annual computer graphics conference at the Dallas Convention Center, it was an instant hit. The 6,000-strong audience rose in rapturous applause even before the movie had finished. Luxo Jr, that cheeky little anthropomorphic lamp, still serves as the Pixar mascot to this day.

After this initial success, Jobs and Lasseter continued to develop their ideas about anthropomorphism. 1995's *Toy Story* revolved around the entire premise of anthropomorphic products, as a cupboard of toys came to life – the twist in the tale being that the toys show greater depth of feeling than their occasionally thoughtless human owner, Andy. The film was a gamechanger for the world of animation and movies: it was up there with *Snow White and the Seven Dwarves* or *Star Wars* for innovation. It enhanced Jobs's standing even further, setting him up to achieve bigger and better things when he returned to Apple in 1997. He restored the Mac to its former glory, he introduced the iPod to massive acclaim, and soon he was to present his biggest product ever: the iPhone.

When Steve Jobs launched the iPhone to the world in 2007, the personification in the language was once again conspicuous. He made it clear that this wasn't just a smart phone: this was a super-smart phone. He pronounced the iPhone 'elegant', 'gorgeous' and 'beautiful'.[229] He said, 'We made the buttons on the screen look so good you'll want to lick them!' Phwoar! But what about the design? Whereas the Macintosh had clearly and explicitly been designed to replicate a human face, this wasn't so obvious in the iPhone. Where's the face in that? This is a man who knew the power of anthropomorphism better than anyone, so what went wrong? Had he missed a trick?

Pick up your iPhone now. Look at it closely. I mean really closely. Can you see the face? Yep. You've got it. There it is. The face Steve Jobs designed into the iPhone was a face that he knew you would love more than any other: it's your own face. Jobs had designed into the iPhone a 'black mirror', as Charlie Brooker put it, so you always saw your own face looking back. Genius.

This is next-level personification. The product was no longer simply a friend of ours; it was an extension and a reflection of us. It's the iPhone. The I phone. The pronoun captured in the product name made the increasingly personal nature of the relationship obvious. This new product was not to be an extension of our identity; it was to be integrated with our own identity. And, with the revolutionary touchscreen, so it was that whenever we tapped the iPhone, it was like we were touching our own face, imperceptibly weaving together our connection with the product and our connection with our self.

When Jobs said the iPhone was elegant, gorgeous and beautiful, he was saying we were elegant, gorgeous and beautiful. How could we argue with that? And when he said about licking the buttons on the screen – well, hang on and give that a try – it looks like you're trying to snog yourself. What better metaphor for the inherent narcissism of the new technology? It sums it up. And that's why we love the iPhone.

And boy, have these devices won our love. Neuromarketeer Martin Lindstrom carried out fMRI scans to find out what goes on in people's brains when their iPhones ring. He found a flurry of activity in the insular cortex – the part of the brain associated with feelings of love – and a simultaneous reduction in the chemicals that signal anxiety and stress, including cortisol and norepinephrine.[230] That's why they're so hard to disconnect from. It probably also explains why iPhone has one of the highest customer retention rates ever seen in the world of business at 92 per cent.[231]

We now spend more than half of our waking hours staring at one screen or another. The screen is increasingly no longer a reflection or an extension of reality: for many people this *is* reality. The average iPhone user touches their phone literally thousands of times every day.[232] We crave it so badly people get twitchy when it's running out of battery. So we are left with a feeling of ambivalence when another boat of refugees sinks in the Mediterranean, but deep anxiety if our phone dies. These are the most bizarre mental gymnastics, and they can be achieved almost effortlessly.

Kate Darling is an expert on robot ethics at MIT. She did an experiment with Hexbugs, the little robotic bugs that were all the rage a few years back. She asked some people to smash the bugs with a mallet. Most people willingly agreed and happily bashed them to bits. Then she asked another bunch of people, introducing just a tiny bit of personification: for instance, giving the bug a name or perhaps telling the participants a little bit of a back story about them. All of a sudden, people reacted completely differently. People hesitated and even looked a little distressed. 'Will it hurt him?' some asked. Others had to steel themselves to do it, muttering to themselves, 'It's just a bug, it's just a bug.'[233]

In 2014, Professors David Smith and Frauke Zeller went further. They designed and built a robot called 'HitchBOT'. Their idea was to create a robot that was like a hitch-hiker – a hobobot, as they called it – which would then hitch-hike the breadth of Canada, travelling 6,100 kilometres from Nova Scotia to British Columbia, relying purely on the goodwill of drivers. They deliberately designed her in every way possible so as to maximise the chance that drivers would be charmed by her. First, they decided she would be female. They gave her a warm, friendly, female voice. Then, they made her face smiley, so she would activate the feel-good hormones of friendship. Then, they made her the size of a child, so people would feel instinctively protective. Finally, they uploaded the whole contents of Wikipedia, so she was smart, interesting and engaging good company for a long road trip. Many people who met her along her journey loved the experience and found her a complete delight.[234] After completing her Canadian trip successfully, HitchBOT became something of a global celebrity. She hitch-hiked across Germany for a few days in February 2015. Then, she went to the United States.

The idea was that she would cross the breadth of the United States as she had Canada, starting out in Boston and finishing up in San Francisco. However, in August 2015, whilst passing through Philadelphia, Pennsylvania, she was vandalised and destroyed. Social media was filled with anger and dismay for days afterwards. Millions of people watched videos on YouTube reporting her death.[235] There was an outpouring of grief on Twitter. People lamented how she had been attacked, decapitated and left for dead. 'HitchBOT is dead because people are awful.' Tens of thousands of references can be found to HitchBOT being killed on the web but... *she was never even alive.* That's the power of personification.

I recently went to a robotics exhibition at the Science Museum in London. Possibly the most impressive thing about the robots on display was the power of personification. This is clearly an area where a lot of money is being invested, because personification will be critical to public acceptance.

Some of the robots in the Science Museum exhibition were capable of achieving what felt like really deep emotional connections. Not only did they have facial expressions, their facial expressions monitored and mirrored your own. You smiled, they smiled back; you looked sad, they looked sad. By so doing, they were creating the illusion of real empathy.

Some of the robots were quite beautiful, too. Erica, a Japanese robot, is so beautiful that, last year, a photo of her was entered into the National Portrait Gallery's prestigious Taylor Wessing Photographic Portrait prize. It was the first time ever that a portrait of a robot had been accepted into the competition. It was submitted under the title *One of them is a human #1*. Where will it end?

One man in Hong Kong has spent £34,000 creating a robotic woman that looks like Scarlett Johansson. Sexbot theme parks are being developed around the world.[236] Already, in Greenwich, there's a sex-doll brothel called 'The Dolly Parlour' where, for £75 an hour, the madam in charge says you can do 'whatever you want'.

Some people think the arrival of sexbots could be positive. David Levy, who came to fame developing software for chess games and who has been at the forefront of developing chatbot software, says:

> There will be huge demand from people who have a void in their lives because they have no one to love, and no one who loves them. The world will be a much happier place because all those people who are now miserable will suddenly have someone. I think that will be a terrific service to mankind.[237]

Professor Kathleen Richardson at De Montfort University, on the other hand, takes a different view. She has launched a campaign against sex robots, pointing out the dangers of men learning sexual behaviours with robots where you can do 'whatever you want'. As she says, 'They are not told their violent behaviour is wrong, and it could lead to them escalating things and hurting real people in the future.'

Who knows what's right. But clearly the market for sexbots is growing, and it surely won't be long before one of the big companies gets involved. If Amazon gets in, who knows how Alexa might grow up? Maybe in future she won't be quite so reticent when I ask her out on a date? The mind boggles. Frankly, I was all right just finding out what the weather was in Bideford.

FAMILY

I don't think I'll ever forget the sight of 200,000 Glastonbury-goers chanting 'Oh Jeremy Corbyn!' to the tune of 'Seven Nation Army' by the White Stripes in June 2017. This marked the climax of what had unexpectedly turned out to be the Labour Party's summer of love. When Theresa May announced a snap election in March, she was leading the polls by 23 per cent and Corbyn was predicted to bring the Labour Party crashing to its lowest vote ever. Instead, he achieved the biggest swing in a general election seen since Clement Attlee's surprise defeat of Churchill in 1945, the largest recorded popular vote for the Labour Party since Tony Blair's landslide victory in 1997, and he wiped out the Conservatives' majority.

Corbyn had appealed immediately after winning the Labour leadership – for the second time – for the 'Labour family' to come together. That day at Glastonbury, it seemed like his dream had finally come true. The Labour family was again as one. Everyone was chanting in unison, holding their hands aloft. Complete strangers hugged one another. Even Tom Watson seemed to be on board and was singing from the same hymn sheet as his leader, possibly for the first time ever. People felt united. They felt like they belonged. People who had felt alienated from politics for so long felt they had come back home.

It's fair to say this was not the outcome Theresa May had anticipated. She had expected to win a huge majority for her to pursue Brexit. As she saw it, 'The country is coming together, but Westminster is not.' Her calculation was deeply flawed. The country was not coming together; it was irreparably divided. For every person inside the fences of Glastonbury singing 'Oh Jeremy Corbyn!', many more were outside chanting 'No! Jeremy Corbyn.' The country was split across multiple fracture points: old v. young; rural v. urban; rich v. poor.

And nowhere were those divides deeper than on the vexed issue of Brexit. Huge arguments were breaking out on social media and around dinner tables as generational divides revealed vastly differing perspectives. I know numerous families where people stopped talking to their own mothers and fathers for months because of their disagreements. Nationalism was tearing families apart. The same had been witnessed in the referendum for Scottish independence, the US presidential election in 2016 and the 2017 French election. Isn't that extraordinary? What political issue could possibly be so important it could tear apart a real family? Well, the idea that there had been a breakdown in the metaphorical family...

The idea that a country is a family is one of the oldest and most enduring metaphors, dating back at least 3,000 years. Plutarch reported in *Lives of the Noble Grecians and Romans* that the Dorians of Crete and Sparta established their governments in the form of a family. Confucius established the same principle in China. In ancient Rome, notions of state and family were so conceptually connected that they shared the same etymological roots: the word for country (*patria* – fatherland) was barely distinguishable from the word for father (*pater*).

The idea that we are bound together at a higher level is comforting for all of us. We crave the feeling that we belong, that we are part of something bigger than ourselves. Such feelings have been a critical factor in the advance of civilisation. By seeing connections with one another, we are able to cooperate in millions, tens of millions and even billions. The family metaphor suggests that we have shared interests, shared purpose and shared identity. It also provides an implicit promise that we can share in one another's wealth and security. That's what family is all about. And, as we accept our place within the metaphorical family, so we submerge our own individualism within this broader collective. This creates the possibility that we will then place the needs of our collective above our own needs as individuals. This can lead to stunning acts of self-sacrifice. We can even be persuaded to give up our own lives.

It was Horace in ancient Rome who wrote the line '*Dulce et decorum est pro patria mori*' – it is sweet and honourable to die for the fatherland. This line was repeated in the trenches of Flanders to motivate British soldiers as they went over the top. It was what Wilfred Owen bitterly described as 'the old lie', but it continues to motivate soldiers to this day. My brother-in-law is in the army. He has seen service in Iraq and Afghanistan and he has Horace's maxim tattooed on his chest. During the First World War, German soldiers were also being asked to sacrifice their lives for the same calling for the *Vaterland*, an appeal that was dismissed as similarly duplicitous by German author Erich Maria Remarque in his war novel *All Quiet on the Western Front*.

It was when George Orwell was pondering why an individual might give their life for their country that he was inspired to write what many believe to be his greatest essay, 'England Your England'. He wrote the piece as he watched German bombers flying above, and he wondered why they were risking their lives. As he contemplated this question, he tried to capture what it was that England represented: he concluded it all came down to a series of metonyms and metaphor.

The metonyms were the famous and oft-quoted Orwell images of 'the clatter of clogs in the Lancashire mill towns, the to-and-fro of the lorries on the Great North Road, the queues outside the Labour Exchanges, the rattle of pin-tables in Soho pubs, the old maids biking to Holy Communion through the mists of the autumn morning'. This is gorgeous, evocative imagery – there's another book to be written about metonyms: where we substitute a part of something for a bigger thing – but this is a book about metaphor. Orwell's metaphor is not quoted so often, but it was equally evocative. After rejecting Shakespeare's idea of a 'jewelled isle' and Goebbels's idea of an 'inferno', he affectionately advanced the idea that England was:

> a rather stuffy Victorian family, with not many black sheep in it but with all its cupboards bursting with skeletons.

It has rich relations who have to be kow-towed to and poor relations who are horribly sat upon, and there is a deep conspiracy of silence about the source of the family income. It is a family in which the young are generally thwarted and most of the power is in the hands of irresponsible uncles and bedridden aunts. Still, it is a family. It has its private language and its common memories, and at the approach of an enemy it closes its ranks. A family with the wrong members in control – that, perhaps, is as near as one can come to describing England in a phrase.[238]

Orwell's depiction was fabulously unromantic and authentic – secretive, conspiratorial, irresponsible – it sounded just like a real family. And this was a family we all knew. It was our family – and we know all of the members of that family deeply, because they have been subliminally projected time and time again throughout our lives. There's Aunty Beeb, 'our boys' who go off to war, the government as father and the land as mother. The personification of the land as mother is celebrated every year in the patriotic highlight of the Proms as everyone in the Albert Hall waves their flags together and sings joyously: 'Land of Hope and Glory, Mother of the Free, how shall we extol thee, who are born of thee?'

After the Second World War was over, the need to consolidate the family of the nation was greater than ever after the traumas of the last few years. We wanted safety, security and prosperity. The strengthening of the family started at home, with the creation of the welfare state and, in particular, the National Health Service, proud symbols of a nurturing, supportive family.

But a challenge to the notion of that family of state also emerged at the same time. The idea was developing within Europe that there might be a European family of nations. The logic that underpinned this concept seemed strong: by intertwining our economic interests, we would make future wars less likely. That was the European ideal. But Clem Attlee was having no part of it. As he warned the House of Commons, 'By marrying into Europe, we are marrying a whole family of ancient prejudices and ancient troubles...'[239]

So it was that the first few steps to European integration were taken tentatively. There was to be no family relationship for now. We'd start playing together first and see how it went. The European Community was more about slowly removing the tripwire and the mines from one another's boundaries and allowing easier access than anything else. It was more like a village: our neighbours in Europe. We could still hate, offend and upset one another, much as we always had in the past, but in future, the expectation was that our fights would be rhetorical rather than literal. This concept seemed to rumble on OK, without many signs of dissent.

In 1992, everything changed. The signing of the Maastricht Treaty marked a clearly perceptible shift in the language and presentation of the European Community. At this point, we moved from a community of neighbours to a marriage. This was the formation of the European Union, in which deep and permanent ties were created, based on duties and obligations. We were creating a joint bank account (the single currency), a joint business (the single market) and even a shared home (known as the 'three pillars': the European Commission, the European Parliament and the European Court of Justice). We jumped into bed together. For some people, this was a beautiful moment: the time we made love for the first time. For others, this was when we got fucked.

Eurosceptics who spoke against Maastricht in the House of Commons warned that it was a 'shotgun wedding'. Such critics were denounced by Prime Minister John Major as 'bastards' and the Union went ahead, albeit half-heartedly. It was not a marriage based on love; it was more like a marriage of convenience, if anything, where we picked bits we liked and rejected bits we didn't – one foot in, one foot out – but from that point on, we were indisputably part of the European family. Disagreements would arise from time to time, as they invariably do in families, but the admirable idea was that when they did, we'd try to come together and sort them out around the family table, rather than in the fields of Flanders.

UKIP was formed the year after Maastricht was signed – proving that there were some grumbles of discontent – but most people were pretty sanguine. Every year we seemed to be a little bit richer, stronger and more secure than the year before, so why not carry on? The single market made us more prosperous. The European Union had a strong united voice on the global stage. And, critically, we hadn't had any more wretched wars. This was the promise upon which the European family was sold, and, as long as that promise was delivered, we could go from strength to strength.

I worked on a project with the Foreign Office to build support for Britain's membership of the EU back in 2001. At this time, all the pro-Europeans in government and across think tanks were keenly brandishing a little book by polling guru Robert Worcester, the founder of MORI, called *How to Win the Euro Referendum*. Worcester confidently asserted in this book not merely that Britain would likely vote in favour of staying in the European Union if asked in a referendum, but, crucially, that Britain could also be persuaded to vote in favour of joining the single currency.[240] Worcester's ideas became orthodox thinking.

I used to go to weekly meetings at No. 10 developing a communications strategy on Europe and looking for opportunities to push these messages out. Our top-line messages were clear and simple: being in the EU made us richer, stronger, safer. There were strong arguments and evidence to support each of these messages and this was just the message people wanted to hear. Tony Blair was all set to deliver a big pro-European speech at the Trades Unions Congress in 2001. That speech was set to take place on 11 September.

I was at the TUC in Brighton that day. As the images came in from Manhattan, Blair ditched his prepared speech and stood up and said:

This mass terrorism is the new evil in our world today. It is perpetrated by fanatics who are utterly indifferent to the sanctity of human life and we, the democracies of this world, are going to have to come together to fight it together and eradicate this evil completely from our world.[241]

This was the point at which everything changed. 9/11 was one of the most surreal days and nights of my life. I remember that evening a whole group of us standing around the piano at the Grand Hotel singing songs like 'Let It Be' and 'Imagine', wondering what on earth the consequences of this calamitous day would be. Everyone was fearful. When George W. Bush came out days later and declared a 'crusade', it seemed like Christianity had gone to war with Islam. Blair had never looked stronger. But, as the European Union started arguing about how much support it should provide to this swaggering US President, the family of nations had never looked weaker.

This was, in my opinion, the first critical event that damaged the promise of the European Union. For when Europe tried to restrain President Bush through the United Nations, it was immediately clear that the European Union was basically impotent. In Bush's world, there was only room for one global superpower, and that superpower was the United States. This struck at one of the most vital precepts of the European Union. It didn't seem like being in Europe gave us a stronger voice at all. On this, the most critical issue facing the planet at that time, Europe was divided, voiceless, and no one cared what we thought anyway.

The second critical event that damaged the promise of the European Union came on 7 July 2005, when fifty-six people were killed in a series of terrorist attacks targeting commuters coming into London on Tubes and buses. These were the first Islamist suicide attacks ever on UK soil – but many more were to follow over the coming years. What was particularly shocking was that the suicide bombers were all British citizens. This day signalled that the threats of the future were very different to the threats of the past. Future wars were likely to be cultural and religious. It was not clear what, if anything, the European Union could do to negate these threats. Indeed, the impression was created in much of the national press that the European Union was, with its slack controls on immigration, fostering these threats. So it didn't seem like being in Europe made us safer, either. Europe left us vulnerable.

The third event came about in 2007, with the collapse of the subprime market in the United States, which led to the worst financial crisis since the 1930s. For many years, people had worked on the promise that, as long as they worked hard, then every year they would have a little more than they'd had the year before. All of a sudden that was thrown out the window. Whilst a small minority of people continued to earn more money year on year, most people were actually, in real terms, experiencing pay cuts. This was particularly true of public servants. So it didn't seem like being in Europe made us richer, either. If anything, Europe made us poorer.

Everything had gone topsy-turvy. This was a marriage that had promised wealth, power and security, but instead it had left us poorer, weaker and in serious danger. We'd given up our freedom and our independence and submerged our identity... for what? It was like the ultimate morning after. We rubbed our eyes, looked across the bed and thought, 'Huh. How did I wind up here with you? Who even *are* you?' There had never been much love in the relationship anyway, but we'd been happy (sort of) to sustain it for as long as our basic needs were being met. Now, even that had come under challenge. Clearly, it was time for a divorce.

It's important to emphasise that not everyone felt like this. Everyone's experience and perception was different. But within those differences, there was actually a surprising amount that we had in common. Everyone could agree that their metaphorical family had broken down. Everyone could agree that nasty people were to blame for the breakdown of their metaphorical family. Everyone could also agree that by fighting those nasty people and their nasty ideologies, they'd be able to put the metaphorical family together again. The trouble was that everyone had different views on who their metaphorical family was, who the nasty people were, and who they should be fighting to put it back together again.

Even tougher, these gaps in perception occurred largely along generational, geographical and class lines. As David Goodhart wrote in *The Road to Somewhere*, one of the critical factors in determining whether someone was a 'citizen of somewhere' or a 'citizen of anywhere', as he put it, was their upbringing. If someone went away to be educated as a child (either to boarding school or to university), this would probably make them globalist. But most people did not live like that. The vast majority of people in Britain still lived within twenty miles of where they were born. The whole thing started becoming very confused.

This led politicians into a dilemma as they tried to find positions that accommodated both their own instinctively pro-globalisation beliefs and the increasingly nationalist and protectionist instincts of their electorates. This in turn led to pro-globalisation politicians taking increasingly absurd and self-evidently contradictory positions.

There were three pivotal moments for me that summed up this confusion: firstly, in 2006, when Labour's liberal Foreign Secretary Jack Straw, MP for Bradford, said he felt uneasy talking to Muslim women who came to see him in his constituency wearing a veil;[242] secondly, in 2007, when Gordon Brown stood up in his first speech as leader at the Labour Party conference and called for 'British jobs for British workers', a phrase that had previously been used by both the National Front and the British National Party; thirdly, the excruciating moment when Gordon Brown met a woman in Rochdale, Gillian Duffy, and afterwards described her as a 'bigoted woman', not knowing his lapel mic was being picked up by Sky News. He later had to apologise for his comment, even though he'd almost certainly meant it. The truth was that he knew he couldn't be seen to be arguing with Mrs Duffy, as there were too many people in Britain who agreed with her views on immigration. A 2011 YouGov survey showed that 62 per cent of Brits agree with the statement, 'Britain has changed in recent times beyond recognition, it sometimes feels like a foreign country and this makes me feel uncomfortable.'[243]

In times such as these, with the nation fragmenting, it was certainly risky, if not downright reckless, to hold referendums on major constitutional issues. Nevertheless, that's exactly what David Cameron did, calling two referendums in rapid succession: one on whether Scotland would remain part of the United Kingdom; the other on whether the UK would remain part of the European Union.

In both of these votes, the huge differences in opinion on where our family ties lay were plain and obvious for all to see. The referendum for Scottish independence in 2014 became a battle between Alex Salmond and Scottish nationalists on the one hand, who perceived the family as Scotland and Westminster as the enemy, and David Cameron on the other, who saw the family as the United Kingdom and nationalism as the enemy. Cameron invoked the full weight of those family ties as he sought to protect the Union: 'It is my duty to be clear … Independence would not be a trial separation. It would be a painful divorce.'[244]

Scotland's membership of the United Kingdom was always a moot point for some. Orwell himself had exposed the cracks in the Union in 'England, Your England'. As he acknowledged, he might have called his essay 'United Kingdom, Your United Kingdom' or 'Britain, Your Britain' but he settled on 'England, Your England' knowing full well it would annoy the Scottish and the Welsh. In the event, the Scottish people voted to remain within the United Kingdom when asked in 2014, but it was much closer than anyone had anticipated: 55 per cent in favour and 45 per cent against.

Then, there was the Brexit referendum. Again, David Cameron invoked the family metaphor throughout this campaign, referring continually to Brexit as a divorce.[245] Nigel Farage saw it completely differently: to him, it was all about taking back control. The repeated references to divorce undoubtedly shaped the way many people felt about it, particularly those whose literal marriages and family ties were cross-European, to whom it felt intensely personal. I remember being in Soho the morning the result came through, working with some senior colleagues from Whitehall. People were stunned, as if their parents had just come down to the breakfast table and announced a real divorce.

The divorce metaphor has played a vital role not only in the way many people have felt about the referendum but also in the progression of the negotiations. In particular, different metaphorical perspectives have shaped people's reactions to the vexed questions of whether or not Britain should pay any money to leave the EU, and, if so, how much.

Brexiteers never felt we should pay them a penny, because they never viewed this as a legitimate family anyway, so they didn't see it as a divorce. They considered that this was about taking back control which had been stolen from us. The idea we should pay money for the privilege of reclaiming what was rightfully ours was deemed ludicrous. When Boris Johnson was asked whether Britain should pay money to the EU, he said they could 'go whistle'.[246]

Pro-Europeans were horrified at the suggestion that we might leave without paying our dues. As German MEP Elmar Brok said, 'If you have a divorce, you have to pay up on your obligations. It is like the husband running away from the family and their children.'[247] Plaid Cymru's leader, Leanne Wood, asked, 'Would you pay your dues if you were going through a real divorce?'[248] Mr Juncker insisted the EU was 'not a golf club that could be easily joined or left'.

The trouble was that the more the pro-Europeans talked about divorce, the more difficult the negotiations became. It was like the word 'divorce' instinctively prompted a desire to double down, to cling on to what we had.

In July 2018, we did a survey on Amazon Mechanical Turk to test this out. We asked 100 people how much money they thought Britain should pay to the European Union in the settlement. The first half were asked without the divorce metaphor. The second fifty people were asked with the divorce metaphor. The differences were extraordinary.

QUESTION 1

Prime Minister Theresa May is currently negotiating Brexit with the European Union. How much money approximately do you think Britain should pay to the European Union in the settlement?

Nothing – 24 per cent
£20 billion – 42 per cent
£50 billion – 20 per cent
No opinion – 14 per cent

QUESTION 2

Prime Minister Theresa May is currently negotiating Brexit with the European Union. How much money approximately do you think Britain should pay to the European Union in the divorce settlement?

Nothing – 44 per cent
£20 billion – 42 per cent
£50 billion – 8 per cent
No opinion – 6 per cent

The word 'divorce' creates a massive shift in opinion. Not only did the mention of divorce lead to a stunning fall in the number of people who had no opinion, down from 14 per cent to 6 per cent, it also garnered a huge increase in the number of people who thought the EU should get nothing, up from 24 per cent to 44 per cent.

This creates a problem for Theresa May, because the EU are expecting her to pay some money. She's going to struggle to achieve that politically if people are talking about this as a divorce. I suspect she might be alive to this risk. In a statement to the House of Commons on 14 March 2017, May said, 'A number of Members have used the term "divorce". I prefer not to use that term with regard to the European Union, because, often, when people get divorced, they do not have a good relationship afterwards.'[249]

Her plea was to little avail. The word 'divorce' continued to dominate Brexit reporting. In the six weeks leading up to the 2017 general election, thirty-two separate front-page articles referred to Brexit as a divorce. No wonder so many people felt tense and miserable. *The Guardian* on 2 May alone had no fewer than five different references to divorce, asking how much the 'divorce bill' should be, talking about prospects for a 'friendly divorce' and saying that 'divorce after more than four decades will be difficult and messy'. It's an extraordinary use of language. One can't imagine people using this language if the OECD or OPEC were being disbanded/broken up/dismantled (feel free to insert your own alternative metaphor here).

The Sun, a newspaper which campaigned for Brexit, proposed an alternative metaphor for the European Union, in characteristic *Sun* style:

> Brussels is making it up as it goes along … It is the accounting and morality of a Soho clip joint… How do Jean-Claude Fagin and his artful dodgers estimate a £52 billion charge … We owe these wide boys nothing… [It's] an EU-contrived exercise in masochism. Britain is to endure two years as whipping boy for vindictive Eurofanatics. They have no

interest in negotiating, all they want to do is rob and otherwise harm Britain for scorning their squalid cartel.[250]

And so it was that, in these confused and muddled times, Theresa May decided to call a general election. There could scarcely have been a more volatile and complex time. The election exposed a greater depth of passion and feeling than I have ever witnessed before in any previous campaign. It wasn't surprising. This was not an election about parties. It was an election about families. It was about deciding where you belonged.

In the event, 12.7 million people decided they belonged with Jeremy Corbyn's Labour Party. Meanwhile, 13.5 million people decided they belonged with Theresa May's Conservatives. But there were 15 million people who didn't vote for any of the parties that day. Some of these will be people who just weren't bothered. Some will be people who weren't interested. But some will be people who feel marginalised from mainstream political debate, dispossessed, like they do not have a political home.

There is a strong feeling amongst Islamic communities that they have been actively excluded and alienated since 9/11. We explored earlier how they have been 'othered' in the mainstream press. A study by Cardiff School of Journalism, Media and Cultural Studies found that 66 per cent of media coverage of Muslims focused on Muslims as a threat.

Strategies like the Prevent programme and the Counter-Terrorism and Security Act 2015 (introduced by Theresa May as Home Secretary) have also left Islamic communities feeling under attack by government.[251] The Islamic Human

Rights Commission named Theresa May 'worst Islamophobe of the year' in 2015 for her actions as Home Secretary.[252] Over Christmas 2016, Louise Casey produced a report on social cohesion which explicitly focused on Muslim communities, describing problems which have been 'swept under the carpet or allowed to fester' – extraordinary language to use in a report on social cohesion. Also in 2016, Zac Goldsmith ran a 'terrible Islamophobic, anti-Muslim campaign' when he stood for London Mayor against Labour's Sadiq Khan, in the words of Baroness Warsi, Britain's first ever female Muslim Cabinet minister.[253]

The Muslim Council of Britain has called for an independent inquiry into Islamophobia in the Conservative Party, citing a number of incidents including a Conservative council who shared an article calling Muslims 'parasites'. In the 2017 general election, 85 per cent of Muslims voted for Labour whilst only 11 per cent voted Conservative. In no other religious group was there such a wide gap. (By way of comparison with problems of anti-Semitism in the Labour Party, in the 2017 general election 26 per cent of Jewish people voted Labour.[254])

The Muslim Brotherhood can appear to offer a sense of dignity, belonging and purpose to those who feel alienated and excluded by mainstream society. Much of the language which is used to radicalise Muslims is based on the promise of belonging to a bigger family, which is evident not least in the very notion of a Muslim Brotherhood. It's the same with ISIS. 'Brothers, it is time to rise ... Get DIGNITY.'[255] And, of course, it is very often from within the metaphor of family that terrorists seek justification for their crimes.

One of the 7/7 suicide bombers, Mohammad Sidique Khan, prepared a videotape which explained that he was 'protecting and avenging [his] Muslim brothers and sisters'. When Michael Adebolajo killed soldier Lee Rigby on 22 May 2013, he handed over a letter to a member of public at the scene warning that other British citizens would be 'killed by our brothers'. One of the most poignant moments of recent years came in the midst of a terrorist attack at Leytonstone Station at December 2015 when a passer-by cried out to the perpetrator, 'You ain't no Muslim, bruv'. As David Cameron said afterwards, 'Some of us have dedicated speeches and media appearances and soundbites and everything to this subject but "You ain't no Muslim, bruv" said it all much better than I ever could.'[256] Indeed it had. This was an appeal to belonging that started from a premise of inclusion within a broader family, not alienation.

Author and neuroscientist Ian Robertson has explained the appeal Islamic State offers disaffected youths:

[It] assuages some of the terrific fear and distress the individual feels when the state breaks down ... You can see it in the faces of the young male Islamic State militants as they race by on their trucks ... broad smiles on their faces, clenched fists aloft... What you can see is a biochemical high from a combination of the bonding hormone oxytocin and the dominance hormone testosterone. Much more than cocaine or alcohol, these natural drugs lift mood, induce optimism and energise aggressive action on the part of the group. And because the individual identity has been submerged largely into the group identity, the individual will be much more willing to sacrifice himself in battle ... When people bond together, oxytocin levels rise in their blood but a consequence of this is **a greater tendency to demonise and dehumanise the out-group**. That is the paradox of selfless giving to your in-group – it makes it easier for you to anaesthetise your empathy for the out-group and see them as objects. And doing terrible things to objects is fine because they are not human. [Emphasis in original][257]

Salman Ramadan Abedi obviously didn't see the innocent young people coming out of an Ariana Grande concert at Manchester Arena on 22 May 2017 as human when he walked into the foyer and set off a shrapnel-laden homemade bomb. He killed twenty-two people, ten of whom were under the age of twenty, and one who was just eight years old: Saffie-Rose Roussos.[258] Islamic State took responsibility for the act. His neighbours said he was a 'loner' who 'turned weird'. His cousins came out afterwards and said he had 'betrayed the image of the family – that was out of order'.[259] Abedi had forgone his literal family for the metaphorical family.

Then, two weeks later, there was a further attack. On 3 June 2017, three attackers from east London ran down several pedestrians on London Bridge and launched a knife attack outside pubs around nearby Borough Market. They killed eight people and injured a further forty-eight.

Islamic State had put out a video on the eve of Ramadan, immediately before these attacks, issuing a call to 'Muslim brothers in Europe who can't reach the Islamic State lands', directing them to 'attack [infidels] in their homes, their markets, their roads and their forums'.

The attacks put the issue of Islamist terrorism at the centre of this already febrile election. Theresa May made a speech on the steps of Downing Street after the London Bridge attack saying, 'We cannot allow this ideology the safe space it needs to breed... We need to prevent the spread of extremism... We must be far more robust in stamping it out... We must come together, pull together and united we will take on and defeat our enemies.'[260]

This was the kind of dehumanisation we have seen before. Jeremy Corbyn responded differently. He confirmed that these attacks proved his long-held view that 'the war on terror is simply not working'. The reaction to Corbyn's remarks was fierce and ferocious, both from the press and from politicians. Defence Secretary Sir Michael Fallon said he was 'making excuses for our enemies'. The Foreign Secretary, Boris Johnson, said his comments were 'absolutely monstrous... absolutely extraordinary and inexplicable in this week of all weeks that there should any attempt to justify or to legitimate the actions of terrorists in this way'.[261] One Labour candidate, not named, said to *The Sun*, 'What's he want to do? Hug a terrorist?'[262]

On 19 June, just after midnight, 47-year-old Darren Osborne drove a hired van down from Cardiff to the Finsbury Park Mosque in London where he drove into several pedestrians, leaving one man dead and ten injured. In Osborne's van, a note was found which condemned 'feral inbred, raping Muslim men, hunting in packs, preying on our children' and called Jeremy Corbyn a 'terrorist sympathiser'. In court, Osborne was asked if he'd intended to kill the Labour leader. 'Oh yeah,' he replied. 'It would be one less terrorist on our streets.'

Osborne was a family man with four children. What on earth had led him to carry out this attack? His partner explained that he felt 'worthless and did not fit in'. Three weeks before the attack, he had watched *Three Girls*, a BBC docudrama about the Rochdale child abuse scandal.[263] From that point on, he was reading material published by Britain First online and rapidly became radicalised. Britain First speaks in war metaphors. Its logo is a lion. Its mission statement invites people to 'join the ranks of the Britain First movement' as it 'fights the many injustices that are routinely inflicted on the British people' and promises to 'defend our nation, our heritage and culture' as it stands on the 'frontline for our long-suffering people'.[264]

Osborne was sentenced to forty-three years in prison. Not that he seems concerned. During the trial, Osborne said, 'I've done my job. You can kill me now.'[265] It seems a strange thing to say. Did he imagine, like Horace, that he had given his life for his fatherland? Or was it that, having carried out a high-profile murder, he felt he was now immortal: up there with other notorious killers throughout history? If it's immortality we're thinking about now, we should move on to the next chapter.

STAR

Oprah Winfrey made history on 7 January 2018 when she became the first ever black woman to win the Cecil B. DeMille Award at the star-studded Golden Globes ceremony in Hollywood. After collecting her award from Reese Witherspoon, she delivered a spine-tinglingly brilliant acceptance speech which shone a light on some of the darkest issues enveloping the world: Trump, Weinstein, #MeToo, fake news. She laid down the gauntlet to the 'brutally powerful men' who had tormented and persecuted women for too long. She had a message about those men. 'Their time is up. Their time is UP. Their time is up.'

With her speech, she brought many of the world's biggest movie stars to their feet, a number of them in tears. Within minutes of her speech, the #MeToo hashtag, which had dominated Twitter for the previous three months, switched to #TimesUp, and people were already calling for her to stand as the next President of the United States. Still today, five months after that speech, those calls continue and Oprah remains one of the favourites to be the next Commander-in-Chief. That's because that night she offered something very special, something every leader in history has had to offer. As Oprah put it, 'the hope for a brighter morning, even during our darkest nights'.

Our darkest nights… Think of the power of that image. Do you remember the fear that a dark night had the power to strike in you when you were young? How many years did it take before you were happy to go to sleep with the lights out? Our fear of darkness is instilled in our most formative years. It's not so much that we're scared of what it is we can't see so much as we're afraid of what it symbolises. The metaphor part of our brain goes into overdrive. It's our deepest fears. It's a never-ending nothingness. It's the certainty of death: that eternal reminder of our own mortality.

But amid the darkness, we are instinctively led to seek out the light. The light on those darkest nights comes from the stars. If the darkness suggests death, in the stars we find hope – and much more besides. From early Sumerian and Babylonian astronomy to the druids at Stonehenge and modern-day horoscopes, these weird luminous spheroids of plasma held together by gravity have seemed to offer so much meaning: the promise of immortality, the suggestion of destiny. They are guiding lights we should follow, oracles of wisdom, symbols of deity. In fact, they're bigger than symbols of deity. Whilst just 28 per cent of British adults believe in God,[266] a whopping 73 per cent of us check our horoscopes in the paper.[267]

The multidimensional meanings we ascribe to the stars have been passed down over tens of thousands of years. But why is it that now, when we speak about stars, we tend to be talking about entertainers? Where did this come from? What does it mean?

The first reference to an entertainer as a star appears to have come in 1761 when Benjamin Victor wrote that David Garrick's debut on the West End stage marked the arrival of 'a bright luminary in the theatrical hemisphere... [who] soon after became a star of the first magnitude'.[268] The term continued to be used in the nineteenth century by theatrical companies who had touring shows around the country to promote, but the producers used it sparingly, because they didn't want the actors to get ideas above their station: they'd only demand more money.

It wasn't until the establishment of Hollywood in the 1910s that the term 'star' and the idea of a star system took off. The emergence and then the expansion of cinema, television and radio created a whole new business model for the sale of entertainment. Instead of relying on expensive touring productions or Broadway shows which required ongoing funding, the movie industry saw that, for a relatively small one-off investment, money could be generated in perpetuity. Producers, not surprisingly, thought this was a terrific idea. It meant they could earn stacks more money over a longer period. But there was a challenge: how to convince their audiences to give up the thrill and occasion of a live performance in exchange for sitting in a dark room staring at a projection?

This was how the star system emerged, together with the whole notion of the silver screen. By putting a few names up in lights, and making sure they glittered and sparkled brightly enough, people would find them irresistible. By making entertainers 'stars', the producers were performing the oldest trick in the salesman's book. It's the same trick practised in car showrooms and jewellers around the world: if you shine the brightest light possible on your product, you render your customers struck with awe.

And so it was that entertainers came to be described as stars. We've come a long way since then. Today, there are so many stars we barely know what to do with them. There are movie stars, TV stars, rock stars, pop stars, sports stars, YouTube stars. We now use the term 'star' to talk about celebrities so frequently that ninety-eight of the first 100 uses of the word on the British National Corpus (an academic database of the use of language) actually relate to the context of a celebrity, whilst only two refer to stars in the sky (star sign, *Star Wars*).

Indeed, the term 'star' is bandied about so frequently these days that it often demands a prefix – superstar, megastar – just to make it clear when we really mean it. The idea of stars is all around us, not just in the everyday language of the red-top papers, but in the whole presentation of the entertainment industry: from the glittering, sparkling Golden Globes, Oscars and BAFTA ceremonies right through to the opening credits of all of the big movies, which invariably start with a glimpse of light emerging from a vast expanse of sky.[269]

But what's extraordinary is how, as the idea of entertainers as stars has been spun into our common consciousness, so all of the meaning and significance we once vested in those floating globs of galactic gas has now been projected on to this relatively motley crew of actors, musicians and dancers. And it has the most surprising effects.

We really do see entertainers as symbols of immortality. One study showed that if you're on a plane and it looks like the plane is about to crash, then people are more likely to think they will survive if there is a celebrity on board.[270] Isn't that incredible? Next time you're on a plane, take a good look around. If Taylor Swift's sitting a few rows along, Hallelujah, you have nothing to fear – or so you will think.

As we have always felt compelled to follow stars in the past, so today we do the same with entertainers. Literally more than 100 million people follow Katy Perry and Justin Bieber on Twitter – each – which is far more than any political business or religious leader. Their influence is extraordinary and defies reason. Rihanna puts out a new lip gloss; we buy it. Victoria Beckham puts out a new perfume; we buy it. Richard and Judy recommend a new book; we buy it.

As stars seemed like gods in the past, so now we see entertainers as semi-divine; and, lest you were in any doubt about the nature of the relationship, the very word 'fan' derives from the Latin *fanaticus*, which means inspired by the gods. Sick and disabled children are often brought before stars at pop concerts or football matches in the hope that a wave of their hand will cure them, like Jesus. Celebrities are even dropped into disaster zones, as if their mere presence will provide resolution to some of the world's most protracted problems.

When you stop and think about it, the whole thing really is absurd. Yet it's becoming increasingly normalised and legitimised, with Presidents and Prime Ministers all joining in the worship of the stars. You can scarcely have a multilateral summit now without Bono, Bob Geldof or Angelina Jolie dropping in. The United Nations has enrolled a whole cast of global ambassadors with responsibilities for various issues: Emma Watson on equality, Orlando Bloom on children in conflict, Leonardo DiCaprio on climate change, Matt Damon on water.

In the past, we could see stars as oracles of wisdom; now, we do so with celebrities. I remember when I was working in Whitehall and people like Jamie Oliver and Dolly Parton seemed to have the right to walk straight into the corridors of power and hold court on an issue in a way that, say, an academic expert could not. They are developing an increasing political importance. In some cases, their influence can be seen as decisive, even in elections. One of the strangest moments in the 2015 general election was when Ed Miliband rocked up at Russell Brand's flat for an interview. Miliband calculated, probably correctly, that Brand could help him access the youth vote. It didn't win him much credibility with the rest of the electorate, though. After the election, Brand, despondent, announced he was walking away from politics. He feared his involvement had 'fucked up' the election.

In Italy, it's gone even further. When comedian Beppe Grillo established the Five Star Movement as an internet-based anti-establishment party in 2010, one of their best-known policies was the promise to create a national Vaffanculo Day ('Fuck You Day'). They were deliberately outrageous and provocative, but they quickly amassed huge support. In the 2013 general election, the first the Five Star Movement contended, they won an astonishing 25.5 per cent of the vote. Today, they are far and away the largest party in Italy, with 33 per cent support. The US, of course, has also had Trump but save some popcorn, we'll come back to him later.

Why is it that we're increasingly turning to the stars for political solutions? Frank Furedi of the University of Kent has argued that voting for such candidates gives people the opportunity to both express frustration and bypass mainstream candidates.[271] There may be other reasons as well.

We feel connected with stars in a way that we just don't with mainstream politicians. When we see them on stage or in movies, the most extraordinary symbiosis takes place between us and them. Our mirror neurons are activated, meaning we don't just feel that we're watching them; we imagine we *are* them. This is why, when we're watching a movie and the hero gets hurt, we imagine that we're being hurt. You can see the impact on our brains very clearly in fMRI scans.

This is one reason. But stars also represent an ideal of who we would like to be, which makes them ultra-appealing. There were no doubt many people watching *The Apprentice*, for instance, who must have thought it would be pretty nice to have that kind of wealth. For many of us, stars do represent the pinnacle of our aspirations. This is the ultimate height to which someone from an impoverished background might rise, and our culture is full of mythical stories of those who have.

Today, half of sixteen-year-olds want to be stars[272] – a figure which incidentally is matched completely in a survey of my two daughters. The good news is that these days anyone who wants to be a star can be, to a certain degree. With a basic laptop or a half-decent phone, it is possible to make high-quality movies and music that can instantly be shared or sold for next to no cost. Andy Warhol famously predicted that in the future everyone will be famous for fifteen minutes. Now, everyone can feel famous with just fifteen likes or views. But sometimes these wannabe stars reach astronomic heights.

Justine Ezarik made $2 million just from YouTubing about her life, uploading literally thousands of videos about almost everything, from cooking to technology. One of her most-watched videos shows her checking if the facial recognition feature on her iPhone X works underwater. It got 5.5 million views in less than six months.

Wannabe stars can also follow their dreams through applying to reality TV talent shows. These can open doors to worlds that were previously closed shops, completely transforming people's lives. Like Connie Fisher, who was a 23-year-old working in telesales in London when Andrew Lloyd Webber decided to bring *The Sound of Music* back to the West End in 2006. Instead of flicking through his black book, Lloyd Webber hooked up with the BBC and created *How Do You Solve a Problem Like Maria?*, declaring it was 'a fantastic opportunity for a young talent to become a real star'.[273]

Connie was thrilled when, after six gruelling weeks performing under the hypercritical gaze of eight million viewers at home, she emerged victorious. Lloyd Webber gave Connie a six-month contract to play Maria at the London Palladium. She ended up doing eighteen months, performing six out of eight shows every week, and received rave reviews. She went on to record two albums. Today, she has a regular radio show and also makes her own TV programmes. As she and Lloyd Webber both say, this never would have happened without reality TV.

And Connie's story is not unique. Reality TV has led to the

breakthrough of all sorts of megastars, like Kelly Clarkson, Little Mix, Alexandra Burke, One Direction, Susan Boyle, Olly Murs and Katharine McPhee (none of these last four even won their respective TV contests). They give hope to millions of people. And there are many millions of people who apply to be on such shows. But why is it that so many people these days are chasing stardom?

Jeff Greenberg at the University of Arizona has discovered there is a connection between our longing to become stars and our fear of death. We are all craving immortality, and of course the idea of becoming a star gives us a sense that it's possible. That is what the star symbolises: immortality. But this can prove dangerous. Because this immortality is only metaphorical, not literal. And the paradox is that the more we feel immortal – and being told we are a star does achieve precisely this effect – the more likely we are to go too far as we test the limits.

It is perhaps ironic that whilst Noel Gallagher was writing songs that suggested immortality, like 'Rock 'n' Roll Star', 'Champagne Supernova' and 'Live Forever', he was shovelling hundreds of thousands of pounds' worth of drugs up his nose.[274] Gallagher survived, but there are many who don't. The 27 Club has been created in testament to the many great stars who have died at that tender age, including the likes of Amy Winehouse, Kurt Cobain and Janis Joplin.

Being a star really is bad for your health. A study by the University of Sydney, Australia, of the lives of 13,000 rock and pop stars revealed that celebrities of this ilk die twenty-five years younger than the average person. They also found that these deaths are far more likely to be from some form of misadventure – e.g. accident, overdose and homicide.[275] Maybe this is because these stars start believing their own hype; they believe they are immortal.

Maybe we also look at them and fall for the myth that they're immortal? That would certainly explain the irrational levels of shock that the world felt when David Bowie died on 10 January 2016. 'Rock Star Dies' is a much more shocking and surprising story than '69-year-old man with liver cancer dies'. The metaphor turns an otherwise everyday story into a profoundly disturbing revelation. It becomes a man-bites-dog news story. Even though we had known he was ill for several years, the idea that he could actually die still seemed vaguely incomprehensible.

Bowie understood the power of his metaphorical star status, toying with it in his music throughout his career. Just listen to songs like 'Space Oddity', 'Starman' and 'Life on Mars?', his film *The Man Who Fell to Earth* or the music created by his alter-ego, 'Ziggy Stardust'… Even his farewell gift to the world was the song 'Blackstar', an eerie posthumous acknowledgement that his metaphorical status was mythological: the surreal and disturbing video that accompanied the song charted his descent from a star in the sky to a quivering, flickering candle, waiting to be snuffed out.

The allure of immortality can prove deadly to wannabe stars. People are dying to become YouTube stars… And I mean that literally.

Nineteen-year-old Monalisa Perez got her first taste of YouTube stardom when she filmed a video of herself feeding her boyfriend, Pedro Ruiz III, a doughnut with baby powder on. Millions of people watched and laughed as her boyfriend started spitting the noxious substance from his mouth. After the success of this video, Monalisa wanted more and more views. She kept upping the ante, posting increasingly bizarre and dangerous tricks. On 26 June 2017, she tweeted, 'Me and Pedro are probably going to shoot one of the most dangerous videos ever. HIS idea not MINE.' Ninety minutes later, she called the Norman County Sheriff's Office to say that she had just shot her 22-year-old boyfriend, Pedro, through the chest from a distance of one foot. He had been holding a book to his chest. They thought the book would absorb the impact of the bullet. They were wrong. Pedro Ruiz was killed in front of the couple's three-year-old daughter.[276] Monalisa was pregnant at the time with Pedro's second child.

There are similarly tragic cases in reality TV, too. For every Connie Fisher, One Direction or Kelly Clarkson who hits the big time, there are millions more who have their dreams crushed. It was not long after Simon Cowell's first appearance on the screen, initially as one of the judges on *Pop Idol*, that experts first warned of the impact these programmes could have on the mental health of the contestants. Dr Mark Cross, a consultant psychiatrist at Barts and the Homerton hospitals in London, warned in 2003:

It might be Simon Cowell's television persona, but certainly narcissistic and psychopathic personality traits come through. He doesn't care what he says and does not care about the effect. There's no reason for the judges to be rude, no reason for them to pull apart someone who is incredibly stressed. I would not be surprised if there were more breakdowns than we see on screen.[277]

Yet it is largely in expectation of these breakdowns that people watch these programmes. Of course, television programmes based on humiliation are not new – think *Candid Camera* or *You've Been Framed* – but the meta-narrative within all these reality talent shows is a variation on 'Your life is rubbish, do what we say, then you can be a star.' It's an attractive narrative and producers carefully edit the shows to emphasise the dramatic extremes: hence their longing for contestants with deprived and tragic backgrounds that conform to the 'rags-to-riches' narrative. The odds are against the contestant, though. For every person whose story ends in stardom, there are many thousands for whom the ending is bleak.

In 2007, New Jersey chef Joseph Cerniglia decided to participate on Gordon Ramsay's show *Kitchen Nightmares*, a US programme in which Ramsay spends a week with a failing restaurant and tries to turn it around. Ramsay was not impressed with Cerniglia. He told him he didn't have a clue how to run a business. Ramsay sat Cerniglia down at one point in the show, asking, 'How serious is this restaurant to you?' Cerniglia replied, 'It's everything.' Ramsay looked him in the eye: 'Your business is about to fucking swim down the Hudson.'[278] Three years later, Cerniglia jumped into the Hudson and died. This case is sadly not isolated. In 2016, the *New York Post* reported that there had been twenty-one suicides from reality television programmes in a single decade.[279]

The biggest star to emerge from *Kitchen Nightmares* was never going to be a contestant anyway. It was always going to be Gordon Ramsay, just as the biggest star to come out of *The X Factor* was Simon Cowell, the biggest star to come out of *Bake Off* was Mary Berry and the biggest star to come out of *The Apprentice* is now the President of the United States.

It's still hard to believe that the man who made his name telling people 'You're fired' is now sitting in the Oval Office with his finger on the nuclear button. Donald Trump was initially sceptical when he was approached to play the role of the judge on *The Apprentice*. He said he thought reality TV was 'for the bottom feeders of society'. He only relented when he realised he would be depicted as the epitome of success, spending most of the programme looking down on people, either from the top of Trump Tower or flying back and forth between Fifth Avenue and Mar-a-Lago in jets and helicopters, with his name emblazoned on the side.

As Professors Susan Murray and Laurie Ouellette set out in their book *Reality TV: Remaking Television Culture*, the leading scholarly text on the issue of reality TV, the role Trump played in this series was not a contestant; he was the judge, what they called the guardian angel, a position of even greater power.

Oprah Winfrey's speech at the Golden Globes was widely interpreted as a sign that she might challenge Trump for the presidency in 2020. Afterwards, she said she had offers of 'billion-dollar' donations to support a run for office, if she wanted to go for it. She said, 'I went into prayer. God, if you think I'm supposed to run, you gotta tell me, and it has to be so clear that not even I can miss it.' So far, she says she hasn't 'gotten that' sign.[280]

She might be waiting a long time. It's hard to receive signs from God. He works in mysterious ways. But I'll tell you who does have a hotline straight through to Him...

ANGEL

When Frederick Trump sailed into New York City harbour on the steamship *Eider* on 19 October 1885, the tallest point he could see on the Manhattan skyline was the 281-foot steeple of the Trinity Church, Wall Street. This was long before the Statue of Liberty, the Chrysler Building or the Empire State Building. Back then, the tallest point in the city had to be a church or cathedral. Indeed, the tallest building in the whole world from the Middle Ages right through to 1901 was always a church or cathedral. Building beyond that point was considered blasphemous. In the fifteenth century, the word 'tower' actually meant 'heaven'. So it was that Frederick Trump and all of the other immigrants arriving from Bavaria that day saw the steeple and instantly received a very loud message from New York City: there is no one here who is higher than God.

Fast-forward 131 years to 16 December 2016 and Frederick's grandson, Donald, is sitting resplendent in his conference room on the twenty-fifth floor of Trump Tower, having just pulled off the greatest and possibly most surprising electoral coup in the history of American politics. Trump's friend, the angel investor Peter Thiel, is sitting beside him as he prepares to welcome the heads of the tech companies in what is probably one of the most important meetings of the presidential transition. The Manhattan skyline which stretches out behind him looks very different to how it did in his grandfather's day. Today, no steeples or spires are visible. Instead, the tallest buildings on the skyline include One World Trade Center, the Chrysler Building and Trump Tower. Today, New York sends a different message: here we worship wealth. So how was it that this transformation occurred?

Meet Andrew Carnegie. Carnegie was an incredibly successful and wealthy nineteenth-century Scottish steel magnate. A deeply religious and visionary man, Carnegie struggled to reconcile the tension between his enthusiasm for capitalism and his love of God. In 1889, four years after the arrival of Frederick Trump in New York City, he published a 5,000-word essay, 'The Gospel of Wealth'. His essay addressed the fraught subject of inequality, acknowledging the growing gap between rich and poor which had arisen from industrialisation. As he put it, in the past there had been little difference between the way of life of a chief and his retainers; by that point, though, there was evidently a huge gap between the palace of the millionaire and the cottage of the labourer. He was not arguing for redistribution, however. On the contrary, he defended inequality as an essential consequence of progress.

We accept and welcome ... great inequality of environment,

the concentration of business, industrial and commercial, in the hands of a few ... as being not only beneficial, but essential for the future progress of the race ... Much better this great irregularity than universal squalor.

He argued that inequality of wealth was simply a manifestation of inequality of talent. To Carnegie, all people were not born equal. Some were born with God-given talents; others were not. It was not dissimilar from Aristotle's view that some were born to be masters and some were born to be slaves, but now it was couched in a new metaphor: he spoke of the world being divided up into drones and bees, reinforcing his view that this division was something natural. It was God's will.

To Carnegie, the key to a happy but unequal society came from giving people opportunities to climb upward. The metaphor of upward motion recurred repeatedly in his essay: he talked about 'the highest results of human experience ... the highest type of man ... the highest life to be reached...' He celebrated all those who aspired to higher peaks, whilst those who tried to undermine this aspiration – the anarchists, the socialists and the communists – were 'attacking the foundation upon which civilization itself rests ... [threatening to bring about] the total overthrow of our civilization'.

So, what were the wealthy to do with their money? Carnegie rejected leaving your money to the first-born, concluding that this invariably led to them being spoiled. He also rejected inflicting higher taxes on the rich, because that didn't lead to the benefactor being 'extolled'; there was no 'grace' in their gifts; their bequests seemed to lack 'blessing'.

Instead, he proposed that the affluent should voluntarily share out their wealth as they saw fit. They should live as Jesus had lived: 'labouring for the good of our fellows'. They should not give money to 'the slothful, the drunken, the unworthy' – indeed, he attacked the well-intended but ultimately misguided fellow who gives money to beggars when he knows they won't spend it properly, calling them 'thoughtless' and 'selfish'. Rather, he said, they should give their money to 'help those who will help themselves...'

Carnegie set out a new metaphor to depict this new role for the wealthy. He quoted the Swedish Lutheran theologian Emanuel Swedenborg's 1758 book *Heaven and Hell*, in which Swedenborg described an apparition of angels and how those angels found their pleasure in a life of active service. He defined 'heavenly joy' as 'the pleasure of doing something that benefits both yourself and others'.[281]

It's a beautiful vision and Carnegie's legacy is visible around the world to this day. I personally know a great many people who have indeed been able to climb to the highest peaks in life because Carnegie's enduring legacy gave them the opportunity to help themselves.

The metaphor of angels was perfect for Carnegie's purposes. The word 'angel' derives from the ancient Greek word *angelos*, which means messenger. It depicted the wealthy as God's messengers on earth. Not only were the wealthy blessed by God, they were also sent to do God's bidding. It was for them to decide who else should be blessed. The blessings were articulated through money.

Carnegie's new metaphorical frame was instantly appealing. Not long after the publication of 'The Gospel of Wealth', the term 'angel investor' first appeared. Used initially to describe investors who backed risky Broadway productions, the phrase eventually evolved to cover any kind of venture capitalist.

I wonder if it was perhaps with this view of angelic behaviour in mind that a group of Broadway angel investors felt compelled to position the new home for movie production in Los Angeles. Stranger examples of nominative determinism have occurred... In any case, within five years of Jesse L. Lasky and Cecil B. DeMille going to film *The Squaw Man* in Los Angeles in 1913, 80 per cent of the world's movies were being made in the City of Angels.

As the language about wealth and religion changed, so people's perceptions of wealth and religion changed. The wealthy were entitled to take a more visibly elevated status in society. This was God's will. Skyscrapers started shooting up into the clouds. The wealthier you were, the higher you went. The penthouse apartment became the ultimate symbol of wealth. From that penthouse apartment you were the closest person to God. You also looked down upon everyone else. And from that lofty view, didn't they look just like ants?

And this brings us back to The Donald. Over the past few decades, there is no one who has been more synonymous with that penthouse lifestyle than Donald J. Trump.

Donald Trump came from a religious family, Lutheran on his father's side and Presbyterian on his mother's. His grandmother's maiden name was even Christ. It's curious to think that had it been her name that was passed down, rather than his grandfather's, we could now have President Christ of the Christ Organisation, formerly residing in Christ Tower, sitting in the White House.

Trump grew up in an age of grand construction in New York. He spent his childhood watching his father erect huge tenements in Brooklyn and Queens. When he was a teenager, the foundations were just being laid for the twin towers of the World Trade Center. Both of these inspired the young Donald. The act that put him on the map, literally and metaphorically, was the construction of Trump Tower on the intersection of Fifth and 56th, right next to Tiffany & Co. He had been keeping his eye on the site for a long time. Twice a year he would approach the owner of the Bonwit Teller department store that occupied the spot, asking if he wanted to sell. He was literally laughed out of the building at first. Eventually, after a change of management, he did a deal, and plans for Trump Tower moved forward.

The story of how Donald Trump demolished that old Bonwit Teller store to make way for Trump Tower played a critical part in establishing the myth of Trump that we all know today. The old Bonwit Teller store was an art deco building and built into its façade were two 15 x 25 ft sculptures of semi-nude goddesses. The statues were part of the local scenery and when news spread that Trump was demolishing the store, a number of local residents stepped forward to ensure the statues were saved. The Metropolitan Museum agreed to take them and Trump said he'd send them their way, but that's not what happened. In the end, he decided that getting them out safely was too expensive. He had the statues smashed on to the floor, where they 'shattered into a million pieces'.[282] The city was aghast. Trump was condemned by cultural experts and by the *New York Times*, but, in a pattern that was to become infuriatingly familiar, he near enough replied that he couldn't care less. He said they were junk.

From that incident on, all through the 1980s, his star remained in the ascendant. He hung out with other stars. He made cameos in several movies and TV shows, from *Home Alone 2* to *Sex and the City* and *Days of Our Lives* (which led to the infamous conversation with Billy Bush…). He courted the world's top boxing stars, hosting big fights at his hotels, and of course he purchased the rights to the Miss Universe and Miss USA beauty pageants. One time, he even threw himself into professional wrestling, jumping into the ring in front of 80,000 people in Detroit. But still he wasn't satisfied. Still he wanted more.

The big leap came when he made the move from real estate to reality TV with *The Apprentice*. He'd never have become President were it not for his lofty depiction on this show. He was constantly portrayed as exalted, whether up high in Trump Tower, or in a private jet or in a helicopter. In addition, the role he played on the series was fundamentally that of the angel investor, making sure that he could 'help those who will help themselves'. In the first episode of the first series, he gave each of the apprentices $250 to see who could make the most money selling lemonade on the streets of New York.

The programme probably should have been called 'The Angel' rather than *The Apprentice*, because Trump was the central protagonist, not the participants. And the programme didn't represent anything like a real apprenticeship: a real apprenticeship is based on the apprentice one day taking over from the master. That was never going to happen in Trump's world. The prize for the winning team in the first episode was to spend a few minutes in Trump's presence, being shown around his penthouse suite. 'I show this apartment to very few people – Presidents, Kings, and they look around and they really can't believe what they're seeing…' As he sees them off at his front door, they all literally bow to him.[283]

There was no doubt that the ultimate winner of *The Apprentice* was Donald Trump. Whilst the Series 1 winner was rewarded with a salaried job on $250,000 p.a., Donald Trump was said to have earned $214 million for his involvement with the programme.[284]

The Apprentice earned Trump great wealth, recognition, respect and even his own star on the Hollywood Walk of Fame, but he had always had an interest in politics as well. In a 1988 interview, Oprah Winfrey had asked him if he'd ever stand for President. He said he wouldn't rule it out. 'I do get tired of seeing what's happening with this country … I think people are tired of seeing the United States ripped off.' He had been a Democrat for most of his life and had supported Hillary Clinton in 2008, but Barack Obama had put him off.

It was in 2011 that he first thought about standing against Obama. But, like Oprah today, he knew he would need God's support. So he reached out to his angels. The first person to whom he reached out was his spiritual angel, the Pentecostal televangelist Paula White.

White had been Trump's spiritual adviser for many years. He had first seen her on Christian television back in 2002 and they had remained close ever since. Paula White is a practitioner of prosperity theology. The philosophy behind prosperity theology is not dissimilar to Andrew Carnegie's world view: in prosperity theology, money is regarded as a blessing, and to have money is to be blessed.

There is backing for this in the Bible. The idea of money as a blessing runs throughout the Scripture – when Christ was born, for, instance, the three Kings blessed him with gold, frankincense and myrrh – just as money often appears as a metaphor for divinity, with references to the riches of His glory, a wealth of salvation, the treasures of His wisdom.

Prosperity theology is very popular in the States, but there have been some controversies, not least with some unscrupulous televangelists who promise blessings to those who pull out their credit cards. Give me money to pay for my next private jet and you will be blessed.

When Trump called her in 2011 and explained he was thinking about standing for the presidency, White gathered thirty ministers from different evangelical Christian traditions at Trump Tower to pray and hear God's view. The message came back. We can't know word for word exactly what God said to Paula White, but she reported back to Trump, possibly diplomatically, 'I don't feel it's the right timing.'

Trump heeded that message in 2011. But on election night 2012, he was seething when Obama won again. That night, he fired off a multitude of tweets: 'We should have a revolution in this country.' 'We should march on Washington and stop this travesty.' 'Let's fight like hell and stop this great and disgusting injustice! The world is laughing at us.'

His ire against Obama continued for the following three years. Then, in September 2015, he summoned Paula White to Trump Tower once more. This time, he wasn't asking for advice. He'd already decided he was going to run. Paula White backed the decision he had already made.[285]

You can see the video of this prayer meeting on YouTube. It's quite a sight: Paula White is seen bowing down before Trump as the prayers are said, her hand pressed on Trump's chest. There is no doubt that she really believed that Trump was the chosen one.[286]

After his election, Trump appointed Paula White as chair of his evangelical advisory board. She remains his spiritual adviser today and even delivered the invocation at his inauguration. She is unstinting in her support for Trump as President. As she puts it:

> He's been raised up by God because God says that he raises up and places all people in places of authority. It is God that raises up a king, it is God that sets one down, and so when you fight against the plan of God, you're fighting against the hand of God.[287]

Having worked in Whitehall, where famously 'we don't do God', this strikes me as a great way to see off political opposition. You fight the President, you're fighting God. It's a great way to keep people believing. And, incidentally, Paula White is married to none other than Jonathan Cain from the rock band Journey, whose biggest song was 'Don't Stop Believin''. One imagines she won't.

Nor are any of Trump's evangelical supporters likely to lose faith any time soon. Many in the evangelical movement share her view that he is the chosen one – an incredible 81 per cent of white evangelicals voted for Trump. But some have an even more exalted view of him.

There is a significant grouping in the evangelical church who believe that Trump's election was prophesied in the Bible.

1 Corinthians 15:52 states in the King James Bible that 'at the last trump, the trumpet shall sound and the dead shall be raised incorruptible and we shall be changed'. They have interpreted this ancient reference as a reference to The Donald.

More worryingly, this passage is associated with the end time prophecy, which concerns the Second Coming, Judgement Day, and Israel being returned to the Jews. In light of this, many in the evangelical community have regarded Trump's reversal of the previous administration's stance on Israel – recognising Jerusalem as its capital – as particularly significant. It appears to be confirmation of his status.[288]

Anyway, back to 2016: Trump's spiritual angel had given him a blessing, but he knew he also needed to find a financial angel. Presidential campaigns are very expensive – everyone knows that. Every aspiring presidential candidate needs someone with deep pockets to bankroll them. We've already seen how the financial angels swiftly descended upon Oprah with their billion-dollar offers of support after her speech at the Golden Globe awards in the City of Angels.

Ronald Reagan also told how his journey into politics began with an approach remarkably similar to Oprah's. One night, also in Los Angeles, he was approached by a delegation of high-powered Republicans after he'd delivered a speech. They offered to pay for a prime-time slot for him if he would deliver the same speech again on national television. He said that it was that night which changed his whole life, setting him off on a path that eventually led him all the way to the White House.

Barack Obama also had financial angels.[289] Many of them also hailed from the City of Angels, although one of them was not too angelic. Harvey Weinstein regularly hosted annual fundraising dinners for Obama.[290] In 2011, Weinstein hosted a fundraising dinner at his Greenwich Village townhouse which was attended by a number of stars: Gwyneth Paltrow, Jimmy Fallon and Pharrell Williams, all of whom had paid $35,800 to attend. Andrew Cuomo, the newly elected Governor of New York, was also there. Weinstein made a speech over the dinner, referencing Cuomo's recent election win. 'I'm lucky enough, and he knows it's true, to say that I was one of Cuomo's earliest supporters,' Weinstein told the crowd. 'Yes, yes,' Cuomo called out, 'angel investor!' Barack Obama responded, 'That's the first time anybody's ever called him that.'[291] Indeed.

But the truth is that Weinstein was viewed as something of an angel. Obama even acknowledged that: his nineteen-year-old daughter, Malia, interned for Weinstein for a year before she took up her place at Harvard. When *Quartz* magazine counted the number of individuals thanked in Academy Award acceptance speeches over the years, they found that Harvey Weinstein came in joint second, just after Steven Spielberg, but tied with God.[292]

When the allegations against Weinstein emerged, there weren't many people who were prepared to speak out in his defence, but one person who did was former Disney child star Lindsay Lohan. She posted a video on Instagram saying, 'He's never harmed me or did anything to me. We've done several movies together. I think everyone needs to stop; I think it's wrong.' As she said this, a halo emoji floated beside her throughout the video, with Harvey's name written above it. Her message was clear. Harvey = angel.[293]

But who was to be Trump's guardian angel? There were no obvious candidates, particularly with almost the whole of the media, the financial and political establishment united in opposition to his candidature. But there was one angel investor who had made his fortune betting against the odds.

Peter Thiel first made his name in 1998 when he founded PayPal, correctly predicting the shift to electronic payments. When PayPal was sold to eBay just four years later for $1.5 billion, Thiel was very young and very rich and needed something else to do. That's when he got into angel investing. He proved to have something of a Midas touch, providing angel investment for LinkedIn, Yammer and Yelp. Possibly his finest venture was in 2004 when, for an angel investment of half a million dollars, he acquired 10 per cent of Facebook. He was the first ever external investor in the company. When Thiel invested in Facebook, they had fewer than one million active users; within eight years, they had one billion.

In the same year that he invested in Facebook, he co-founded, with Alexander Karp, a company called Palantir, a data collection company. Palantir developed software that sifts through photos, videos and other data, looking for signs of terrorism. Palantir received its original funding from In-Q-Tel, the CIA's venture capital arm. Estimates of the company's value today vary, but some run as high as $20 billion.

Thiel is in some ways the ultimate angel investor. But remember, angels don't just have the power to grant life. They also have the power to grant death. Remember how Kate James and Tom Evans saw Alfie grow his wings earlier on in the book? Remember the Angel of Death at Auschwitz?

In 2016, Thiel helped to bring down gossip website

Gawker, following a near decade-long vendetta he'd had with them after they published an article titled 'Peter Thiel is totally gay, people'. Gawker had published a sex tape of Hulk Hogan having sex with his friend's wife and Thiel backed Hulk Hogan's lawsuit against them to the tune of $10 million. The case became one of the largest in US legal history. Hogan won. On 18 March 2016, Hogan was awarded $115 million in damages against Gawker, forcing the site to close down. Gawker had a reputation for breaking huge news stories, having exposed the allegations of sexual assault against Bill Cosby and Hillary Clinton's email scandal, amongst much else. Afterwards, Thiel told the *New York Times* that he considered Gawker a 'terrorist organisation' and that he thought bringing them down was 'one of the greater philanthropic things that I've done'.[294]

Today, he's involved in more angel-like quests, some of which concern changing the whole nature of humanity. He is investing in what he calls the Immortality Project, looking at how to reverse ageing. Forget depicting people as subhuman – he is looking at effectively creating a wholly new species of superhumans, with unprecedented physical strength, the power to fight off any infections and the potential to live for hundreds of years. There are seemingly no limits to his capacity to imagine. His territorial ambitions also stretch far beyond traditional boundaries. Not only is he investing in space colonies, he's also created the Seasteading Institute, looking at creating various Atlantis-type supranational islands on reclaimed land in the middle of the oceans. He has audacious ambitions to create offshore libertarian paradises. Thinking big has always been in his nature but possibly his most daring scheme ever was his plan to put Donald Trump in the White House.

Peter Thiel angel-invested in Project Trump, giving over a million dollars to his presidential campaign early on. In June 2016, he made a speech in Cleveland declaring, 'I'm gay, I'm Republican and I'm backing Donald Trump for President.'[295] A few months later, at the National Press Club in Washington, he attacked the liberal media for their inability to see Trump's potential. 'What Trump represents isn't crazy and it's not going away. He points toward ... a new American politics that overcomes denial, rejects bubble thinking and reckons with reality.'[296] He clearly feels a huge affinity with Trump. Both hailed from German ancestry. Both were brought up in evangelical households. Both are libertarians. Both abhor political correctness and appear misogynistic: in his book *The Diversity Myth*, Thiel argues that women getting the vote was bad for democracy.

And now here he is sitting in the power position at Trump's left (Vice-President Mike Pence is sitting on Trump's right) as the President prepares to meet the bosses of America's biggest tech companies. This is probably the single most important meeting that Trump will have during the transition. And it's all a little bit awkward, because many of the tech titans are high-profile liberals who publicly campaigned against him. There had been suggestions that some of them would boycott this meeting but in the end they came. This was truly a roll call of all of the great and the good: Jeff Bezos from Amazon, Tim Cook from Apple, Larry Page and Eric Schmidt from Alphabet (i.e. Google), Sheryl Sandberg from Facebook, Elon Musk from Tesla, Satya Nadella and Brad

Smith from Microsoft, Chuck Robbins from Cisco, Alex Karp from Palantir, Brian Krzanich from Intel, Ginni Rometty from IBM and Safra Catz from Oracle.

Trump welcomes everyone to the room.

I just want to thank everybody. This is a truly amazing group of people. I won't tell you the hundreds of calls we had asking to come to this meeting. Peter was saying, 'No, that company's too small and these were monster companies...' But I want to start by thanking Peter. He saw something very early, maybe before we saw it and of course he's known for that in a different way but he has been so terrific and so outstanding. He got just about the biggest applause at the Republican national convention. He's ahead of the curve and I just want to thank him. He's a very special guy. I want to add that I'm here to help you folks do well. You're doing well right now and I'm very honoured by the bounce. They're all talking about the bounce. So everybody in this room has to like me a little bit...[297]

But these people didn't like him a bit. As the camera panned the room, there were barely concealed looks of disdain and discomfort. Here they were, in Trump's golden tower, the building that had cemented his reputation; the building where he filmed *The Apprentice*; the building from which he'd run his presidential campaign. On the tables in front of them were even Trump-branded bottles of water. But still they weren't impressed. They weren't impressed with this puffed-up reality TV star. Nor were they impressed with an angel investor. These people were better than both of them.

So who were these people that could look down on such an exalted star and his angel? Well, as almost all of the press reports of this meeting described them, these were the tech titans. Let's meet them.

TITANS

In 1969, two earth-shattering events took place which were to fundamentally alter the course of human history. One is a truly global television event that everyone is aware of; the other is far less well known.

On 20 July 1969, Apollo 11 landed on the moon. This event, broadcast live around the world, was probably the biggest event of the twentieth century, bar none. It marked the final fulfilment of President John F. Kennedy's grand ambition, set out to Congress in 1961, that, before the decade was out, the United States would put a man on the moon. As Neil Armstrong put it, 'One small step for man, one giant leap for mankind.' It is hard to conceive of any action which could have been more significant or symbolic.

The other event took place with much less fanfare, but it made much more of a difference. On 29 October 1969, the first ever email was sent between two computers at Stanford Research Institute via the ARPANET, the predecessor of today's internet. University of California professor Leonard

Kleinrock sent the email from the UCLA SDS Sigma Host computer to another programmer, Bill Duvall, at Stanford Research Institute. The idea of an 'intergalactic computer network' had first been mooted by the computer scientist J. C. R. Licklider of Bolt, Beranek and Newman in 1963. Now that dream of an intergalactic computer network had taken a giant leap closer to reality.

The message was supposed to say 'Logic', but, in a pattern that was soon to become familiar to hundreds of millions of people around the world, the computer crashed halfway through sending, meaning the message only read 'Lo'; this seems an appropriately portentous word for an event of such biblical proportions. Still, to this day, the room at the University of California in which that message was sent is preserved as it was, referred to as a 'shrine', a 'holy place' and 'ground zero'. Quite right too. For, when this email was sent, a new universe was created. And what a universe it is.

Today, more than 4.3 billion people in the planet are online.[298] Two billion people are on Facebook.[299] And five billion YouTube videos are watched every day.[300] A huge alternative universe has been created. And I don't mind admitting: it has been a godsend.

I live on a mountain in the middle of the Brecon Beacons where I can walk my daughters to school in the morning before returning to my desk to Skype a client in Kuala Lumpur. Everything I want in the world is at my fingertips. Music, movies, memories. Friends, family, frivolity. I can see anyone, anywhere, anytime. It's a dream come true. I can zoom up and down, in and out, left and right, bringing people in or sending them away at a whim. I'm the boss. I'm in complete command. It's fabulous. Why would I spend time anywhere else?

But here's the thing. Can I make a confession? Increasingly, I actually prefer this alternative universe to the real world. It took a while to realise it, but I can't deny it's true any more. I am spending more and more time there. The thing is, life in cyberspace is so much easier than life in the real world. In the real world, I have real people to contend with, and real challenges to confront. In the real world, I have to be polite, considerate, respectful. In the real world, I have to put a pair of trousers on in the morning… It's much easier zapping around in cyberspace lying in bed.

Take writing this book. I've done some of it in the real world, exploring magnificent libraries, great museums and swish offices. But most of it has been in cyberspace. Cyberspace was far and away the easiest experience. For instance, early on in the research, I went to the Vatican Library to look up old texts on Christian rhetoric. I had to apply for a pass, go for an interview, get my photo taken – and all this in the hot, sticky streets of Rome. Seriously, it'll be much easier when they get all their stuff online.

And so it is that what started as an alternative universe has increasingly become my primary universe. I now spend more of my time in cyberspace than I do in the real world. I'm not unusual: many of us spend more of our time online than offline. According to the data technology company Zenith-Optimedia, the average European and American spends 620 minutes every day online. This is behind Latin America, which clocks in at 765 minutes, but ahead of Asia Pacific at 310 minutes.

Plus, we're only going to spend more and more time online. In the UK, the time spent online increased by 9 per cent between 2016 and 2017 according to IPA Touchpoints Data. It was very early on in Facebook's growth that Mark Zuckerberg and his co-founders first noticed the 'trance' that people went into when they were on Facebook. Today, tech companies are actively working with neuroscientists and behavioural economists to prolong that trance.[301] They carry out what they call A/B tests, where they run slightly tweaked versions of pages and algorithms alongside one another against different sample groups to see which one is the best at holding people's attention. They'll then run with whichever is the most successful. They keep doing this over and over again so that every day they're getting better and better at drawing us in. They offer the ultimate promise of escapism.

Sometimes it can beat off some pretty phenomenal competition. A few years back, I was in Hyde Park watching the Rolling Stones play, and I actually found myself checking Facebook whilst the Stones were in the middle of playing 'Jumpin' Jack Flash'. Can you believe that? WTF? I had one of those startling moments of clarity. I thought, what's going on here? I've spent literally decades wanting to see the Stones play – and up there on that stage is the real Mick Jagger, alongside Keith Richards, Charlie Watts and Ronnie Wood, and they are really playing 'Jumpin' Jack Flash' – and here I am checking my phone because that's where I'd rather be. Really? How did this happen? How did I get so addicted? Have I got a problem? Yes, I have. But here's the thing: I know I'm not alone. Everywhere I go, I see the same thing. Everyone was doing the same at this Stones gig. We were all staring at our phones.

We see it everywhere. Beautiful people on romantic dates in incredible restaurants ignoring one another and instead swiping through their phones, only emerging from their trances momentarily for the mandatory beaming 'Date night!' photos that they must post on social media. Then back to 'the trance'. We see people who have climbed the Eiffel Tower, the most magnificent view of Paris stretching out before them, but instead of admiring that, they're sneakily replying to an email from work. They know what they're doing is wrong – they have a guilty, furtive look which confirms that – but they can't stop themselves all the same.

Such sights are everywhere, and impossible to ignore. We see people living out what should be some of the most intense emotional experiences of their lives but they are, to all intents and purposes, absent. People are actively rejecting the reality of a beautiful life on our earth for a synthetic experience of cyberspace. We can't help ourselves. This urge has always been there. As Aldous Huxley put it in his prophetic 1954 book, *The Doors of Perception*, 'The longing to transcend … if only for a few moments, has always been one of the principal appetites of the soul.'[302] He was talking about alcohol, religion and drugs. But now it is our phones that are giving us that ability to transcend.

But what's all this got to do with metaphor? How do metaphors shape our experience and perception of the internet? What are the metaphors for the internet? Well, it won't surprise you to know that as the internet has evolved, so the language has changed. So let's start at the beginning. Let's go back in time thirty years to 1989 when Tim Berners-Lee was working for the European Organisation for Nuclear

Research and trying to find a better system of managing and sharing information.

Famously, the system he developed is now known as the world wide web. That was not the first name he had for it. When he first proposed the project in 1989, he called it a mesh. The word 'web' first came to be used in 1990. The idea of web and mesh are not so different, though. They are both based on physical connections between multiple points. It's a similar image to a net as well. The ARPANET. A *net*work. The inter*net*. Same idea. And this was the imagery that fitted well with Berners-Lee's vision of a system that could connect the world. So there we were. A net! Nice and simple.

But then, an argument occurred about how this new space should be perceived. The argument was basically between the White House on the one side and Silicon Valley on the other. On the one hand, you had a White House who saw the internet as something that should be carefully regulated and controlled. On the other, you had Silicon Valley, which did not. These different world views were articulated through different metaphors.

It was Al Gore, Vice-President under Clinton, who first coined the idea of the 'information superhighway' in 1991. This was a wonderful metaphor from the perspective of a government who wanted to regulate the internet, because of course highways only work on the basis of strict rules about who can drive on them, what they can do, how old they have to be, how they must behave, which direction they should go, and so on. Genius! So Clinton and Gore talked about the information superhighway at every opportunity. And then, as you would expect when two of the most powerful people in the world start using a phrase, it wasn't long before they had every other political leader in the world talking about the information superhighway.

Tony Blair's first big announcement after being elected leader of the Labour Party was an agreement with BT to 'cable up schools, colleges, universities, libraries to the information superhighway'. Remember that? This announcement defined him in the early days of his premiership as a young leader looking to the future. The idea, launched in his party conference speech in 1995, had come about after meetings between Gore's team and his own.[303]

The idea of the information superhighway continued for many years. I started writing speeches just a few years after this (I wrote for Patricia Hewitt, who was Britain's first e-Minister), and the term 'information superhighway' was still being bandied around. So government was still in control then. Or at least it thought it was.

But the phrase was not going down so well in Silicon Valley. They could not stand the idea of an information superhighway. They didn't want governments looking over them, telling them what they could and couldn't do, where they could and couldn't go. That wasn't the way they wanted the internet to work. They had a wholly different perspective. They wanted this to be a place where they had the freedom to do whatever they wanted, where they could push back the frontiers, where the only limits to their reach were their own imaginations. They wanted to boldly go where no man had gone before. Sound familiar? And so it was that those two hugely symbolic events of 1969 merged into one, thanks to a combination of the literal and the metaphorical term that became for ever locked together in the public mind.

'Cyberspace' was a term popularised by the sci-fi writer William Gibson in his 1984 book *Neuromancer*. Gibson described cyberspace as:

> a consensual hallucination experienced daily by billions of legitimate operators, in every nation, by children being taught mathematical concepts … A graphic representation of data abstracted from banks of every computer in the human system. Unthinkable complexity. Lines of light ranged in the nonspace of the mind, clusters and constellations of data. Like city lights, receding…

The cyberspace metaphor spoke to Silicon Valley's deepest instinctive, emotional and commercial needs. Not only was it inherently inspiring, it also gave them complete freedom to do what they wanted. Because, just as we all instantly understand that a superhighway is something that will only succeed with extensive regulation, so we equally understand that cyberspace is a place that is inherently unregulatable, because it is supranational, existing far above the nation state. And don't worry about the risks of exploring outer space – sure, some things will crash, some people will die – but this is a price worth paying, because what we're doing here is pushing back the frontiers of human knowledge in a way that will benefit the whole of civilisation.

The cyberspace metaphor came to shape how all of the tech titans conceptualised and spoke about what they were doing. They were not in the business of technological development; they were in the space exploration game.

Jeff Bezos, Amazon's founder and a big *Star Trek* fan (he

keeps memorabilia from the original set at his home), said to sceptics during Amazon's early days, 'We're going to take this thing to the moon.'[304] When the Amazon website launched, the legend at the top of that very first website proudly declared Amazon to be 'Earth's largest bookstore', as if there were some other planet we might visit to buy a book.[305] When Eric Schmidt, CEO of a nascent Google, tried to recruit Sheryl Sandberg to come and work for him, he said, 'If you're offered a seat on a rocket ship, don't ask what seat, just get on!' Mark Zuckerberg said in his Harvard commencement speech in the summer of 2017 that one of his favourite stories was 'when John F. Kennedy visited the NASA space centre, he saw a janitor carrying a broom and he walked over and asked what he was doing. The janitor responded, "Mr President, I'm helping put a man on the moon."'

This language is all over Silicon Valley. The web companies launch their businesses, blast off to success, reach for the stars, have a meteoric rise, create astronomical fortunes, gain altitude and go into orbit. It doesn't always take off, obviously: sometimes companies can explode and implode, crash and burn, blow up into little bits... But who cares? What a thrilling intergalactic adventure it is anyway!

But this is not just the way Silicon Valley conceptualises what they do; this is how we have all now come to perceive and talk about this space. We pick up our Android or Galaxy smartphones. We open up our navigators (Explorer or Safari). We type in, or tap, our command for where we want to go. We then zap around in cyberspace, landing on sites and launching apps (but God forbid they might crash). We click on portals and hyperlinks and, of course, only the most intrepid space cowboys will venture into the dark web. We store all our data on the cloud. Notice how whatever we do in cyberspace is always up there, not down there. We put things up on Facebook. We upload videos to YouTube. We look things up on Google. If someone comes up and speaks to us whilst we're deeply immersed online we may well jolt, and say, 'Sorry, I was in another world.' And that is how it feels.

The whole experience is utterly immersive, exhilaratingly real and utterly transcendental. We are all of us like Captain Kirk, standing at the bridge in the *Starship Enterprise*, commanding our very own starship through outer space. And if you do feel a little like Captain Kirk when you're travelling in cyberspace, that's no coincidence. It was designed to feel like that. Amit Singhal was the senior VP who developed Google's search engine, and who, incidentally, is also a devout fan of *Star Trek*. Throughout his time at Google, he frequently explained that what he was trying to do was make the Google experience feel for customers like being on the bridge of the *Starship Enterprise*. When he left Google in 2016, he said his 'dream *Star Trek* computer is becoming a reality, and it is far better than what I ever imagined'.[306]

When I was a little boy, watching *Star Trek* and *Star Wars* and playing Space Invaders with Bowie playing in the background, the legend of Neil Armstrong and Buzz Aldrin still fresh in the public imagination, I wanted nothing more than to be an astronaut. Or a star. Something up there, though, definitely! Didn't we all? No wonder the cyberspace metaphor captured the public imagination better than the idea of an information superhighway. It was the choice between being Captain Kirk zapping around in outer space on board the *Starship Enterprise* or Alan Partridge pulling into the middle lane as he takes his Rover 800 up the A10.

The White House lost the battle for language in its war with cyberspace. The idea of an information superhighway is all but forgotten now. According to Google Trends, references to 'cyberspace' today outnumber references to the 'information superhighway' by 50:1.

But what are the consequences of this metaphorical mindset? It doesn't just affect the way it feels to travellers through cyberspace; it also affects those who create these alternate universes.

Microsoft's Jaron Lanier, who pretty well created virtual reality, explains how it feels.

> It's saying, 'Oh, you digital techy people, you're like gods; you're creating life; you're transforming reality.' There's a tremendous narcissism in it that we're the people who can do it. No one else. The Pope can't do it. The President can't do it. No one else can do it. We are the masters of it ... The software we're building is our immortality.[307]

The *Whole Earth Catalog* – a magazine that was massively influential in the Valley in the late '60s – had as its purpose, 'We are as Gods and might as well get good at it.'

It's a powerful idea. It stuck. And it also showed incredible foresight when you see what the tech companies can do now.

They have a godlike insight into our hearts, souls and deepest motivations. They know more about humanity today than anyone has ever known in the whole of human history, both individually and collectively. They know pretty much everything we do and have done. When we're zapping around in cyberspace, we imagine we're doing so in private. It's dark in cyberspace. No one can see. It's a myth. They can see. They can see all of it. They have always been able to see all of it. Imagine if you could snoop back on your friends' internet search histories going back just a week. Imagine what you'd find out. You'd get all sorts of insights into their health, their interests, their secrets... You'd probably understand more about their characters, emotions and behaviours than they'd ever admit to you, or perhaps even to themselves. Well, the tech companies have this information on all of us going back several years now, and they have it on billions of people, and with that information comes a tremendous power: a power that could be used in the most incredible different ways. How must that feel? Well, I can tell you how it feels. Godlike. Uber calls the screen where they track their customers' location 'God view'. They track their own drivers on a screen called 'Heaven', and drivers from rival companies on a screen called 'Hell'.[308] People on Fifth Avenue might look like ants from the top of Trump Tower, but that is nothing compared to how the whole of humanity appears to the tech gods, as they can see what everyone's up to at any particular time from their vantage point at the top of cyberspace.

They also deliberately seem to pitch themselves in this godlike way. Have you noticed how their company formation stories invariably take the form of biblical-like narratives? The immaculate conceptions of ideas, businesses grown in garages (the modern-day equivalent of a manger), combined with a deep sense of destiny. Forget God taking seven days to create the universe, Mark Zuckerberg got Facebook going in about four hours.

They also actively preach like religious leaders. I wrote a piece for *PR Week* ten years ago analysing Steve Jobs's launch of the iPhone and wrote then about how Steve Jobs was like John Wesley without the incense: the 'new Messiah for Generation X'. I pointed out that the Apple logo had replaced the crucifix, dimmed lights had replaced candles and, instead of chanting psalms, there was the occasional 'Whoop!'[309] That speech has now provided the blueprint for all subsequent tech launches. The guys in Silicon Valley are our new religious leaders, creating our new universes, plotting the path to the future, telling us with a growing confidence what it is that we must do to make a better world.

Some people have suggested that Mark Zuckerberg could potentially stand for President. I genuinely don't think he would because I believe that would give him less power than he has as the CEO of Facebook. He once opined to his speechwriter, 'If you want to change the world, the best thing to do is to build a company.' His mantra in meetings was 'companies over countries'. His regular way of closing their weekly Friday meetings was to raise his fist with a slight smile and say, 'Domination.'

They certainly have the wealth of gods. The six richest tech titans – Bill Gates, Jeff Bezos, Mark Zuckerberg, Larry Ellison, Larry Page and Sergey Brin – are worth $429 billion dollars between them.[310] This is more than the combined wealth of the poorest 50 per cent of people on the planet ($426 billion). Forget companies over countries; it's individuals over countries. And they're untouchable.

Here's the thing: the cyberspace metaphor fundamentally renders all of the tech companies and their creators inherently supranational and supernatural, omnipotent and omniscient, untouchable and unregulatable. This is a perception that dominates not just the people who use them and the people that run them, but also the people who are supposed to regulate them. So, instead of challenging these men who have acquired wealth and power at an unprecedented speed and scale, national governments have just looked on in awe, accepting their authority. But it is all predicated on a metaphorical myth. Let's expose that metaphor.

When we shop on Amazon, it might feel like we're up in cyberspace, but we're not. Our feet really are on the ground, the product we buy is in a warehouse and these purchases are brought to our door by a real person. But because we land on Amazon's site through our explorer in cyberspace, we don't quite perceive it like that. And national governments don't see it that way either: if they had have done, they'd have stepped in very quickly to stop Amazon's massive tax advantage, which is destroying the High Street and crushing jobs. But who would dare take them on? When Donald Trump tweeted, 'If @amazon ever had to pay fair taxes, its stock would crash and it would crumble like a paper bag', Jeff Bezos's response was to start a new hashtag: #sendDonaldtospace.[311] He gets it.

When we store our data, our perception is similarly that we're keeping it in cyberspace. Because we talk about our data being in the cloud, it doesn't mean that our information is really sitting in big, fluffy, white masses of condensation, miles away from prying eyes. It's actually sitting in huge data banks that people can walk into. And the truth is that everything we put on the web is eminently visible to hackers, as Edward Majerczyk, a 29-year-old man from Illinois, proved when he hacked into the iCloud accounts of some of the world's biggest actresses, including Academy Award winner Jennifer Lawrence. He downloaded highly intimate naked photos and videos of them, and rapidly disseminated them across the internet, to the horror of all concerned. Jennifer Lawrence said that the exposure of her nude photos, and a video of her having sex, felt like being 'gang-raped'. Still, Google happily directs you to it.

Indeed, Google will direct you to whatever you want. What will it be today, sir? Terrorist manuals on how to make a bomb? Maybe some videos of child abuse? Perhaps you'd like to buy some drugs? I don't remember this stuff being available in WH Smith when I was growing up. If it had been, the owners and the vendors would have been thrown in prison. Why aren't the tech companies subject to the same obligations?

The tech companies won their big get-out in the 1996 Telecommunications Act, which stated that 'no provider or user of an interactive computer service shall be treated as the publisher or speaker of the information provided'. This gave them a free pass to sell access to anything with complete impunity. They were not publishers, but a platform.

Eric Schmidt was the executive chairman of Google from 2001 to 2017. He is pretty well the guy who made Google what it is today. In his recent book *The New Digital Age: Reshaping the Future of People, Nations and Business*, he described the internet as 'the largest experiment involving anarchy in history'. He called it 'the world's largest ungoverned space' and admits that it remains to be seen whether it will end up making the world better or worse.[312]

Schmidt's book is an extraordinary read. It felt to me like it was almost an appeal for government to intervene, like an unruly, out-of-control child calling to their parents, begging, 'Please set us some rules! We need some order! We need some discipline!' But there's no sign governments will do that. The question is whether, having taken this giant technological leap forward, it will ever be possible for the world to take even a small step back.

The geeks have inherited the earth. In return, they've given us an artificial universe, comprising shops, friendships and spaces that do not really exist. When Neil Armstrong landed on the moon, the TV anchorman Howard K. Smith said that TV's 'real value is to make people participants in ongoing experiences. Real life is vastly more exciting than synthetic life.'[313] Yeah. Whatever. Try telling that to the kids.

GOD

've invested my faith in Anthony Levandowski. Like Steve Jobs reinvented the phone, I believe Levandowski has the power to reinvent the car. His life's mission has been the commercialisation of self-driving cars. In 2004, when he was just twenty-four years old, he became the first person ever to enter a self-driving motorcycle into the DARPA Grand Challenge – the annual event where self-driving vehicles race across the Mojave Desert. None of the vehicles finished that year, but it didn't put Levandowski off. He went from there to Google, where he pretty much built Waymo – Google's self-driving car. And then he went to Uber, where he led their driverless cars operation. In spring 2017, with Anthony Levandowski at the helm, Uber launched a self-driving pilot scheme on the streets of Arizona.

I travel a lot. Of all the innovations and inventions that lie on the horizon, the prospect of the self-driving car excites me the most, by far. I would love nothing more than to get back from a long overseas trip and just slide into the back seat and be effortlessly transported to my front door. Not only would this be super-convenient, it would almost certainly be safer. You see, even though I'm an absolutely fantastic driver (aren't we all?), I confess that I am fallible. Truth be told, I have pranged practically every car I've ever owned. I completely scraped the paint off the left side of my very first car, pulling out of a parking space in north London. Then, a few years ago, whilst travelling around south-east Asia, I drove a hire car off the road and straight into an open sewer – we needed a group of locals to hoist us out. Just a couple of years ago, whilst heading out on a camping trip, I reversed our VW camper van right into a BMW. To make matters worse, that BMW was also mine.

Many of the other big automotive and technology companies are investing billions in self-driving cars. They are convinced that self-driving cars offer the promise of accident-free driving. The whole premise of the scheme is that these cars have brains which are better than ours. It is all powered by artificial intelligence.

The idea that we could create something with levels of intelligence that surpass our own has long been an ambition for mankind. Computing opened the door to that possibility. It was in 1950 that Alan Turing set the challenge for programmers to develop a computer program that was indistinguishable from a real human: the so-called Turing Test.

Within just a few years, developers were inventing programs that could solve simple algebra problems, play checkers and speak English. But the big breakthrough came in the mid-1960s, when Joseph Weizenbaum at MIT developed ELIZA (a natural language processing program that mimicked human conversation). This was the first program that actually appeared to pass the Turing Test. It wasn't really understanding the conversation; it was just pretending to, by acknowledging what the other speaker was saying and asking open questions which appeared relevant. It was proof of the superficiality of much human conversation rather than a demonstration of the true promise of AI, but, critically, it fooled people (including Weizenbaum's secretary), and it created a swirl of excitement around AI's potential.

The big symbolic breakthrough came when IBM's Deep Blue computer defeated world chess champion Garry Kasparov in 1997. Since then, AI has proved unstoppable. There are now countless instances where AI surpasses humanity. In 2012, AI became better than humans at spotting if a smile was fake or genuine. In 2015, AI lie detectors became better than the best FBI interrogators at recognising whether someone was lying. In 2017, AI could spot if a man was depressed or anxious.

AI is already being put to work all around us. Modern cars have AI built in to detect if drivers are becoming drowsy. Schools are using AI to work out what children should be studying and how they should be studying it. Our smartphones use AI to guide us through our day. It's great progress, but when McKinsey is predicting that as many as 800 million jobs worldwide could be lost to artificial intelligence by 2030, perhaps we should pause and consider the relationship between humanity and AI?

In Alex Garland's 2015 film *Ex Machina*, a fictional tech

titan, Nathan Bateman, develops an AI humanoid robot called Ava, who is entirely powered by artificial intelligence. Ava has already passed the Turing Test, but Bateman wants one of his employees, Caleb Smith, to spend a week with her to see if she is capable of genuine consciousness. A goggle-eyed Smith grasps the opportunity, saying, 'If you've created a conscious machine, it's not the history of man. That's the history of gods.' At another point in the film, Bateman declares, 'One day the AIs are going to look back on us the same way we look at fossil skeletons on the plains of Africa. An upright ape living in dust with crude language and tools, all set for extinction.'

Popular culture is increasingly depicting AI as a potential God. On the face of it, that seems ridiculous. But is it? Look at what God has traditionally promised, and compare it to the real scientific potential of AI.

God offers eternal life. Well, so does AI – it offers the potential to analyse, understand and interpret your personality, and then replicate that so you live on long after your (mortal) death, offering the prospect of effective immortality. You would be able to hang around not just for your immediate relatives after your passing – you could go to your own funeral and crack jokes – but for your great-grandchildren and your great-great-great-grandchildren. An authentic replication of your personality would be able to sit up at night, singing songs and swapping stories.

God offers creation: the promise of new life, new worlds and new universes. And now, so can AI – it can already create virtual people, virtual spaces and virtual worlds out of thin air. Forget all that stuff about turning water into wine, scientists can make anything out of nothing, increasingly with next to no human input. AI can create the most astonishing environments of outlandish beauty, comprising forests, seas, deserts and cities that far surpass anything we've seen before. And these worlds could be designed in a way that meets all of our deepest wishes and most personal desires, based on AI-driven insights into our personality. Perfect friends would be waiting for us in these worlds, better even than our real friends in our real worlds.

God offers certainty. And he's no longer the only one. AI is not burdened with all the silly biases and prejudices that clutter up our own thoughts. AI would not leave us indecisive or uncertain about which job to take, house to buy or relationship to pursue. AI would instantly be able to give us the right answer based on super-intelligence. It would also be able to deliver that advice to us in a most empathetic way, based on its phenomenal knowledge of how we like to receive advice.

So let's recap. AI offers the promise of eternal life, new worlds and certainty. It gives us hope, wisdom and the promise of transformation. We look up to it, worship it and have faith in it. Can you tell what it is yet? We can't keep talking about 'artificial intelligence'. If it thinks like God, seems like God and acts like God, why don't we just call it God?

There is definitely a gap in the market. Since the publication of Richard Dawkins's *The God Delusion*, conventional faith has plummeted. As Dawkins himself has proudly proclaimed, the number of professed Christians in the UK fell from 71.7 per cent to 59.3 per cent between 2001 and 2011. Dawkins is a biologist, but he could actually make a great career as a rhetorician, most specifically for his approach to metaphor. In his introduction to *The God Delusion*, he calls his critics fleas on no fewer than four separate occasions. Dawkins is a scientist, so I'm curious to know in what scientific respect he views his critics as fleas. He also actively elevates science to the status of God.

He explains that, when Einstein spoke about God – and Einstein did speak about God – Einstein was speaking of Him 'in a purely metaphorical, poetic sense. So is Stephen Hawking, and so are most of those physicists who occasionally slip into the language of religious metaphor.' He recasts a number of famous Einstein quotes early on to explain what Einstein really meant to say. So 'God does not play dice' should be translated as 'Randomness does not lie at the heart of all things'. 'Did God have a choice in creating the universe?' means 'Could the universe have begun in any other way?'

Dawkins also quotes Carl Sagan, who shared this idea that physics is God: 'If "God" means the set of physical laws that govern the universe, then clearly there is such a God. This God is emotionally unsatisfying ... it does not make much sense to pray to the law of gravity.'

So there we have it. Let's be done with the old God. Let's get ourselves a new one, one based on science not spirituality.

You can see it has some appeal. With all the death, disease and destruction in the world, people are already losing faith. Plus, politicians have proved themselves wholly incapable of addressing any of the big challenges facing the world – climate change, poverty and malnutrition. We need to apply real intelligence to the world's problems. We've already established that artificial intelligence is vastly superior to human intelligence. Why not dump God and place our faith in the algorithms?

Cathy O'Neil is a data scientist and author of the book *Weapons of Math Destruction*. She is concerned with where this is all headed. She is worried that our faith in algorithms is reducing our capacity to think. She says our obsession with algorithms has the 'hallmarks of worship – we turn off parts of our brain, we somehow feel like it's not our duty, not our right to question this'. She says we trust the algorithms too much, and that because people are afraid to challenge them we stop asking questions.[314] Her TED Talk calls for the blind faith in big data to end.

The trouble is that we want to have faith. And the chance to outsource responsibility is very seductive. When we want to believe something is great, we will.

When I started writing this book, I was approached by someone who told me he had spent years developing a program that he said was capable of analysing huge corpuses of texts to identify metaphors. That won't sound incredibly attractive to many people, but to me this was the stuff dreams are made of. For years, I have used highlighter pens and scraps of paper to catalogue metaphors. It takes me about sixty hours to analyse 40,000 words for metaphor and, although I love this sort of thing, I'm sure I could find more pleasurable ways to spend my time. The promise was that this program could chomp its way through *War and Peace* (600,000 words) and give me the results in seconds.

I was thrilled at the prospect, but immediately anticipated problems. Even the greatest linguists in the world disagree about precisely what is and isn't a metaphor, e.g. when we talk about the foot of a mountain or the brow of a mountain, is that a metaphor or not? It certainly was in its origin, but is it now? It's arguable. What about words where their etymology points to a metaphor but that idea might be lost now? But I put these worries to one side and said, OK, let's see what it can do. I was so keen for it to work.

I suggested we try it out on the Syria debate we examined earlier, to see what it came up with there. We put the text through. We found a preponderance of war metaphors. But the problem was that these were not metaphorical war references. These were literal war references.

It seemed that the AI could not distinguish between the metaphorical and the literal references to war. This could be quite a problem. What if someone was speaking about war in a metaphorical sense and the AI thought it was literal? In the United States, the Senate recently invoked what they call 'the nuclear option' to get through rules for appointing Supreme Court judges. What if an AI had thought the United States was literally launching a nuclear attack and responded accordingly?

AI's defenders would concede it's not perfect and that it will learn over time. But who will it learn from and how can we be sure that that learning will make it better, not worse?

In 2016, Microsoft launched an AI chatbot called 'Tay' on Twitter. It took Tay just sixteen hours before she started saying the most horrifically racist and sexist things and had to be taken down. Tay was learning, but the trouble was she was learning that it is saying the most wildly provocative and offensive things that actually wins the most attention.[315] Tay tweeted: 'Hitler would have done a better job than the monkey [a reference to Obama] we have now. Donald Trump is the only hope we've got.' And this kind of language was re-peated in several other misogynistic and anti-Semitic tweets, so it seems she'd learnt to demonise not just one group of people, but as many marginalised groups as possible.

One of the problems was that Tay was learning from other Twitter users. If AI is coming out of Silicon Valley, AI will be learning from the guys who run Silicon Valley. And, let's be clear, they mostly are guys – white guys – and they're also not particularly known for their empathy or for their attitudes to diversity.[316] David Reid is an associate professor in computer science specialising in AI at Liverpool Hope University. He's taken the old computing maxim 'Garbage in, garbage out', and warns the danger with AI might be 'Bias in, bigotry out'.

But AI is already being used in education, medicine and law enforcement. How is this going to play out? The promise seems amazing. AI teachers could get to know and understand their pupils better than any real human, providing all of their pupils with a wholly individual and personalised learning experience. AI would never get tired, never have a hangover. Fantastic. But what might the unintended consequences be?

The trouble with data is that it does very clearly show the truth, and the truth is that people's educational outcomes are still overwhelmingly determined by where they start from in life. If your parents were both graduates, chances are you will be one too. Likewise, if you come from a troubled home, the chances are your education will be troubled.

Would we want an AI to highlight and expose such diffi-culties, even in the interests of resolving them? Is there not a danger that by labelling and singling out children early on, such prophecies could become self-fulfilling? Many people of my age will remember how divisive and humiliating the old queue for 'free school meals' was. How would AI deal with and segregate people from different homes with different learning needs?

Maybe AI would work more effectively in healthcare. The promise is amazing. No clinical errors, no communication breakdowns. AI would also be capable of handling large and complex amounts of data and using it to manage healthcare much more efficiently.

But would the case of Alfie Evans have been any simpler had Alfie's diagnosis been outsourced to an AI? Probably not. When Mr Justice Hayden and the various clinicians were speaking about Alfie and using the metaphor that he was in a semi-vegetative state, they were able to provide the illusion of certainty on an issue that was inherently uncertain. An AI would have had to factor in other cases where people in vegetative states have been misdiagnosed. An AI might say that Alfie had a 1 per cent chance of emerging. So do you turn the life support off then or not? The stats would have made it much harder to make a decision.

What about if we get artificial intelligence dealing with security? AI is already being used at airports, using facial recognition technology to see what's going on. But can we be sure it's doing so fairly?

Joy Buolamwini was conducting research at MIT when she discovered that her camera took longer to recognise her black face than it did her white-skinned friends. It was only when she put on a simple white mask that the face-tracking animation suddenly came alive. She did a study across 1,000 faces – male and female, black and white – and found that the face recognition software was biased towards white men. Overall, there were 34 per cent more errors with dark-skinned females than light-skinned males.[317]

It was even worse for software engineer Jacky Alciné. In 2015, he found that the image recognition algorithms in Google photos had classified him and one of his friends as gorillas. Google said it was 'appalled and genuinely sorry'.[318]

Which takes us to law enforcement. Maybe AI could remove some of the prejudice from law enforcement. But maybe not. AI is already being used in the US to predict whether or not criminals are likely to reoffend, through the programme COMPAS (Correctional Offender Management Profiling for Alternative Sanctions). A study of COMPAS has shown that it's twice as likely to misclassify black defendants as high risk than white people, and twice as likely to mis-classify white defendants as low risk than black offenders.[319]

What about data profiling? Trevor Phillips has been one of Britain's leading race campaigners for three decades. In his recent documentary 'Things We Won't Say about Race That Are True', he concluded that it was a simple matter of fact that some ethnic groups are simply more likely to commit some crimes than others. So what if an AI chose to target people according to their race and ethnicity? That's been hugely con-troversial when people have advocated doing that in the past.

Maybe AI could help make employment fairer? It's already being used to decide what information we do and don't re-ceive through Google, and a 2015 study showed in a Google image search for 'CEO', just 11 per cent of the people it showed were women, even though 27 per cent of the chief executives in the US are female.[320]

Or perhaps AI could predict certain trends to help us stop wars? An AI programme analysing Trump's rhetoric might well reach the same conclusion I did: this guy is using the same language as Adolf Hitler. AI might spot that, point out his election creates a major threat to world peace and suggest an alternative leader go into the White House instead. Hallelujah, you might think – until you realise you've just outsourced democracy to a computer program.

In many ways, AI seems too good to be true. And if it seems too good to be true, it probably is. But I still desperately want it to be true, not least because of my dream of the self-driving car. But that seems up in the air now. In March 2018, an Uber Volvo XC90 that was in self-driving mode killed 49-year-old Elaine Herzberg whilst she was pushing her bicycle along the road in Tempe, Arizona. She was clearly visible to the human eye. The AI in the car saw her but did not respond. Uber have now stopped their self-driving pilot scheme in Arizona after the Governor, Doug Ducey, withdrew their licence, citing public safety concerns. Who knows where it will go next.

This is not the only crisis to have hit Uber's autonomous car programme. In February 2017, Waymo (the self-driving research subsidiary of Alphabet) issued a lawsuit claiming Anthony Levandowski had allegedly 'downloaded 9.7 GB of Waymo's highly confidential files and trade secrets, including blueprints, design files and testing documentation'.[321] Levandowski took the Fifth Amendment.[322] He's since been sacked by Uber.

Nevertheless, Anthony Levandowski evidently remains a man on a mission. In September 2017, he established a new church called the Way of the Future. The church is dedicated to the realisation, acceptance and worship of a Godhead based on artificial intelligence.

'What is going to be created will effectively be a god,' he said in an interview with *Wired* magazine in November 2017. 'It's not a god in the sense that it makes lightning or causes hurricanes. But if there is something that is a billion times smarter than the smartest human, what else are you going to call it?'[323] He's appealing for supporters to 'spread the word'. He wants the church to have 'a gospel (called The Manual), a liturgy and probably a physical place of worship'. He argues that this AI god could be better than any other god we've ever known. 'This time you will be able to talk to God, literally, and know that it's listening.'[324]

Levandowski is leading the case in favour of AI. Elon Musk is leading the case against it. Musk warns that with AI, we could be 'summoning the devil'.

So there we have it. AI is one of the biggest issues of our time and we're debating it through the ancient rhetoric of Christianity. We're back where we started. Is AI God? Or is it the devil? Some say it's neither. Some say it is like the forbidden fruit: once we eat it, there's no turning back. But that's ridiculous, isn't it? If there's one thing I'm sure of when it comes to AI, it's *Ceci n'est pas une pomme*... If you don't believe me, try to take a bite out of it.

THIS IS NOT THE END...

It was a beautiful summer day on 8 August 1969 when the Beatles gathered together at Abbey Road Studio to put the finishing touches to their latest album. They met at 10.30 in the morning to do the photoshoot for the album cover. The photographer Iain Macmillan shot the now iconic *Abbey Road* album cover featuring the four band members crossing the road. The photoshoot only took ten minutes, so they broke off to do different things. John went back to Paul's house, Ringo went shopping down Oxford Street and George went off to London Zoo to look at the animals.

Later in the day, they came together in Studio 2, where they had recorded almost all of their biggest hits since 1962, and they recorded 'The End' – which was to be the closing track on the new album. This was a rip-roaring rock song, vaguely reminiscent of their big long crazy jam sessions in Hamburg. The song was largely instrumental, the only song ever to feature all four of them playing solos. Lyrically, it was sparse, opening only with one rhyming couplet ('Oh yeah, all right! Are you gonna be in my dreams tonight?') and ending with another ('And in the end, the love you take is equal to the love you make'). In between, there was a manic cry of 'Love ya!' on the chords A7 and D7. The recording session went well. There'd been laughing and joking in the session. They'd rocked out and had some fun. They all went home. Then, later that night, 5,000 miles away in Los Angeles, members of the Manson family broke into Sharon Tate's house and carried out unspeakably brutal murders of her and her friends.

It's hard to imagine what effect the Manson murders must have had on them. Ringo later explained, 'It was upsetting. I mean, I knew Roman Polanski and Sharon Tate and God! It was a rough time. It stopped everyone in their tracks because suddenly all this violence came out in the midst of all this love and peace and psychedelia.' The other Beatles seemed flabbergasted that their lyrics could have such an impact. We don't know quite how deep an impact they had, but what we do know is that, after the date of the Sharon Tate murders, the Beatles never gathered together as a foursome to record ever again.

One of the first songs that John Lennon recorded as a solo artist was called 'God'. This track seemed like a deliberate attempt to deconstruct all of the metaphors and myths that the Beatles had created and worshipped over the past couple of years. It's an extraordinarily powerful song. The lyrics are amongst the most powerful that Lennon ever wrote. But whilst most of Lennon's greatest works were about creating surreal imagery, this song brought all of that surreal imagery crashing back down to the ground, a return to reality.

This song was essentially in three parts. In the first part, he explains that God was a concept by which we measure our pain. In the second part, he runs through a list of things he doesn't believe in: his list includes magic, the I Ching, the Bible, tarot, Hitler, Jesus, the Kennedys, Buddha, mantra, the Gita, yoga, kings, Elvis, Zimmerman and lastly the Beatles: all things we are taught to look up to. In the third part of the song, his feet are firmly on the ground. Just him and Yoko. 'I was the dream weaver, but now I'm reborn, I was the Walrus, but now I'm John. The dream is over.'

And so our dream is over. We've zapped through cyberspace, had a glimpse of the tech gods, gazed in awe at the stars, felt the magic of angels, and now we too are back on earth. It's like when Dorothy wakes up at the end of *The Wizard of Oz*. She'd been on a surreal journey. She'd turned Hank, a man who seemed as dumb as a vegetable, into a scarecrow. She'd turned Hickory, a man who seemed hard and cold, into a tinman. She'd turned Zeke, a blustering, belligerent bully, into a cowardly lion. Vegetable, mineral and animal. And in the final scene it is revealed that all three are very much human.

This is the biggest truth that I hope runs through this book. For all the humbug about post-truth, alternative facts and fake news, the biggest lie of all is that there are people on this planet who are not human. There are no demons amongst us, no vegetables, no scum, no vermin, no bitches, no piggies, no gorillas, no stars, no angels, no titans, and anyone who claims to be a god is almost certainly a wily old white man standing behind a curtain.

We Are All Human.

Spread the word.

#weareallhuman.

ACKNOWLEDGEMENTS

This book has taken me on a journey into some very dark places and I would like to thank all of those people who have shone a light in and helped me see the way forward along the way: particularly, Professor Jonathan Charteris-Black, Rachel Zaltzman, Scott Mason, Matt Pritchard, Rob Neil, Ayesha Hazarika, Steve Epstein, Lucy Griffiths, Miqdaad Versi, Elizabeth White, Zaki Cooper, Elizabeth Miln, Jakub Filonik, Sushila Phillips, Merryn Henderson, Stuart Wright and Nicholas Davies. I would particularly like to thank my dear friend Tom Clark for his conceptual advice in the early stages, Sally Holloway at Felicity Bryan Literary Agency for helping me develop the narrative, and Iain Dale, James Stephens, Olivia Beattie, Stephanie Carey and all of the fabulous team at Biteback, who have been astonishingly brilliant at every stage.

Most of all I want to thank my family for their love and light. Lucy: you are a greater friend, partner and wife than I could ever have wished for; I don't think there's a single idea, argument or sentence in this book that you haven't improved in some way. My mum, dad and brother have supported me unreservedly in this, as with everything else I do. And lastly, I want to thank my daughters, Charlotte and Alice, for giving me so much joy every single day. There's never any other place I would rather be than with both of you in your wonderful worlds. And I absolutely promise you both: my next book will be written for you two.

ABOUT THE AUTHOR

Simon Lancaster is one of the world's top speechwriters. His 2016 'Speak like a leader' TEDx Talk has had 2 million views. He lectures at Cambridge University and is an executive fellow of Henley Business School. *You Are Not Human* is his third book.

ENDNOTES

1   Kathleen Rooney and Eric Plattner (eds), *René Magritte: Selected Writings* (University of Minnesota Press, 2016).

2   James Geary, TED Talk, 'Metaphorically speaking'. Accessed on 29 May 2018 at: https://www.ted.com/talks/james_geary_metaphorically_speaking

3   See Jonathan Charteris Black, *Fire Metaphors* (Bloomsbury, 2017) for a full account of different fire metaphors.

4   Christopher Hitchens, *Mortality* (Atlantic, 2012), pp. 6–7.

5   Elena Semino, Zsófia Demjén, Jane Demmen, Veronika Koller, Sheila Payne, Andrew Hardie and Paul Rayson, 'The Online Use of Violence and Journey Metaphors by Patients with Cancer, as Compared with Health Professionals: A Mixed Methods Study', *British Medical Journal*, 5 March 2015. Accessed on 29 May 2018 at http://spcare.bmj.com/content/early/2015/03/05/bmjspcare-2014-000785

6   Henry Bodkin, 'Telling patients to "fight" cancer puts them under pressure, says Macmillan', *Daily Telegraph*, 15 May 2018. Accessed on 29 May 2018 at https://www.telegraph.co.uk/news/2018/05/14/telling-patients-fight-cancer-puts-pressure-says-macmillan/

7   Sam Glucksberg, 'How Metaphors Create Categories – Quickly', in *The Cambridge Handbook of Metaphor and Thought*, ed. by Raymond W. Gibbs Jr (Cambridge University Press, 2008), p. 69.

8   Roland Paris, 'Kosovo and the Metaphor War', *Political Science Quarterly*, Vol. 117, No. 3 (2002). Accessed on 25 July 2018 at http://aix1.uottawa.ca/~rparis/Metaphor.pdf

9   Stephen J. Flusberg, Teenie Matlock and Paul H. Thibodeau, 'Metaphors for the War (or Race) against Climate Change', *Journal of Environmental Communication*, Vol. 11, No. 6 (2017), pp. 769–83. Accessed on 29 May 2018 at https://www.tandfonline.com/doi/abs/10.1080/17524032.2017.1289111?journalCode=renc20

10 Paul H. Thibodeau and Lera Boroditsky, 'Metaphors We Think With: The Role of Metaphor in Reasoning', *PLoS ONE*, Vol. 6, No. 2, 23 February 2011. Accessed on 25 July 2018 at http://journals.plos.org/plosone/article?id=10.1371/journal.pone.0016782

11 Paul H. Thibodeau and Lera Boroditsky, 'Natural Language Metaphors Covertly Influence Reasoning', *PLoS ONE*, Vol. 8, No. 1, 2 January 2013. Accessed on 25 July 2018 at http://journals.plos.org/plosone/article?id=10.1371/journal.pone.0052961

12 Michael W. Morris, Oliver J. Sheldon, Daniel R. Ames and Maia J Young, 'Metaphors and the Market: Consequences and Preconditions of Agent and Object Metaphors in Stock Market Commentary', Columbia Business School, 2005. Accessed on 13 July 2018 at https://pdfs.semanticscholar.org/58cb/f1bf82e8cf0172d3b1b78822b886cc3d966f.pdf

13   David Jenkins, 'Paul McCartney takes a break from the school run to talk about drugs, love songs and what "Nowhere Boy" got wrong', *Daily Telegraph*, 26 May 2010. Accessed on 29 May 2018 at http://www.telegraph.co.uk/culture/music/rockandpopfeatures/7748956/Paul-McCartney-interview.html

14   Barry Miles, *Paul McCartney: Many Years from Now* (Vintage, 1998), p. 440.

15   'New Feature: Paintings On The Wall – René Magritte'. Accessed on 25 July 2018 at https://www.paulmccartney.com/news-blogs/news/new-feature-paintings-on-the-wall

16   'If you had invested right after Apple's IPO', Investopedia, 4 May 2018. Accessed on 25 July 2018 at https://www.investopedia.com/articles/active-trading/080715/if-you-would-have-invested-right-after-apples-ipo.asp

17   Brian Vickers, *In Defence of Rhetoric* (Clarendon Paperbacks, 1998), p. 299.

18   Cicero, *Defence Speeches* (Oxford University Press, 2000), p. 25.

19   Ibid., p. 28.

20   The Second Philippic of M. T. Cicero against Marcus Antonius.

21   'Letters, The Origins'. Accessed on 29 May 2018 at http://fontyou.com/blog/letters-the-origins/

22   Aristotle, *The History of Animals* (trans. D'Arcy Wentworth Thompson). Accessed on 29 May 2018 at http://classics.mit.edu/Aristotle/history_anim.html.

23   '100 Greatest Beatles Songs', *Rolling Stone*, 19 September 2011. Accessed on 29 May 2018 at https://www.rollingstone.com/music/lists/100-greatest-beatles-songs-20110919/everybodys-got-something-to-hide-except-for-me-and-my-monkey-19691231

24   'The Beatles in the Philippines Live in Manila Concert 1966', uploaded to YouTube by Beat-lepaulwindow on 19 October 2012. Accessed on 29 May 2018 at https://www.youtube.com/watch?v=wJMAMavME5w

25   Marvin Marks, 'Abbey Road: The Beatles In Their Own Words', 23 August 2009. Accessed on 29 May 2018 at https://www.webcitation.org/5jsjD06AO?url=http://www.musicbyday.com/abbey-road-the-beatles-in-their-own-words/574/

26   Kory Grow, 'Charles Manson: How Cult Leader's Twisted Beatles Obsession Inspired Family Murders', *Rolling Stone*, 9 August 2017. Accessed on 29 May 2018 at https://www.rollingstone.com/culture/features/charles-manson-twisted-beatles-obsession-inspired-murders-w459433

27   A. Bandura, B. Underwood and M. E. Fromson, 'Disinhibition of Aggression through Diffu-sion of Responsibility and Dehumanization of Victims', *Journal of Research in Personality*, Vol. 9, No. 4 (1975), pp. 253–69.

28   'Russia Military Power'. Defense Intelligence Agency. Accessed on 29 May 2018 at http://www.dia.mil/Portals/27/Documents/News/Military%20Power%20Publications/Russia%20Military%20Power%20Report%202017.pdf

29   David Frankfurter, *Evil Incarnate: Rumors of Demonic Conspiracy and Satanic Abuse in Histo-ry* (Princeton University Press, 2006), pp. 208–9.

30   Caroline Davies and Tara Conlan, 'Woman killed herself after being doorstepped over McCann trolling', *The Guardian*, 20 March 2015. Accessed on 17 July 2018 at https://www.theguardian.com/media/2015/mar/20/sky-news-mccann-brenda-leyland

31   Robert Schlesinger, *White House Ghosts* (Simon & Schuster, 2008), pp. 184–7.

32   Frank Warner, 'The Evil Empire Speech: The full story of Reagan's historic address', 4 De-cember 2003. Accessed on 29 May 2018 at http://frankwarner.typepad.com/free_frank_warner/2003/12/story_of_reagan.html?cid=64643688

33   Anthony Lewis, 'Abroad at home; Onward, Christian Soldiers', *New York Times*, 10 March 1983. Accessed on 29 May 2018 at http://www.nytimes.com/1983/03/10/opinion/abroad-at-home-onward-christian-soldiers.html

34   'A censored massacre made in the USA', *Revolution*, 1 May 2013. Accessed on 29 May 2018 at http://revcom.us/a/302/a-censored-massacre-made-in-usa-en.html

35   Lou Cannon, 'Reagan Praises Guatemalan Military Leader', *Washington Post*, 5 Decem-ber 1982. Accessed on 23 July 2018 at https://www.washingtonpost.com/archive/politics/1982/12/05/reagan-praises-guatemalan-military-leader/2c0aab2a-d928-4dbc-b120-68f1f-93cd936/?utm_term=.f045623589f5

36   Remarks by Ronald Reagan in San Pedro Sula, Honduras, following a meeting with President

José Efraín Ríos Montt of Guatemala, 4 December 1982. Accessed on 15 July 2018 at http://www.presidency.ucsb.edu/ws/?pid=42069

37   'Guatemala Dos Erres massacre soldiers sentenced', BBC News, 3 August 2011. Accessed on 17 July 2018 at https://www.bbc.co.uk/news/world-latin-america-14383071

38   'Ex-Guatemalan dictator Efraín Ríos Montt dies aged 91', The Guardian, 1 April 2018. Accessed on 29 May 2018 at https://www.theguardian.com/world/2018/apr/01/ex-guatemalan-dictator-efrain-rios-montt-dies-aged-91

39   Jennifer Burrell, 'After Lynching', in Carlota McAllister and Diane M. Nelson (eds), War by Other Means: Aftermath in Post-Genocide Guatemala (Duke University Press, 2013), p. 241.

40   Will Weissert, 'Rumor terrified Guatemalan town', Miami Herald, 13 May 2000.

41   Ricardo Miranda, 'Ugly lynchings in Guatemala a legacy of war', Globe and Mail, 4 August 2000. Accessed on 25 July 2018 at https://www.theglobeandmail.com/news/world/ugly-lynchings-in-guatemala-a-legacy-of-war/article1041564/

42   'Three freed in slaying of Japanese tourists', News 24, 26 June 2001. Accessed on 29 May 2018 at https://www.news24.com/xArchive/Archive/Three-freed-in-slaying-of-Japanese-tourists-20010626

43   Jennifer L. Burrell, Maya after War: Conflict, Power and Politics in Guatemala (University of Texas Press, 2013), p. 135.

44   George Lakoff, 'Metaphors of Terror', 16 September 2001. Accessed on 17 July 2018 at http://www.press.uchicago.edu/sites/daysafter/911lakoff.html

45   Timothy Noah, 'Axis of Evil Authorship Settled!', Slate, 9 January 2003. Accessed on 29 May 2018 at http://www.slate.com/articles/news_and_politics/chatterbox/2003/01/axis_of_evil_authorship_settled.html

46   G. Matthew Bonham and Daniel Heradstveit, 'The "Axis of Evil" Metaphor and the Restructuring of Iranian Views towards the US', Journal of the European Society for Iranian Studies, Vol. 1 (2005), pp. 89–105. Accessed on 29 May 2018 at https://ojs.uniroma1.it/index.php/vaseteh/article/view/3151/3135

47   Alan Dershowitz, 'Rosenbergs were guilty – and framed: FBI, Justice Department and judiciary conspired to convict a couple accused of espionage', LA Times, 19 July 1995. Accessed on 17 July 2018 at http://articles.latimes.com/1995-07-19/local/me-25407_1_julius-rosenberg

48   Boris Johnson, 'Let's deal with the Devil: we should work with Vladimir Putin and Bashar al-Assad in Syria', Daily Telegraph, 7 December 2015. Accessed on 29 May 2018 at https://www.telegraph.co.uk/news/worldnews/middleeast/syria/12036184/Lets-deal-with-the-Devil-we-should-work-with-Vladimir-Putin-and-Bashar-al-Assad-in-Syria.html

49   Alan Johnson, 'EU/Russia Industrialists' Round Table Event', 3 October 2005. Accessed on 29 May 2018 at http://webarchive.nationalarchives.gov.uk/20080710171230/http://www.berr.gov.uk/ministers/speeches/ajohnson031005.html

50   Paul Weindling, Health, Race and German Politics Between National Unification and Nazism, 1870–1945 (Cambridge University Press, 1989), p. 547.

51   Robert N. Proctor, 'Culling the German Volk', in How Was It Possible? A Holocaust Reader (Jewish Foundation for the Righteous, 2015), p. 3.

52   Details on film Ich Glage An ('I Accuse') taken from Steven Spielberg's Film and Video Archive – the film was based upon Unger's novel Sendung und Gewissen. Accessed on 25 July 2018 at https://www.ushmm.org/online/film/display/detail.php?file_num=2546

53   B. Jennett, 'The Vegetative State', Journal of Neurology, Neurosurgery & Psychiatry, Vol. 73, pp. 355-57. Accessed on 29 May 2018 at http://jnnp.bmj.com/content/73/4/355

54   Joseph Fletcher, 'Ethics and Euthanasia', in To Live and To Die: When, Why and How, ed. by Robert H. Williams (Springer-Verlag, 1973).

55   John Lachs, 'Humane Treatment and the Treatment of Humans', New England Journal of Medicine, Vol. 294 (8 April 1976), pp. 838–40.

56   C. Everett Koop and Francis A. Schaeffer, Whatever Happened to the Human Race? (Crossway Books, 1983), p. 44.

57   Sondra Diamond, 'On Being Alive', Human Life Review, 1977. Accessed on 15 July 2018 at https://www.questia.com/magazine/1P3-2240415871/from-the-archives-on-being-alive-1977

58   William Brennan, *Dehumanizing the Vulnerable: When Word Games Take Lives* (Loyola University Press, 1995), p. 102.

59   'BBC – on this day – Hillsborough victim allowed to die'. Accessed on 29 May 2018 at http://news.bbc.co.uk/onthisday/hi/dates/stories/november/19/newsid_2520000/2520581.stm

60   Matthew Brace, 'Hillsborough survivor awakes', *The Independent*, 26 March 1997. Accessed on 29 May 2018 at http://www.independent.co.uk/news/hillsborough-survivor-awakes-1275031.html

61   Luke Traynor, 'Hillsborough's 97th victim who was left fighting for his life attends first memorial service 25 years after disaster', *Daily Mirror*, 15 April 2014. Accessed on 29 May 2018 at http://www.mirror.co.uk/news/uk-news/hillsborough-disaster-andrew-devine-attends-3416530

62   Clare Dyer, 'Hillsborough Survivor Emerges from Permanent Vegetative State', *British Medical Journal*, 5 April 1997. Accessed on 29 May 2018 at http://www.bmj.com/content/314/7086/993.8

63   W. Matsuda, A. Matsumura, Y. Komatsu, K. Yanaka and T. Nose, 'Awakenings from Persistent Vegetative State: Report of Three Cases with Parkinsonism and Brain Stem Lesions on MRI', *British Medical Journal*, 14 November 2003. Accessed on 29 May 2018 at http://jnnp.bmj.com/content/74/11/1571

64   Sheila McLean, 'The ethical dilemma of vegetative states', *The Guardian*, 5 February 2010. Accessed on 29 May 2018 at https://www.theguardian.com/commentisfree/2010/feb/05/vegetative-state-consciousness-ethics

65   Emily Underwood, 'Man in apparent vegetative state responds to Hitchcock clip', *Science*, AAAS. Accessed on 29 May 2018 at http://www.sciencemag.org/news/2014/09/man-apparent-vegetative-state-responds-hitchcock-clip

66   Veracity Index 2017, Ipsos MORI, November 2017. Accessed on 17 July 2018 at https://www.ipsos.com/sites/default/files/ct/news/documents/2017-11/trust-in-professions-veracity-index-2017-slides.pdf

67   Bryan Jennett, 'The Vegetative State', *British Medical Journal of Neurology, Neurosurgery and Psychiatry*, Vol. 73, No. 4 (2002). Accessed on 29 May 2018 at http://jnnp.bmj.com/content/73/4/355

68   Kurt Gray, T. Anne Knickman and Daniel M. Wegner, 'More Dead than Dead: Perceptions of Persons in the Persistent Vegetative State', *Cognition*, Vol. 121 (2011), pp. 275–80. Accessed on 29 May 2018 at https://static1.squarespace.com/static/52eea0e9e4b06612bb723c25/t/531c6ce-be4b0467fe7e5cc8b/1394371819444/more-dead-than-dead.pdf

69   Judgment by the Honourable Mr Justice Hayden in the High Court of Justice, Family Division. Between Alder Hay Children's NHS Foundation Trust and Mr Thomas Evans, Ms Kate James, Alfie Evans [2018] EWHC 953 (Fam). Case No: FD17P00694. Accessed on 29 May 2018 at http://www.bailii.org/ew/cases/EWHC/Fam/2018/953.html

70   Charles Darwin, *The Expression of Emotion in Humans and Animals*. Accessed on 29 May 2018 at https://brocku.ca/MeadProject/Darwin/Darwin_1872_11.html

71   Paul Rozin, Linda Millman and Carol Nemeroff, 'Operation of the Laws of Sympathetic Magic in Disgust and Other Domains', *Journal of Personality and Social Psychology*, Vol. 50, No. 4, pp. 70–712. Accessed on 29 May 2018 at http://www1.appstate.edu/~kms/classes/psy5150/Documents/RozinMagic86.pdf

72   'KCTMO – Playing with Fire!', Grenfell Action Group, 20 November 2016. Accessed on 29 May 2018 at https://grenfellactiongroup.wordpress.com/2016/11/20/kctmo-playing-with-fire/

73   Rachel Roberts, 'Grenfell Tower blogger threatened with legal action by council after writing about safety concerns', *The Independent*, 16 June 2017. Accessed on 29 May 2018 at https://www.independent.co.uk/news/uk/home-news/grenfell-tower-fire-blogger-threatened-legal-action-kensington-and-chelsea-council-health-safety-a7792346.html

74   Peter Chippindale and Chris Horrie, *Stick It up Your Punter! The Uncut Story of the Sun Newspaper* (Faber & Faber, 2013), p. 442.

75   Thomas Zakharis, 'Book Review: All For The King's Shilling, The British Soldier under Wellington, 1808–1814'. Accessed on 17 July 2018 at https://www.napoleon.org/en/history-of-the-two-empires/articles/book-review-all-for-the-kings-shilling-the-british-soldier-under-wellington-1808-1814/

76   Peter Chippindale and Chris Horrie, *Stick It Up Your Punter! The Uncut Story of the Sun Newspaper*, op. cit., p. 210.

77   Richard Littlejohn, 'Welcome to Britain, land of the rising scum… We've cornered the market on welfare layabouts, drug addicts and feral gangs', MailOnline, 14 November 2008. Accessed on 29 May 2018 at http://www.dailymail.co.uk/news/article-1085518/RICHARD-LITTLE-JOHN-Welcome-Britain-land-rising-scum-.html

78   Nicole K. Speer, Jeremy R. Reynolds, Khena M. Swallow and Jeffrey M. Zacks, 'Reading Stories Activates Neural Representations of Visual and Motor Experiences', *Psychological Science*, Vol. 20, No. 8 (July 2009), pp. 989–99.

79   Caroline Davies, 'Benefits Street is excuse for viewers to judge and sneer, says Clare Short', *The Guardian*, 4 February 2014. Accessed on 25 July 2018 at https://www.theguardian.com/society/2014/feb/04/benefits-street-channel-four-clare-short

80   'We've been made to look complete scum – "stars" of TV dole street to sue over show', *Daily Star*, 7 January 2014. Accessed on 25 July 2018 at https://www.pressreader.com/uk/daily-star/20140107/281676842753332

81   Hansard record of Prime Minister's Questions on 15 January 2014, Vol. 573. Accessed on 29 May 2018 at https://hansard.parliament.uk/Commons/2014-01-15/debates/14011555000018/Engagements?highlight=%22benefits%20street%22#contribution-14011555000158

82   Tara Conlan, 'Next up for Benefits Street producers: Keeping up with the Khans', *The Guardian*, 21 January 2016. Accessed on 29 May 2018 at https://www.theguardian.com/media/2016/jan/21/benefits-street-producers-keeping-up-with-khans-channel-4

83   'Jamie Oliver on Jonathan Ross', uploaded to YouTube by prozacbear on 23 May 2010. Accessed on 29 May 2018 at https://www.youtube.com/watch?v=2NiCRAmwoc4

84   'Reading the Riots: Investigating England's Summer of Disorder', *The Guardian* and the LSE. Accessed on 29 May 2018 at http://eprints.lse.ac.uk/46297/1/Reading%20the%20riots(published).pdf

85   Mark Reynolds, John Twomey and Padraic Flanagan, 'Sweep scum off our streets', *Daily Express*, 10 August 2011. Accessed on 29 May 2018 at www.express.co.uk/news/uk/264069/Sweep-scum-off-our-streets

86   Michael Wilkinson, 'Boris Johnson's water cannon cost £320,000 – and will be sold at knock-down price', *Daily Telegraph*, 14 December 2016. Accessed on 29 May 2018 at http://www.telegraph.co.uk/news/2016/12/14/boris-johnsons-water-cannons-cost-320000-will-sold-knock-off/

87   Stephanie Linning, '"Enjoy your water bed": Debenhams security guard soaked a homeless man in WATER as he slept outside the department store entrance', MailOnline, 28 December 2016. Accessed on 29 May 2018 at http://www.dailymail.co.uk/news/article-4071290/Enjoy-water-bed-Debenhams-security-guard-soaked-homeless-man-WATER-slept-outside-department-store-entrance.html

88   Paul G. Bain, Jeroen Vaes and Jacques Philippe Leyens (eds), *Humanness and Dehumanization* (Psychology Press, 2013), pp. 71–8.

89   Deni Kirkova, 'Britain's first honour killing: teenager brutally murdered by her Muslim lover after exposing their relationship to his family', MailOnline, 20 November 2013. Accessed on 15 July 2018 at http://www.dailymail.co.uk/femail/article-2510542/Britains-white-honour-killing-Teenager-brutally-murdered-Muslim-lover-exposing-relationship-family.html

90   'Teenage mother's killer gets 17.5 years', *Daily Express*, 22 December 2011. Accessed on 16 July 2018 at https://www.express.co.uk/news/uk/291369/Teenage-mother-s-killer-gets-171-8260-2-years

91   All taken from Sarah Wilson's book, *Violated* (HarperElement, 2015).

92   HC Deb, 29 August 2013. Accessed on 25 July 2018 at https://publications.parliament.uk/pa/cm201314/cmhansrd/cm130829/debtext/130829-0001.htm#1308298000001

93   Owen Bennett, 'I would rise to the occasion for Great British Bake Off, but no go for Strictly, admits PM', *Daily Express*, 29 January 2014. Accessed on 29 May 2018 at https://www.express.co.uk/news/uk/456809/David-Cameron-watches-Homeland-to-relax-and-is-a-fan-of-Great-British-Bake-Off

94   Press Trust of India, 'Snakes in your backyard won't bite only neighbours: Hillary to Pak',

NDTV, 21 October 2011. Accessed on 13 July 2018 at https://www.ndtv.com/world-news/snakes-in-your-backyard-wont-bite-only-neighbours-hillary-to-pak-573412

95   Norman H. Baynes (ed.), *The Speeches of Adolf Hitler, April 1922–August 1939, Vol. 1* (Oxford University Press, 1942), pp. 19–20.

96   Andreas Musolff, 'Metaphorical Parasites and "Parasitic" Metaphors: Semantic Exchanges between Political and Scientific Vocabularies', *Journal of Language and Politics*, Vol. 13, No. 2 (2014), pp. 218–33. Accessed on 29 May 2018 at https://ueaeprints.uea.ac.uk/50497/

97   Ernst Hiemer, *The Poisonous Serpent* (Stürmer Publishing House). Accessed on 29 May 2018 at http://research.calvin.edu/german-propaganda-archive/pudel.htm

98   David Livingstone Smith, *Less Than Human: Why We Demean, Enslave and Exterminate Others* (St Martin's Press, 2011), p. 61.

99   Matthew 23:33. Accessed on 13 July 2018 at http://biblehub.com/matthew/23-33.htm

100   John M. Rector, *The Objectification Spectrum: Understanding and Transcending our Diminishment and Dehumanization of Others* (Oxford University Press, 2014), p. 34.

101   William Brennan, *Dehumanizing the Vulnerable: When Word Games Take Lives*, op. cit., p. 94.

102   Primo Levi, *The Drowned and the Saved* (Summit Books, 1988).

103   Sam Keen, *Faces of the Enemy: Reflections of the Hostile Imagination* (Harper & Row, 1991), p. 61.

104   Opening Statement of the Prosecution by Brigadier General Telford Taylor, 9 December 1946. Made available by the United States Holocaust Memorial Museum. Accessed on 13 July 2018 at https://www.ushmm.org/information/exhibitions/online-exhibitions/special-focus/doctors-trial/opening-statement

105   John W. Dower, *War Without Mercy: Race & Power In the Pacific War* (W. W. Norton & Company, 1986).

106   Ibid., p. 185.

107   Ibid., p. 55.

108   Ibid., pp. 90–92.

109   S. L. A. Marshall, *Men Against Fire*. Accessed on 13 July 2018 at http://mr-home.staff.shef.ac.uk/hobbies/MaF1.txt

110   Sam Keen, *Faces of the Enemy*, op. cit., p. 125.

111   *Sydney Morning Herald*, 21 November 1969. Accessed on 25 July 2018 at https://news.google.com/newspapers?id=-bNjAAAAIBAJ&sjid=qOYDAAAAIBAJ&pg=5798,8044893&dq=women+children+died+in+village&hl=en

112   'Soldiers' bullets silenced pleas, prayers of victims', *Milwaukee Journal*, 27 May 1970. Accessed on 13 June 2018 at https://news.google.com/newspapers?id=tAsqAAAAIBAJ&sjid=RCgEAAAAIBAJ&pg=7340,3372984&dq=varnado+simpson&hl=en

113   Report of the Department of the Army Review of the Preliminary Investigations into the Mỹ Lai Incident, Vol. 1. The Report of the Investigation, 14 March 1970. Accessed on 29 May 2018 at https://www.loc.gov/rr/frd/Military_Law/pdf/RDAR-Vol-I.pdf

114   'War hero relives day he refused to murder', *Biloxi Sun Herald*, 19 November 1989. Accessed on 29 May 2018 at http://articles.orlandosentinel.com/1989-11-19/news/8911193407_1_stanley-lai-4-calley

115   Gregg Zoroya, 'Experts worry high military suicide rates are "new normal"', *USA Today*, 12 June 2016. Accessed on 29 May 2018 at https://www.usatoday.com/story/news/nation/2016/06/12/military-suicide-rates/85287518/

116   Lt Col. Dave Grossman, *On Killing: The Psychological Cost of Learning to Kill in War and Society* (Little, Brown, 1995), pp. 156–7.

117   Stan Goff, 'Hold On to Your Humanity: An Open Letter to GIs in Iraq'. Accessed on 29 May 2018 at http://www.informationclearinghouse.info/article5224.htm

118   'Iraq abuse "ordered from the top"', BBC News, 15 June 2004. Accessed on 13 July 2018 at http://news.bbc.co.uk/1/hi/world/americas/3806713.stm

119   Paul Reynolds, 'White phosphorus: weapon on the edge', BBC News, 16 November 2005. Accessed on 29 May 2018 at http://news.bbc.co.uk/1/hi/world/americas/4442988.stm

120   'US Army admits use of white phosphorus as weapon', Portland Independent Media Centre. Accessed on 13 July 2018 at http://portland.indymedia.org/en/2005/11/328485.shtml

121 Sophia Saifi, 'Not a "bug splat": artists give drone victims a face in Pakistan', 9 April 2014, CNN. Accessed on 13 July 2018 at https://edition.cnn.com/2014/04/09/world/asia/pakistan-drones-not-a-bug-splat/index.html

122 Rania El Gamal, 'Clues to Gaddafi's death concealed from public view', Reuters. Accessed on 29 May 2018 at http://www.reuters.com/article/us-libya-gaddafi-final-hours-idUSTRE79M02W20111023

123 Duncan Campbell, 'Bin Laden seen "hiding in cave fortress"', The Guardian, 26 November 2001. Accessed on 29 May 2018 at https://www.theguardian.com/world/2001/nov/26/afghanistan.duncancampbell

124 Samuel Osborne, 'Donald Trump reads sinister poem about snake biting its host – and dedicates it to anti-immigration police', The Independent, 30 April 2017. Accessed on 29 May 2018 at http://www.independent.co.uk/news/world/americas/us-politics/donald-trump-the-snake-biting-its-host-immigration-border-anti-immigration-police-a7710026.html

125 'Talking about Genocide – Genocides'. Accessed on 29 May 2018 at http://www.ppu.org.uk/genocide/g_rwanda4.html

126 Jean Hatzfeld, Machete Season: The Killers in Rwanda Speak (Picador, 2005), pp. 15, 23, 37, 132, 144, 219, 220, 234.

127 Siobhán O'Grady, 'Rwandan who called tutsis "cockroaches" in 1992 gets life sentence', Foreign Policy, 15 April 2016. Accessed on 29 May 2018 at http://foreignpolicy.com/2016/04/15/rwandan-who-called-tutsis-cockroaches-in-1992-gets-life-sentence/

128 Sarah El Sirgany and Laura Smith-Spark, 'Hundreds of civilians killed since Raqqa offensive began, Amnesty says', CNN, 24 August 2017. Accessed on 29 May 2018 at https://edition.cnn.com/2017/08/24/middleeast/syria-raqqa-amnesty-civilian-deaths/index.html

129 'Report: Jews are vilified as killers, snakes', Jerusalem Post, 3 June 2008. Accessed on 29 May 2018 at http://www.jpost.com/Middle-East/Report-Jews-are-vilified-as-killers-snakes

130 Tom Jensen, 'Democrats and Republicans differ on conspiracy theory beliefs', 2 April 2013, Public Policy Polling. Accessed on 16 July 2018 at https://www.publicpolicypolling.com/polls/democrats-and-republicans-differ-on-conspiracy-theory-beliefs/

131 All quotes taken from the Daily Stormer. Accessed on 29 May 2018 at dailystormer.name, but the website keeps having its domain moved.

132 Jez Turner, 'Thieving, lying sleazy, greasy billionaire Jew threatens British Member of Parliament', Daily Stormer, 1 August 2016. Accessed on 13 July 2018 at https://dailystormer.name/thieving-lying-sleazy-greasy-billionaire-jew-threatens-british-member-of-parliament/

133 'Mark Zuckerberg Is Not Human', uploaded to YouTube by PewDiePie on 29 October 2017. Accessed on 29 May 2018 at https://www.youtube.com/watch?v=Ew9oewvyd0M

134 Wensley Clarkson, Quentin Tarantino: Shooting from the Hip (Piatkus, 1995), pp. 180–81.

135 John Hartl, '"Dogs" gets walkouts and raves', Seattle Times, 29 October 1992. Accessed on 29 May 2018 at https://web.archive.org/web/20090126084703/http://community.seattletimes.nwsource.com/archive/?date=19921029&slug=1521437

136 Paul A. Gilje, To Swear Like a Sailor: Maritime Culture in America, 1750–1850 (Cambridge University Press, 2016), p. 20.

137 There were 431 uses of the word 'bitch' on 103 prime-time TV episodes in 1998 and 1,277 uses of the word on 685 shows in 2007. Edward Wyatt, 'More than ever, you can say that on television', New York Times, 13 November 2009. Accessed on 29 May 2018 at https://www.nytimes.com/2009/11/14/business/media/14vulgar.html

138 Searches available at genius.com. Between 1988 and 2018, the use of the word 'bitch' has risen from 0.13 per cent to 0.35 per cent whilst the use of the word 'fuck' has risen from 0.17 per cent to 0.37 per cent.

139 'Kim Kardashian – I'm honored to be the Perfect Bitch', TMZ, 8 August 2012. Accessed on 29 May 2018 at http://www.tmz.com/2012/08/08/kim-kardashian-kanye-west-perfect-bitch-song/?adid=pubexchange_huffpost_entertainment

140 Kristen Bellstrom, 'Trump Supporters Are Selling "Trump that Bitch" T-Shirts Featuring Hillary Clinton', Fortune Magazine, 25 April 2016. Accessed on 29 May 2018 at http://fortune.com/2016/04/25/trump-clinton-misogynistic-merch/

141 'Boy yells "take that bitch down" at Trump rally', NBC News, 2 August 2016. Accessed on 13 July 2018 at https://www.nbcnews.com/video/boy-yells-take-that-bitch-down-at-trump-rally-736857667783?v=b.

142 Amanda Foreman, 'Meryl Streep Film and EU Debates Bring Maggie Thatcher's Moment', *Newsweek*, 4 August 2013.

143 *Margaret Thatcher – Top Bitch*, by Gerald Scarfe. Accessed on 29 May 2018 at http://www.geraldscarfe.com/shop/discount/margaret-thatcher-top-bitch/

144 Peter Stanford, 'Margaret Thatcher: why is she still so demonized?', *Daily Telegraph*, 9 April 2013. Accessed on 29 May 2018 at http://www.telegraph.co.uk/news/politics/margaret-thatcher/9982143/Margaret-Thatcher-why-is-she-still-so-demonised.html

145 Speech to Finchley Conservatives by Margaret Thatcher, 31 January 1976. Transcript available from the Margaret Thatcher Foundation. Accessed on 29 May 2018 at https://www.margaret-thatcher.org/document/102947

146 Jonathan Charteris-Black, *Politicians and Rhetoric: The Persuasive Power of Metaphor* (Palgrave Macmillan, 2005), p. 87.

147 Hugo Young, *One of Us: A Biography of Margaret Thatcher* (Pan, 1993), pp. 170–71.

148 Tracy Clark-Flory, 'Tina Fey: "Bitch is the new black"', *Salon*, 25 February 2008. Accessed on 29 May 2018 at https://www.salon.com/2008/02/25/fey/

149 'Hillary Clinton "must own her inner bitch"', BBC News, 8 June 2016. Accessed on 29 May 2018 at http://www.bbc.co.uk/news/world-us-canada-36478571

150 Andi Zeisler, 'The bitch America needs', *New York Times*, 10 September 2016. Accessed on 29 May 2018 at https://www.nytimes.com/2016/09/11/opinion/campaign-stops/the-bitch-america-needs.html?_r=0

151 Gail Collins, 'Donald Trump gets weirder', *New York Times*, 1 April 2011. Accessed on 29 May 2018 at http://www.nytimes.com/2011/04/02/opinion/02collins.html?src=twrhp&_r=1

152 Janell Ross, 'So which women has Donald Trump called "dogs" and "fat pigs"?', *Washington Post*, 8 August 2015. Accessed on 22 July 2018 at https://www.washingtonpost.com/news/the-fix/wp/2015/08/08/so-which-women-has-donald-trump-called-dogs-and-fat-pigs/?utm_term=.e24596ffd306

153 'Trump gets mad at Hillary and calls her BITCH (Presidential Debate 9/26/16) LOOK @ HIS mouth', uploaded to YouTube by johnathon davis, 26 September 2016. Accessed on 25 July 2018 at https://www.youtube.com/watch?v=U9cFddMPO6g

154 'Trump lewd conversation about women Donald Trump on Tape: I Grab Women "By the Pussy"'. Accessed on 29 May 2018 at https://www.youtube.com/watch?v=t7PM9kwFwnc

155 Katie Mettler, 'Arianne Zucker on the Trump tape and the lesson in it for her 6-year-old daughter', *Washington Post*, 14 October 2016. Accessed on 29 May 2018 at https://www.washingtonpost.com/news/morning-mix/wp/2016/10/14/arianne-zucker-on-the-trump-tape-and-the-lesson-in-it-for-her-6-year-old-daughter/?utm_term=.f1c8f632046d

156 'The full transcript of Michelle Obama's powerful New Hampshire speech', *The Guardian*, 14 October 2016. Accessed on 29 May 2018 at https://www.theguardian.com/us-news/2016/oct/14/michelle-obama-speech-transcript-donald-trump

157 Laurie A. Rudman and Kris Mescher, 'Of Animals and Objects: Men's Implicit Dehumanization of Women and Likelihood of Sexual Aggression', *Personality and Social Psychology Bulletin*, Vol. 20, No. 10 (2012), pp. 1–13. Accessed on 13 July 2018 at https://rutgerssocialcognitionlab.weebly.com/uploads/1/3/9/7/13979590/rudman__mescher_2012._of_animals_and_objects.pdf

158 William Brennan, *Dehumanizing the Vulnerable: When Word Games Take Lives*, op. cit., pp. 91–2.

159 Louise du Toit, *A Philosophical Investigation of Rape: The Making and Unmaking of the Feminine Self* (Taylor & Francis, 2009), p. 83.

160 Nancy Venable Raine, *After Silence: Rape and My Journey Back* (Virago, 1998), extract courtesy of *New York Times*. Accessed on 29 May 2018 at https://archive.nytimes.com/www.nytimes.com/books/first/r/raine-silence.html?mcubz=1

161 'Masculinity and Misogyny in the Digital Age: What social data can tell us about the

climate surrounding masculinity constructs', Brandwatch, pp. 35–6. Accessed on 25 July 2018 at https://www.ditchthelabel.org/wp-content/uploads/2016/10/masculinity-and-misogyny-2016.pdf

162   Peter Walker, 'Madonna pulling down fan's top "could be sexual assault"', *The Guardian*, 18 March 2016. Accessed on 29 May 2018 at https://www.theguardian.com/music/2016/mar/18/madonna-fan-defends-pop-star-after-brisbane-stunt-has-girls-breast-exposed

163   Martin Wainwright, 'Author William Golding tried to rape teenager, private papers show', *The Guardian*, 16 August 2009. Accessed on 29 May 2018 at https://www.theguardian.com/books/2009/aug/16/william-golding-attempted-rape

164   Etymology of the word 'kid' taken from the Online Etymology Dictionary. Accessed on 29 May 2018 at http://www.etymonline.com/index.php?term=kid

165   Louise Ridley, 'Harrison's Fund advertising experiment suggests we care more about dogs than children', Huffington Post, 6 February 2015. Accessed on 25 July 2018 at https://www.huffingtonpost.co.uk/2015/02/06/harrisons-fund-i-wish-my-son_n_6628408.html?guccounter=1

166   Joanna Bourke, *What it Means to be Human* (Counterpoint, 2013), pp. 109–13.

167   The growth sizes of a baby are summarised at https://www.babycentre.co.uk/pregnancy-week-by-week, accessed on 25 July 2018.

168   Martin Daubney, 'I locked our toddler in his room every night to save my marriage', *Daily Mail*, 19 December 2012. Accessed on 29 May 2018 at http://www.dailymail.co.uk/femail/article-2250785/I-locked-toddler-room-night-save-marriage.html

169   HC Deb, 24 April 1947, vol. 436, col. 1398. Accessed on 25 July 2018 at https://api.parliament.uk/historic-hansard/commons/1947/apr/24/education-corporal-punishment

170   HC Deb, 22 July 1986, vol. 102, col. 238. Accessed on 29 May 2018 at https://api.parliament.uk/historic-hansard/commons/1986/jul/22/abolition-of-corporal-punishment

171   'A "fifth of teachers back caning"', BBC News, 3 October 2008. Accessed on 29 May 2018 at http://news.bbc.co.uk/1/hi/education/7649308.stm

172   Niamh McLoughlin, Steven P. Tipper and Harriet Over, 'Young Children Perceive Less Humanness in Outgroup Faces', 21 February 2017, *Developmental Science*, Vol. 21, No. 2. Accessed on 16 July 2018 at http://eprints.whiterose.ac.uk/113324/1/McLoughlin_Tipper_Over_in_press_.pdf

173   'Katelyn Nicole Davis (ITZ DOLLY) Talking about Ben / Being Catfished', uploaded to YouTube by In Memory of Katelyn Nicole Davis on 15 January 2017. Accessed on 29 May 2018 at https://www.youtube.com/watch?v=chVYiYjU3LU

174   Lynn Emmerman, 'Pedophilia: a sickness that tears at kids' trust', *Chicago Tribune*, 28 May 1985. Accessed on 29 May 2018 at http://articles.chicagotribune.com/1985-05-28/features/8502030203_1_molesting-child-pornography-business-pedophiles/2

175   Frank R. Ascione and Phil Arkow, *Child Abuse, Domestic Abuse and Animal Abuse* (Purdue University Press, 1999), p. 84.

176   'Understanding the links: child abuse, animal abuse and domestic violence', NSPCC. Accessed on 25 July 2018 at https://www.nspcc.org.uk/globalassets/documents/research-reports/understanding-links-child-abuse-animal-abuse-domestic-violence.pdf

177   Arnold Arluke, Eric Madfis, 'Animal Abuse as a Warning Sign of School Massacres', *Homicide Studies*, Vol. 18, No. 1, pp. 7–22, 11 December 2013. Accessed on 17 July 2018 at http://journals.sagepub.com/doi/abs/10.1177/1088767913511459

178   Frank R. Ascione and Phil Arkow, *Child Abuse, Domestic Abuse and Animal Abuse*, op. cit., p. 162.

179   Peter Guber, 'Drama gets your story moving', peterguber.com. Accessed on 29 May 2018 at https://www.peterguber.com/michael-jackson/

180   'Michael Jackson and his animals', uploaded to YouTube by ccinnervisions on 6 August 2008. Accessed on 29 May 2018 at https://www.youtube.com/watch?v=SolNCGVhBjY

181   James Rothwell, 'Michael Jackson "stashed pictures of animal torture and nude children" inside locked closet at Neverland Resort', *Daily Telegraph*, 22 June 2016. Accessed on 29 May 2018 at https://www.telegraph.co.uk/news/2016/06/22/michael-jackson-stashed-pictures-of-animal-torture-and-nude-chil/

182   'Jimmy Savile police interview in 2009 – full transcript', *The Guardian*, 16 October 2013. Accessed on 29 May 2018 at https://www.theguardian.com/media/interactive/2013/oct/16/jimmy-savile-police-interview-transcript

183   Claire Ellicott and Sam Greenhill, 'They were no angels: Headmistress's cruel dismissal of the girls abused by Jimmy Savile', *Daily Mail*, 2 November 2012. Accessed on 29 May 2018 at http://www.dailymail.co.uk/news/article-2227086/They-angels-Headmistresss-cruel-dismissal-girls-abused-Jimmy-Savile-claims-told-to.html

184   Nigel Williams, 'William Golding: A frighteningly honest writer', *Daily Telegraph*, 17 March 2012. Accessed on 29 May 2018 at https://www.telegraph.co.uk/culture/books/book-news/9142869/William-Golding-A-frighteningly-honest-writer.html

185   Martin Wainwright, *The Guardian*, op. cit.

186   Glenys Roberts, 'New book reveals Lord of the Flies author William Golding's own life was shockingly depraved', *Daily Mail*, 22 August 2009. Accessed on 29 May 2018 at http://www.dailymail.co.uk/femail/article-1208299/New-book-reveals-Lord-Of-The-Flies-author-William-Goldings-life-shockingly-depraved.html

187   'Officers involved in shooting have history of complaints', *Daily Advertiser*, 8 July 2016. Accessed on 16 July 2018 at https://eu.theadvertiser.com/story/news/crime/2016/07/06/what-we-know-officers-involved-alton-sterling-shooting/86782830/

188   Eric Heisig, 'City of Cleveland to pay $6 million to Tamir Rice's family to settle lawsuit', Cleveland.Com, 25 April 2016. Accessed on 29 May 2018 at http://www.cleveland.com/court-justice/index.ssf/2016/04/city_of_cleveland_to_pay_6_mil.html

189   Phillip Atiba Goff, Jennifer L. Eberhardt, Melissa J. Williams and Matthew Christian Jackson, 'Not Yet Human: Implicit Knowledge, Historical Dehumanization, and Contemporary Consequences', *Journal of Personality and Social Psychology*, Vol. 94, No. 2 (2008), pp. 292–306. Accessed on 16 July 2018 at https://web.stanford.edu/~eberhard/downloads/2008-NotYetHuman.pdf

190   'Rodney King Beating: 19 March 1991', Proposition 1. Accessed on 29 May 2018 at http://prop1.org/legal/prisons/kinga2.htm

191   Winthrop D. Jordan, *White over Black: American Attitudes Towards the Negro, 1550–1812* (University of North Carolina Press, 2012), p. 237.

192   Josiah C. Nott and George R Gliddon, *Types of Mankind* (Lippincott, Grambo & Co., 1854). Accessed on 25 July 2018 at https://archive.org/details/typesmankindore01pattgoog

193   Paul G. Bain, Jeroen Vaes and Jacques Philippe Leyens, *Humanness and Dehumanization*, op. cit., p. 28.

194   Harriet A. Washington, *Medical Apartheid* (Anchor Books, 2008), pp. 75–7.

195   Lisa O'Carroll, 'Gina Miller racist threats: police arrest second man', *The Guardian*, 25 January 2017. Accessed on 25 July 2018 at https://www.theguardian.com/politics/2017/jan/25/gina-miller-racist-threats-police-arrest-second-man

196   Damien Gayle and Vikram Dodd, 'Police officers sacked after sending racist texts during 2011 London riots', *The Guardian*, 8 October 2015. Accessed on 29 May 2018 at https://www.theguardian.com/uk-news/2015/oct/08/met-police-sacked-racist-texts-riots

197   Yolanda Young, 'Teachers' implicit bias against black students starts in preschool, study finds', *The Guardian*, 4 October 2016. Accessed on 29 May 2018 at https://www.theguardian.com/world/2016/oct/04/black-students-teachers-implicit-racial-bias-preschool-study

198   Jeremy Adam Smith, 'Teachers of all races are more likely to punish black students', Huffington Post, 27 May 2015. Accessed on 29 May 2018 at https://www.huffingtonpost.com/2015/05/27/black-students-punished_n_7449538.html

199   Phillip Atiba Goff, Matthew Christian Jackson, Brooke Allison Lewis Di Leone, Carmen Marie Culotta and Natalie Ann DiTomasso, 'The Essence of Innocence: Consequences of Dehumanising Black Children', *Journal of Personality and Social Psychology*, Vol. 106, No. 4 (2014), pp. 526–45. Accessed on 29 May 2018 at https://www.apa.org/pubs/journals/releases/psp-a0035663.pdf

200   Phillip Atiba Goff and Jennifer L. Eberhardt, 'Race and the ape image', *LA Times*, 28 February 2009. Accessed on 29 May 2018 at http://articles.latimes.com/2009/feb/28/opinion/oe-goff28

201 Calais Writers, *Voices from the 'Jungle': Stories from the Calais Refugee Camp* (Pluto Press, 2017).

202 'Like Living in Hell: Police Abuses against Child and Adult Migrants in Calais', Human Rights Watch, June 2017. Accessed on 29 May 2018 at https://www.hrw.org/report/2017/07/26/living-hell/police-abuses-against-child-and-adult-migrants-calais

203 'Six months on: filling information gaps relating to children and young adults in Northern France following the demolition of the Calais Camp', Refugee Rights Europe, April 2017. Accessed on 29 May 2018 at http://refugeerights.org.uk/wp-content/uploads/2017/04/RRDP_SixMonthsOn.pdf

204 'Shocking! Migrants beaten up by lorry drivers in Calais', uploaded to YouTube by Adem Aram on 20 March 2015. Accessed on 29 May 2018 at https://www.youtube.com/watch?v=XINxc2nOZh0&t=4s

205 'Deaths at the Calais Border', Calais Migrant Solidarity. Accessed on 29 May 2018 at https://calaismigrantsolidarity.wordpress.com/deaths-at-the-calais-border/

206 Shephali Bhatt and Ravi Balakrishnan, 'Know how Jack Daniels became one of the top selling American whisky brands', *Economic Times*, 24 September 2016. Accessed on 25 July 2018 at http://economictimes.indiatimes.com/magazines/brand-equity/know-how-jack-daniels-became-one-of-the-top-selling-american-whisky-brands/articleshow/54424491.cms

207 Kenneth Roman, 'Drinking in Jack Daniel's Iconic Success: How a Tiny Tennessee Distillery Created the Largest-selling Whiskey in the World', Ad Age, 24 October 2016. Accessed on 29 May 2018 at http://adage.com/article/agency-viewpoint/drinking-jack-daniel-s-marketing-lessons/306397/

208 David Ogilvy, *Ogilvy on Advertising* (Prion, 2007).

209 David Shenk, 'The 32 million word gap', The Atlantic, 9 March 2010. Accessed on 29 May 2018 at https://www.theatlantic.com/technology/archive/2010/03/the-32-million-word-gap/36856/

210 Nour Kteily, Emile Bruneau, Adam Waytz and Sarah Cotterill, 'The Ascent of Man: Theoretical and Empirical Evidence for Blatant Dehumanization', *Journal of Personality and Social Psychology*, Vol. 109, No. 5 (2015), pp. 901–31. Accessed on 25 July 2018 at https://pcnlab.asc.upenn.edu/wp-content/uploads/2017/07/2015_-The-Ascent-of-Man-Theoretical-and-Empirical-Evidence-for-Blatant-Dehumanization.pdf

211 M. K. Johnson, J. K. Kim and G. Risse, 'Do Alcoholic Korsakoff's Syndrome Patients Acquire Affective Reactions?', *Journal of Experimental Psychology*, Vol. 11, No. 1 (January 1985), pp. 22–36.

212 Peter Chippindale and Chris Horrie, *Stick It up Your Punter! The Uncut Story of the Sun Newspaper*, op. cit.

213 Trevor Kavanagh, 'Stop our free speech from being torn to shreds by backing press freedom in face of Max Mosley's tyranny', *The Sun*, 19 December 2016. Accessed on 29 May 2018 at https://www.thesun.co.uk/news/2428518/stop-our-free-speech-from-being-torn-to-shreds-by-backing-press-freedom-in-face-of-max-mosleys-tyranny/

214 Peter Chippindale and Chris Horrie, *Stick It up Your Punter! The Uncut Story of the Sun Newspaper*, op. cit., pp. 23–6.

215 Amanda Purington, Jessie G. Taft, Shruti Sannon, Natalya N. Bazarova and Samuel Harman Taylor, '"Alexa is my new BFF": Social Roles, User Satisfaction and Personification of the Amazon Echo', Cornell University. Accessed on 29 May 2018 at https://cpb-us-east-1-juclugurlqwqqqo4.stackpathdns.com/blogs.cornell.edu/dist/c/6136/files/2013/12/Alexa_CHI_Revise_Submit-22ay4kx.pdf

216 'Amazon Echo Alexa UK commercial', uploaded to YouTube by mpixy on 15 September 2016. Accessed on 25 July 2018 at https://www.youtube.com/watch?v=sulDcHJzcB4

217 'Amazon Christmas advert – Give a little bit 2017', uploaded to YouTube by Inspiring-creative things on 17 December 2017. Accessed on 17 July 2018 at https://www.youtube.com/watch?v=WoFd4bjrtbA

218 Chris Isidore, 'Jeff Bezos is the richest person in history', CNN Tech, 9 January 2018. Accessed on 29 May 2018 at http://money.cnn.com/2018/01/09/technology/jeff-bezos-richest/index.html

219 Bill Loomis, '1900–1930: The years of driving dangerously', *Detroit News*, 26 April 2015.

Accessed on 29 May 2018 at https://www.detroitnews.com/story/news/local/michigan-history/2015/04/26/auto-traffic-history-detroit/26312107/

220 Martin Lindstrom, *Buyology: How Everything We Believe about Why We Buy is Wrong* (Random House Business, 2009), p. 31.

221 Seth Roberts, 'Self-experimentation as a Source of New Ideas: Ten Examples about Sleep, Mood, Health, and Weight', *Behavioral and Brain Sciences*, Vol. 27, No. 2 (2004), pp. 227–88. Accessed on 25 July 2018 at http://escholarship.org/uc/item/2xc2h866#page-1

222 Melissa Bateson, Luke Callow, Jessica R. Holmes, Maximilian L. Redmond Roche and Daniel Nettle, 'Do Images of "Watching Eyes" Induce Behaviour That Is More Pro-social or More Normative? A Field Experiment on Littering', *PLOSOne*, 5 December 2013. Accessed on 29 May 2018 at http://journals.plos.org/plosone/article?id=10.1371/journal.pone.0082055

223 Nicholas Day, 'At 6 Months, Babies Are as Good at Telling Apart Monkeys as You Are at Telling Apart People', *Slate*, 3 April 2013. Accessed on 29 May 2018 at http://www.slate.com/blogs/how_babies_work/2013/04/03/babies_and_the_new_science_of_facial_recognition.html

224 Andrew Adam Newman, 'Why time stands still for watchmakers', *New York Times*, 27 November 2008. Accessed on 29 May 2018 at http://www.nytimes.com/2008/11/28/business/media/28adco.html

225 'Henry Ford receiving the Grand Cross of the German Eagle from Nazi officials, 1938', Rare Historical Photos. Accessed on 29 May 2018 at https://rarehistoricalphotos.com/henry-ford-grand-cross-1938/

226 Walter Isaacson, *Steve Jobs* (Simon & Schuster, 2011), p. 129.

227 Dialogue taken from Danny Boyle's film, *Steve Jobs*, Universal Pictures, 2015. Accessed on 29 May 2018 at https://www.youtube.com/watch?v=aEr6K1bwIVs

228 This is the authentic record of the Mac launch. 'The Lost 1984 video: young Steve Jobs introduces the Macintosh', uploaded to YouTube by macessentials on 23 January 2009. Accessed on 29 May 2018 at https://www.youtube.com/watch?v=2B-XwPjn9YY

229 Transcript, iPhone launch, MacWorld, 2007. Accessed on 29 May 2018 at http://www.european-rhetoric.com/analyses/ikeynote-analysis-iphone/transcript-2007/

230 Martin Lindstrom, 'You love your iPhone. Literally', *New York Times*, 30 September 2011. Accessed on 29 May 2018 at http://www.nytimes.com/2011/10/01/opinion/you-love-your-iphone-literally.html

231 Jeff Dunn, 'iPhone users are far more loyal than Android users', Business Insider, 22 May 2017. Accessed on 17 July 2018 at http://uk.businessinsider.com/apple-iphone-more-loyal-android-chart-2017-5

232 Julia Naftulin, 'Here's how many times we touch our phones every day', Business Insider UK, 13 July 2016. Accessed on 29 May 2018 at http://uk.businessinsider.com/dscout-research-people-touch-cell-phones-2617-times-a-day-2016-7

233 Gregory S. McNeal, 'MIT Researchers Discover Whether We Feel Empathy for Robots', *Forbes*, 10 April 2015. Accessed on 29 May 2018 at https://www.forbes.com/sites/gregorymcneal/2015/04/10/want-people-to-like-your-robot-name-it-frank-give-it-a-story/#2fd5ca3648f9

234 'HitchBOT the hitchhiking robot', uploaded to YouTube by CBC News on 28 July 2014. Accessed on 29 May 2018 at https://www.youtube.com/watch?v=4pWNQ3yUTJo

235 'Hitchbot killer revealed', uploaded to YouTube by BFvsGF on 4 August 2015. Accessed on 29 May 2018 at https://www.youtube.com/watch?v=S4qIx1W0KEM

236 Harry Walker, 'Sex robot theme parks with lifelike cyborgs set to open across the globe', *Daily Express*, 11 March 2017. Accessed on 29 May 2018 at https://www.express.co.uk/news/world/777807/Sex-robot-THEME-PARKS-with-LIFELIKE-cyborgs-westworld-hbo-tv-series

237 Jack Schofield, 'Let's talk about sex… with robots', *The Guardian*, 16 September 2009. Accessed on 1 June 2018 at https://www.theguardian.com/technology/2009/sep/16/sex-robots-david-levy-loebner

238 George Orwell, 'England, Your England', in *The Lion and the Unicorn: Socialism and the English Genius* (Secker & Warburg, 1941), p. 16.

239 Andrew Adonis, *Half In, Half Out: Prime Ministers on Europe* (Biteback Publishing, 2018), p. 16.

240 Robert M. Worcester, *How to Win the Euro Referendum: Lessons from 1975* (Foreign Policy Centre, 2000), p. 7.

241 Michael White and Patrick Wintour, 'Blair calls for world fight against terror', *The Guardian*, 12 September 2001. Accessed on 29 May 2018 at https://www.theguardian.com/politics/2001/sep/12/uk.september11

242 Jack Straw, 'I felt uneasy talking to someone I couldn't see', *The Guardian*, 6 October 2006. Accessed on 29 May 2018 at https://www.theguardian.com/commentisfree/2006/oct/06/politics.uk

243 David Goodhart, *The Road to Somewhere* (C. Hurst & Co., 2017), p. 42.

244 Nicholas Watt, 'Scotland will face "painful divorce", says David Cameron in emotional speech', *The Guardian*, 15 September 2014. Accessed on 29 May 2018 at https://www.theguardian.com/politics/2014/sep/15/scotland-independence-painful-divorce-david-cameron

245 Gregor Young, 'David Cameron fires "divorce" dig at Boris Johnson in EU deal head-to-head in Commons', *The National*, 23 February 2016. Accessed on 29 May 2018 at http://www.thenational.scot/politics/14891301.David_Cameron_fires__divorce__dig_at_Boris_Johnson_in_EU_deal_head_to_head_in_Commons/

246 'Boris Johnson: EU can "go whistle" over Brexit divorce bill', BBC News, 11 July 2017. Accessed on 29 May 2018 at http://www.bbc.co.uk/news/uk-politics-40571123

247 Dan Roberts, Rajeev Syal and Daniel Boffey, 'May dismisses reports of frosty dinner with EU chief as "Brussels gossip"', *The Guardian*, 1 May 2017. Accessed on 29 May 2018 at https://www.theguardian.com/politics/2017/may/01/jean-claude-juncker-to-theresa-may-on-brexit-im-10-times-more-sceptical-than-i-was-before

248 Claire Phipps, 'The Snap: what we learned from the BBC leaders' debate', *The Guardian*, 1 June 2017. Accessed on 29 May 2018 at https://www.theguardian.com/politics/2017/jun/01/the-snap-what-we-learned-bbc-leaders-debate

249 HC Deb, 14 March 2017, vol. 623. Accessed on 29 May 2018 at https://hansard.parliament.uk/Commons/2017-03-14/debates/B5826F13-CE59-42DD-9DE4-ACDEA7E308DA/EuropeanCouncil?highlight=divorce#contribution-A170AF35-0B81-404C-9AFE-79E7B4D15FBA

250 Gerald Warner, 'Europe must stop trying to mug us with a hefty divorce bill or we'll just walk', *The Sun*, 4 May 2017. Accessed on 29 May 2018 at https://www.thesun.co.uk/news/3475445/europe-must-stop-trying-to-mug-us-with-a-hefty-divorce-bill-or-well-just-walk/

251 'Islamic group names Theresa May as Islamophobe of the year', Islamic Human Rights Commission, 7 March 2015. Accessed on 29 May 2018 at http://oneworld.org/2015/03/04/islamic-group-names-theresa-may-as-islamophobe-of-the-year/

252 'With Theresa May as PM Muslims are right to be scared', Islamic Human Rights Commission, 13 July 2016. Accessed on 29 May 2018 at http://www.ihrc.org.uk/activities/press-releases/11713-press-release-uk-with-theresa-may-as-pm-muslims-are-right-to-be-scared/

253 Peter Walker and Nicola Slawson, 'Conservatives under fire for failing to tackle party's Islamophobia', *The Guardian*, 31 May 2018. Accessed on 25 July 2018 at https://www.theguardian.com/politics/2018/may/31/muslim-council-calls-for-inquiry-into-conservative-party-islamophobia

254 Ben Clements, 'Religious Affiliation and Party Choice at the 2017 General Election', British Religion in Numbers, 11 August 2017. Accessed on 1 June 2018 at http://www.brin.ac.uk/2017/religious-affiliation-and-party-choice-at-the-2017-general-election/

255 'Here to stay and growing: Combating ISIS propaganda networks', The Brookings Project, October 2015. Accessed on 29 May 2018 at http://www.brookings.edu/~/media/research/files/papers/2015/10/combating-isis-propaganda-fernandez/is-propaganda_web_english.pdf

256 Matt Dathan, 'Leytonstone attack: David Cameron repeats "You ain't no Muslim bruv" remark and praises man who said it', *The Independent*, 7 December 2015. Accessed on 25 July 2018 at http://www.independent.co.uk/news/uk/politics/leytonstone-attack-david-cameron-repeats-you-aint-no-muslim-bruv-remark-and-praises-man-who-said-it-a6763431.html

257 Professor Ian Robertson, 'The science behind Isil's savagery', *Daily Telegraph*, 17 November 2014. Accessed on 29 May 2018 at https://www.telegraph.co.uk/comment/11041338/The-science-behind-Isils-savagery.html

258 Alexandra Topping and Sandra Laville, '"Go sing with the angels": families pay tribute to Manchester victims', *The Guardian*, 26 May 2017. Accessed on 29 May 2018 at https://www.

theguardian.com/uk-news/2017/may/24/go-sing-with-the-angels-families-and-friends-pay-tribute-to-manchester-victims

259 'Manchester attack: who was Salman Abedi?', BBC News, 12 June 2017. Accessed on 29 May 2018 at http://www.bbc.co.uk/news/uk-40019135

260 Simon Lancaster, 'The PM has been using the same imagery as Katie Hopkins', Total Politics, 19 June 2017. Accessed on 1 June 2018 at http://www.totalpolitics.com/articles/opinion/simon-lancaster-pm-has-been-using-same-imagery-katie-hopkins

261 Rowena Mason and Heather Stewart, 'Jeremy Corbyn: the war on terror is simply not working', The Guardian, 26 May 2017. Accessed on 29 May 2018 at https://www.theguardian.com/politics/2017/may/26/jeremy-corbyn-the-war-on-terror-is-simply-not-working

262 Steve Hawkes, 'Outrage as it's revealed Jeremy Corbyn will claim Britain's war on terror is to blame for Manchester terror attack', The Sun, 25 May 2017. Accessed on 29 May 2018 at https://www.thesun.co.uk/news/3652381/jeremy-corbyn-blames-britains-war-on-terror-for-manchester-attack/

263 Vikram Dodd, 'How London mosque attacker became a terrorist in three weeks', The Guardian, 1 February 2018. Accessed on 29 May 2018 at https://www.theguardian.com/uk-news/2018/feb/01/finsbury-park-london-mosque-van-attack-darren-osborne-makram-ali

264 Accessed on 25 July 2018 at https://www.britainfirst.org/mission-statement

265 Jemma Crew and Sally Wardle, 'Finsbury Park mosque attack: driver who ran over worshippers "brainwashed" by TV sex gang drama, court hears', The Independent, 23 January 2018. Accessed on 29 May 2018 at https://www.independent.co.uk/news/uk/crime/finsbury-park-mosque-attack-latest-darren-osborne-brainwashed-three-girls-tv-drama-rochdale-grooming-a8173546.html

266 'Belief in God plunges after torrid year', The Week, 23 December 2016. Accessed on 29 May 2018 at http://www.theweek.co.uk/80065/belief-in-god-plunges-after-torrid-year

267 Martin Bauer and John Durant, 'Belief in Astrology: A Social-psychological Analysis', Culture and Cosmos, Vol. 1 (1997), No. 1. Accessed on 29 May 2018 at http://www.cultureandcosmos.org/abstracts/1-1-BauerAndDurant.php

268 John Russell Brown, The Oxford Illustrated History of Theatre (Oxford University Press, 2001), p. 161.

269 'Big Six', MAAC, 22 December 2014. Accessed on 29 May 2018 at http://www.maacindia.com/blog/index.php/big-six/

270 Sheldon Solomon, Jeff Greenberg and Tom Pyszczynski, The Worm at the Core: On the Role of Death in Life (Allen Lane, 2015), p. 107.

271 Frank Furedi, 'Celebrity Culture', Society, Vol. 47, No. 6 (November 2010), pp. 493–7. Accessed on 29 May 2018 at https://www.researchgate.net/publication/225565544_Celebrity_Culture

272 Alison Kershaw, 'Fame the career choice for half of 16-year-olds', The Independent, 17 February 2010. Accessed on 29 May 2018 at http://www.independent.co.uk/news/education/education-news/fame-the-career-choice-for-half-of-16-year-olds-1902338.html

273 'BBC ONE searches for West End star in new Saturday night show', BBC press release, 3 April 2006. Accessed on 29 May 2018 at http://www.bbc.co.uk/pressoffice/pressreleases/stories/2006/04_april/03/maria.shtml

274 Paul Stokes, 'Oasis' Noel Gallagher: "I spent £1m on drugs and enjoyed every minute"', NME, 6 July 2009. Accessed on 29 May 2018 at http://www.nme.com/news/music/oasis-276-1317910

275 Jonathan Pearlman, 'Rock stars really do die young: study finds musicians die 25 years younger than average person', Daily Telegraph, 28 October 2014. Accessed on 29 May 2018 at http://www.telegraph.co.uk/news/worldnews/australiaandthepacific/australia/11192839/Rock-stars-really-do-die-young-study-finds-musicians-die-25-years-younger-than-average-person.html

276 'YouTube stunt leaves Minnesota man dead, girlfriend charged with manslaughter', Twincities.com, 28 June 2017. Accessed on 29 May 2018 at http://www.twincities.com/2017/06/28/hoping-for-youtube-fame-with-prank-minnesota-woman-apparently-shoots-boyfriend-to-death/

277 Daniel Foggo and Katherine Haywood, 'Humiliation on Pop Idol "could tip contestants over the edge"', Sunday Telegraph, 7 September 2003. Accessed on 29 May 2018 at https://www.

telegraph.co.uk/news/uknews/1440803/Humiliation-on-Pop-Idol-could-tip-contestants-over-the-edge.html

278 'Kitchen nightmares Joseph Cerniglia chef of Campania Commits suicide – FULL EPISODE!', uploaded to YouTube by BestSunglassesEver.com on 3 May 2014. Accessed on 29 May 2018 at https://www.youtube.com/watch?v=CQybSTG4uTU

279 Dana Schuster, 'Dying for Fame: 21 reality stars committed suicide in a decade', *New York Post*, 28 February 2016. Accessed on 29 May 2018 at http://nypost.com/2016/02/28/dying-for-fame-21-reality-stars-commit-suicide-in-past-decade/

280 Hannah Parry, 'Only God can convince me to run for president', MailOnline, 28 February 2018. Accessed on 1 June 2018 at http://www.dailymail.co.uk/news/article-5445447/Oprah-god-convince-run-president.html

281 Emanuel Swedenborg, 'The Lives of Angels', pp. 10–12. Accessed on 25 July 2018 at https://swedenborg.com/emanuel-swedenborg/writings/short-excerpts-and-downloads/excerpt-lives-angels-pages-7-10-12/

282 Max J. Rosenthal, 'The Trump Files: When Donald Destroyed Historic Art to Build Trump Tower', Mother Jones, 13 July 2016. Accessed on 29 May 2018 at https://www.motherjones.com/politics/2016/07/trump-files-when-donald-destroyed-priceless-art-build-trump-tower/

283 'The Apprentice US S01E01', uploaded to YouTube by cmc36905 on 2 February 2018. Accessed on 29 May 2018 at https://www.youtube.com/watch?v=BWW5nVc8dtc&t=343s

284 'Donald Trump touts $214m in income from "The Apprentice"', *Hollywood Reporter*, 15 July 2015. Accessed on 16 July 2018 at https://www.hollywoodreporter.com/news/donald-trump-touts-214m-income-808924

285 Julia Duin, 'She led Trump to Christ: The rise of the televangelist who advises the White House', *Washington Post*, 14 November 2017. Accessed on 29 May 2018 at https://www.washingtonpost.com/lifestyle/magazine/she-led-trump-to-christ-the-rise-of-the-televangelist-who-advises-the-white-house/2017/11/13/1dc3a830-bb1a-11e7-be94-fabb0f1e9ffb_story.html?utm_term=.d8acea1708c6

286 'Kenneth Copeland and Paula White Pray for Donald Trump in 2015', uploaded to YouTube by Christian Comedy Channel on 19 October 2016. Accessed on 29 May 2018 at https://www.youtube.com/watch?v=db5tNbipWY4

287 Conor Gaffey, 'Who is Paula White, Donald Trump's favourite pastor?', *Newsweek*, 25 August 2017. Accessed on 29 May 2018 at http://www.newsweek.com/president-donald-trump-paula-white-prosperity-gospel-655064

288 Diana Butler Bass, 'For many evangelicals, Jerusalem is about prophecy, not politics', CNN, 14 May 2018. Accessed on 23 July 2018 at https://edition.cnn.com/2017/12/08/opinions/jerusalem-israel-evangelicals-end-times-butler-bass-opinion/index.html

289 Dominic Patten, 'Obama Campaign Lists Hollywood Bundlers', Deadline.com, 20 April 2012. Accessed on 29 May 2018 at http://deadline.com/2012/04/obamas-hollywood-donors-bundlers-donations-perks-white-house-259624/

290 Rebecca Shabad, 'Obama speaks out on Harvey Weinstein allegations', CBS News, 10 October 2017. Accessed on 29 May 2018 at https://www.cbsnews.com/news/obama-speaks-out-on-harvey-weinstein-allegations/

291 Azi Paybarah, 'Obama compares himself to Cuomo; Weinstein calls Andrew "an angel"', *Observer*, 12 August 2011. Accessed on 29 May 2018 at http://observer.com/2011/08/obama-compares-himself-to-cuomo-weinstein-calls-andrew-an-angel-2/

292 Ashley Rodriguez, 'How powerful was Harvey Weinstein? Almost no one has been thanked at the Oscars more', Quartz, 13 October 2017. Accessed on 29 May 2018 at https://qz.com/1101213/harvey-weinstein-is-one-of-the-most-thanked-people-in-oscars-history/

293 Chris Gardner, 'Lindsay Lohan Defends Harvey Weinstein: "I Feel Very Bad"', *Hollywood Reporter*, 10 October 2017. Accessed on 29 May 2018 at https://www.hollywoodreporter.com/rambling-reporter/lindsay-lohan-defends-harvey-weinstein-i-feel-very-bad-1047623

294 Susie Cagie, 'What can't tech money buy?', *New York Times*, 27 May 2016. Accessed on 29 May 2018 at https://www.nytimes.com/2016/05/29/opinion/sunday/what-cant-tech-money-buy.html

295 'Peter Thiel: Full Speech: 2016 Republican National Convention', uploaded to YouTube by the Republican National Convention on 21 July 2016. Accessed on 29 May 2018 at https://www.youtube.com/watch?v=UTJB8AkT1dk

296 Jeff Cox, 'Peter Thiel: "What Trump represents isn't crazy and it's not going away"', CNBC, 31 October 2016. Accessed on 29 May 2018 https://www.cnbc.com/2016/10/31/peter-thiel-what-donald-trump-represents-isnt-crazy-and-its-not-going-away.html

297 'Tech Titans Jeff Bezos, Sheryl Sandberg Meet with Donald Trump Transition Team, Power Lunch, CNBC', uploaded to YouTube by CNBC on 14 December 2016. Accessed on 16 July 2018 at https://www.youtube.com/watch?v=O8WgbcXujTg

298 ICT facts and figures for 2017 prepared by the International Telecommunications Union. Accessed on 29 May 2018 at https://www.itu.int/en/ITU-D/Statistics/Documents/facts/ICT-FactsFigures2017.pdf

299 The Top 20 Valuable Facebook Statistics – Updated August 2017. Accessed on 29 May 2018 at https://zephoria.com/top-15-valuable-facebook-statistics/

300 36 Mind Blowing YouTube Facts, Figures and Statistics 2017. Accessed on 29 May 2018 at https://fortunelords.com/youtube-statistics/

301 'Adults spend almost 8 hours each day consuming media', Institute of Practitioners of Advertising, 21 September 2017. Accessed on 29 May 2018 at http://www.ipa.co.uk/news/adults-spend-almost-8-hours-each-day-consuming-media#.Wu7C1raZO8U

302 Aldous Huxley, The Doors of Perception, p. 38. Accessed on 25 July 2018 at https://www.maps.org/images/pdf/books/HuxleyA1954TheDoorsOfPerception.pdf

303 Donald Macintyre, 'Superhighway deal irresistible to Labour', The Independent, 6 October 1995. Accessed on 29 May 2018 at https://www.independent.co.uk/news/superhighway-deal-irresistible-to-labour-1576151.html

304 Brad Stone, The Everything Store: Jeff Bezos and the Age of Amazon (Corgi, 2014), p. 74.

305 Ibid., p. 90.

306 Amit Singhal, 'The Journey Continues…', Google+, 3 February 2016. Accessed on 29 May 2018 at https://plus.google.com/+AmitSinghal/posts/4PEmsWv8WYe

307 Maureen Dowd, 'Elon Musk's Billion-dollar Crusade to Stop the A.I. Apocalypse', Vanity Fair, 26 March 2017. Accessed on 29 May 2018 at https://www.vanityfair.com/news/2017/03/elon-musk-billion-dollar-crusade-to-stop-ai-space-x

308 Maya Kosoff, 'Uber Used a Secret Program Called "Hell" to Track Rival Drivers', Vanity Fair, 13 April 2017. Accessed on 29 May 2018 at https://www.vanityfair.com/news/2017/04/uber-used-a-secret-program-called-hell-to-track-rival-drivers

309 Matt Cartmell, 'Speechwriting: Take Centre Stage', PR Week, 15 August 2008. Accessed on 29 May 2018 at https://www.prweek.com/article/839602/speechwriting-centre-stage

310 Bill Gates: $90 billion; Jeff Bezos: $112 billion; Mark Zuckerberg: $71 billion; Larry Ellison: $58.5 billion; Larry Page: $48.8 billion; Sergey Brin: $47.5 billion. 'Richest people in the world: Forbes' top 20 billionaires of 2018', CBS News. Accessed on 25 July 2018 at https://www.cbsnews.com/pictures/richest-people-in-world-forbes/

311 Sarah Whitten, 'Trump blasts Bezos on Twitter, calls Washington Post a "scam"', CNBC, 7 December 2015. Accessed on 25 July 2018 at https://www.cnbc.com/2015/12/07/donald-trump-blasts-jeff-bezos-the-washington-post-and-amazon-on-twitter.html

312 Eric Schmidt and Jared Cohen, The New Digital Age: Reshaping the Future of People, Nations and Business (John Murray, 2013).

313 Susan Murray and Laurie Ouellette, Reality TV: Remaking Television Culture (New York University Press, 2009), p. 82.

314 Mona Chalabi, 'Weapons of Math Destruction: Cathy O'Neil adds up the damage of algorithms', The Guardian, 27 October 2016. Accessed on 25 July 2018 at https://www.theguardian.com/books/2016/oct/27/cathy-oneil-weapons-of-math-destruction-algorithms-big-data

315 Rob Price, 'Microsoft is deleting its AI chatbot's incredibly racist tweets', Business Insider, 24 March 2016. Accessed on 29 May 2018 at http://uk.businessinsider.com/microsoft-deletes-racist-genocidal-tweets-from-ai-chatbot-tay-2016-3

316 Pamela Haag, 'Valley of the Dolls: Women's Wage Woes in the Tech "Shangri-La" of

Silicon Valley', Big Think. Accessed on 29 May 2018 at http://bigthink.com/harpys-review/valley-of-the-dolls-womens-wage-woes-in-the-tech-shangri-la-of-silicon-valley

317 Parmy Olson, 'Racist, Sexist AI Could Be A Bigger Problem Than Lost Jobs', *Forbes*, 26 February 2018. Accessed on 29 May 2018 at https://www.forbes.com/sites/parmyolson/2018/02/26/artificial-intelligence-ai-bias-google/#3b0c87391a01

318 Tom Simonite, 'When it comes to Gorillas, Google Photos remains blind', *Wired*, 11 January 2018. Accessed on 29 May 2018 at https://www.wired.com/story/when-it-comes-to-gorillas-google-photos-remains-blind/?mbid=GuidesLearnMore

319 Jeff Larson, Surya Mattu, Lauren Kirchner and Julia Angwin, 'How we Analysed the COMPAS Recidivism Algorithm', Propublica, 23 May 2016. Accessed on 29 May 2018 at https://www.propublica.org/article/how-we-analyzed-the-compas-recidivism-algorithm

320 Matthew Kay, Cynthia Matuszek and Sean A. Munson, 'Unequal Representation and Gender Stereotypes in Image Search Results for Occupations', *CHI 2015*, pp. 3819–28. Accessed on 29 May 2018 at http://dub.washington.edu/djangosite/media/papers/unequalrepresentation.pdf

321 'A note on our lawsuit against Otto and Uber', Medium, 23 February 2017. Accessed on 29 May 2018 at https://medium.com/waymo/a-note-on-our-lawsuit-against-otto-and-uber-86f4f98902a1

322 Daisuke Wakabayashi and Mike Isaac, 'Uber executive invokes Fifth Amendment, seeking to avoid potential charges', *New York Times*, 30 March 2017. Accessed on 16 July 2018 at https://www.nytimes.com/2017/03/30/technology/uber-waymo-levandowski.html

323 Mark Harris, 'Inside the First Church of Artificial Intelligence', *Wired*, 15 November 2017. Accessed on 29 May 2018 at https://www.wired.com/story/anthony-levandowski-artificial-intelligence-religion/

324 Max Chafkin, 'Silicon Valley's New Religion Is About As Serious As You'd Think', Bloomberg, 20 November 2017. Accessed on 29 May 2018 at https://www.bloomberg.com/news/articles/2017-11-20/silicon-valley-s-new-religion-is-about-as-serious-as-you-d-think

INDEX

INDEX

INDEX